JOHN W. WEEKS
1860–1926

THE LIFE OF
JOHN W. WEEKS

BY

CHARLES G. WASHBURN

WITH AN INTRODUCTION BY

CALVIN COOLIDGE
President of the United States

AND WITH ILLUSTRATIONS

BOSTON AND NEW YORK
HOUGHTON MIFFLIN COMPANY
The Riverside Press Cambridge
1928

COPYRIGHT, 1928, BY HOUGHTON MIFFLIN COMPANY

The Riverside Press
CAMBRIDGE · MASSACHUSETTS
PRINTED IN THE U.S.A.

TO
THE WIFE, THE CHILDREN
AND THE GRANDCHILDREN
OF
JOHN WINGATE WEEKS

'*Statesman, yet friend to truth! of soul sincere,*
In action faithful, and in honour clear;
Who broke no promise, serv'd no private end.'

PREFACE

THIS book is really a composite production in which many friends have had a part. Some of the contributions appear substantially as they were written.

Members of the family have aided in many ways. Major-General George Barnett, Dr. F. M. Bunts, Mr. W. H. Stayton, Honorable O. E. Weller, classmates at the Naval Academy, have given me their impressions of John Weeks. Mr. Henry Hornblower and Mr. Henry N. Sweet, former partners, and Mr. Daniel G. Wing, formerly associated with Mr. Weeks in the First National Bank of Boston, have supplied much information in regard to business activities. Judge Charles Thornton Davis has contributed an account of the 'Wardroom Club.' Judge Alonzo Rogers Weed, of Newton, has related Mr. Weeks's services as Alderman and Mayor of that City. The late Edward W. Baker, of Brookline, Secretary of the 'Faithful Ten,' has depicted the activities of that militant organization. I must assume the responsibility for what is said of the service in the National House and Senate and contemporary happenings. Vice-President Charles G. Dawes, Secretary of War Dwight F. Davis, General Pershing, Major-General James G. Harbord, retired, the late Governor-General of the Philippines, Leonard Wood, all bear testimony to the value of Mr. Weeks's service as Secretary of War. Mr. Louis H. Warner, for many years secretary to Mr. Weeks, has been extremely useful in his intelligent examination of the correspondence and selection of letters that were of importance. Mr. John W. Martyn, his secretary both before and after Mr. Weeks became Secretary of War, has been most helpful. I have had the aid of Governor W. P. G. Harding, of the Federal Reserve Bank of Boston, in treating the monetary legislation, in the framing of which Mr. Weeks had so large a part.

It has been a great pleasure to collect this material and to mould it into its present form.

I served with Mr. Weeks in the Fifty-Ninth, Sixtieth, and Sixty-First Congresses. He was my closest friend there and our intimacy continued to the end. It has been my aim to have him interpret himself through his speeches and letters. It is a matter of very little importance to chronicle what the biographer thinks; it is a matter of very great importance to record what the subject of the biography says and does. The political period treated covers the last twenty years or more, during which time there have been great changes in the electorate and a great increase in the responsibilities assumed by the National Government. Four amendments have been added to the Federal Constitution. Legislation has been had upon a great variety of new subjects. Most important and certainly the most unusual, that incident upon our participation in the World War, our recovery from those conditions, and the reforming of our archaic monetary system fastened upon the country by the necessities of the Civil War.

During this period annual appropriations have increased from a billion dollars a year to nearly four times that amount. The interest requirements of the National debt in 1927 about equal the annual net cost of administering the Government in 1907.

As legislator and Secretary of War, Mr. Weeks had a large part in favoring or opposing what was done.

CHARLES G. WASHBURN

WORCESTER, MASSACHUSETTS

CONTENTS

ILLUSTRATIONS

INTRODUCTION

BY

PRESIDENT CALVIN COOLIDGE

IT is now nearly twenty-four years since I first came in
contact with John W. Weeks. He was in Northampton
to speak at a Republican rally. While there were other,
and then better known, speakers I cannot recall what
they said, but I have a very distinct impression of the
argument which he made. It was this quality of being
able clearly to demonstrate the correctness of his own
conclusions to others which constituted his greatness.
He was a business man, and a successful one, because he
saw clearly and judged accurately. During his long service in the National House he brought these qualities of
his mind and the results of his experience to the solution
of the many problems of government. He rose to a very
important place, both in the organization and the esti-
mation of the House of Representatives. For six years
he served Massachusetts in the United States Senate. I
was a member of the General Court when he was chosen,
and after casting a complimentary vote or two in the
caucus for our own Congressman, who was not a candidate, thereafter continued my support of Mr. Weeks
until he was elected.

It was during his service in the Senate that I came
into more intimate contact with him. The more I saw
of him, the more I admired him. While he was in no
sense a pugnacious man, and always desired to compose
differences, he never failed to have the courage of his
convictions. He was willing to assert what he thought

to be right and take the consequences of supporting the principles in which he believed. He was not lacking in tact, but there was no element of evasion in his nature.

During his service in the House and Senate he gained a wide reputation. The National Republican Convention in 1916 showed that there were a large number of delegates desirous of nominating him for the Presidency. During the War he was of great service to his country by reason of his technical education as a naval officer and his broad business experience. President Wilson had come to recognize his ability in his dealing with the Federal Reserve Act, and the Democratic members of the Senate always had a great deal of confidence in his judgment.

At the same time I came to Washington as Vice President, Mr. Weeks was made Secretary of War. Although he had been educated in the Naval Academy he was recognized by Army officers as a man who had made very broad studies of land operations. He had the reputation of having a thorough knowledge of the military history of the battles in the war between the North and South. I saw him constantly in the Cabinet meetings and know the great confidence that President Harding had in him and the success with which he administered his office.

After I became President he continued as my Secretary of War. Due to his ill health, he notified me in the spring of 1925 that he felt he must retire. I persuaded him not to relinquish his office then, and he made no formal resignation until late in the summer. Even then he continued for some weeks to hold the office at my earnest solicitation.

He was for many years a great help to his Party, serving at headquarters in the conduct of national campaigns. He had a very wide acquaintanceship and was able to gain and hold the confidence of a very important following. For a number of years I was closely associated with him and numbered him among my friends. His influence in the Congress, even after he had retired from the body, always remained very great. He was blessed with wisdom and discretion, great energy and deep patriotism. He had about him the vigor of the hills combined with the culture of the city. The knowledge that America produces men of his eminent qualities and sturdy character will always be a source of hope and confidence.

THE LIFE OF
JOHN W. WEEKS

.﹒.

CHAPTER I

Boyhood days in Lancaster, New Hampshire — Life at the Naval Academy — A surveyor in Florida — Marriage — Business career — Service in the Spanish War — The Naval Militia, the Naval Brigade, the Wardroom Club.

WE are informed by the town history of Lancaster, New Hampshire, that one David Page, of Petersham, Massachusetts, having become dissatisfied with an allotment of land in Haverhill, New Hampshire, of which he was one of the grantees, in company with sixty-nine other persons procured, in 1763, a charter for a town, in the upper Coös country, in very rich meadow land along the Connecticut River.

One of the original grantees was, as his name appears, Reverend Mr. Joshua Wingate Weeks, brother of Captain John and son of Dr. John Weeks. His great-grandfather, Leonard Weeks, the immigrant, first of the line in this country, came from Wells, Somerset, England. He came to America about 1650 and settled in or near Portsmouth, New Hampshire. In 1660 he received grants of land in what is now Greenland, New Hampshire, near Portsmouth, where he settled with his family of eight children. He was a selectman of Portsmouth, a constable, and for several years sheriff. He died in 1707.

One of his sons, Samuel, built, about 1710, what has always been known as the 'Old Brick House' in Greenland, on land originally granted to his father, Leonard Weeks. This house still stands in excellent repair and is now occupied by Mr. John Williams Weeks, the direct descendant of Samuel. The house has never been out of the family nor in the hands of any but a direct male descendant.

Another son of Leonard was Joshua. Joshua was born in 1674 and died in 1758. He lived in Greenland, New Hampshire. In 1699, he married Comfort Hubbard, sister of Thomas Hubbard, a prosperous Boston merchant and at one time Treasurer of Harvard College. They had ten children, one of whom was Dr. John Weeks (1716–63). He studied medicine in this country and in England and practiced in Greenland and Hampton, New Hampshire. He is spoken of as a popular physician; colonel of a military regiment, and Justice of the Peace. In 1737 he married Martha Wingate, daughter of Colonel Joshua Wingate, a prominent resident of Hampton. The latter was a selectman, member of the Legislature, and active in military affairs. He commanded a company at the siege of Louisburg (1745). Of the ten children born of this marriage, Captain John Weeks (1749–1818) was one.

As a young man, he had hunted on the Kennebec River, and on one of his trips was so attracted by the upper Connecticut River valley that he moved from Greenland, New Hampshire, to Lancaster in 1786. He left his wife behind until he could get settled, but brought with him his son John Wingate, a boy of six, and his daughter Patty. Early in 1787, he wrote to his wife:

'We shall move into our log house this week. It will be a very comfortable one. The logs, all peeled, are smooth and clean. The house is eighteen feet wide and twenty feet long. We shall have one comfortable room and two bed rooms. Our family now consists, besides myself, of one hired man, one girl [Patty, his daughter], one boy [John Wingate], one cow, one heifer, one sheep, one hog, one pig, one dog, one cat, one hen, and one chicken. We also have a pair of geese ... which we shall take home in the fall. You would be pleased to see our little family and Patty's management of it.'

Mrs. Weeks followed her husband in the autumn of that year, making the journey on horseback through the White Mountain Notch, carrying her seven-months-old daughter in her arms while her younger son, James Brackett Weeks, rode behind her on the same horse.

Captain John was spoken of as a 'zealous patriot.' During the Revolution, he was a Second Lieutenant in Captain Jonathan Robinson's Company, which reënforced the army at New York.

He became one of the most influential citizens of Lancaster; was Selectman, Representative in the General Court, a delegate to the New Hampshire Convention in which he was one of fifty-seven to vote to ratify the Federal Constitution, forty-six being recorded in the negative.

Major John W. Weeks (1781–1853) who came to Lancaster with his father, Captain John, in 1786, had a distinguished career. In the War of 1812 he held the commission of Captain in the Eleventh United States Infantry and had a part in nearly all the hard fighting on the Northern frontier. He was promoted to the rank of Major for gallantry in action at the battle of Chippewa.

In politics, he was a Jacksonian Democrat and a man of great influence. He held many offices: was Selectman of Lancaster for ten years; Town Moderator, Sheriff, Representative in the General Court; one of the Commissioners appointed to survey the Maine-New Hampshire boundary in 1828; member of Congress for two terms, 1829–33; a man, as one of his contemporaries wrote, 'whose opinions upon public questions were respected in State and Nation.'

James Brackett Weeks (1784–1858), a younger son of Captain John and brother of Major John Wingate was a farmer and settled on the south slope of Mount Prospect which lies in the valley to the south of the village of Lancaster. He cleared the land and built the house which is still standing. It was on this farm that he shot fifteen deer in one season. He was one of the founders of the First Congregational Society in 1854.

He had seven children. The oldest, James W. Weeks, had a long and useful career. He was a land surveyor, manufacturer, and public official. Under Major Pope (later General Pope of Bull Run fame) he helped survey, in 1845, from Hall's Stream to Lake Champlain and personally made the preliminary sketches and surveys for the topographical maps of the entire line.

He was a school teacher, Selectman, Town Moderator, Judge of Probate, member of the Board of County Commissioners and of the State Board of Agriculture. He was also one of the incorporators of the White Mountain Railroad in 1848, a member of the first Board of Directors of the White Mountain Bank, chartered in 1852, President and Trustee of the Savings Bank of Coös County, President and Treasurer of the Lancaster Academy.

BIRTHPLACE AT LANCASTER, N.H.

The second son of James B. was William D. Weeks (1818–85), spoken of as 'one of Lancaster's most honorable men.' Although a farmer, he had many other interests. He was a Selectman, Judge of Probate for many years, Deputy Collector of Internal Revenue, first President of the Coös and Essex Agricultural Society. In 1844, at the age of twenty-six, he was sent, as a Whig, to the General Court at Concord. He was Lieutenant and then Lieutenant-Colonel in the Twenty-Fourth and Forty-Second Regiments of the New Hampshire Militia.

Of this long line of ancestors, prominent in the service of the Nation, State, County, and Town, John Wingate Weeks, the subject of this biography, named for his great-uncle, Major John Wingate Weeks, was born on April 11, 1860, the male line of his descent running as follows: Leonard Weeks, ———–1707; Joshua Weeks, 1674–1758; Dr. John Weeks, 1716–63; Captain John Weeks, 1749–1818; James Brackett Weeks, 1784–1858; William D. Weeks, 1818–85; John Wingate Weeks, 1860–1926. In the maternal line, his great-great-grandfather, Major Earl Clapp, served with the Colonial troops at Louisburg, Nova Scotia, in 1758. Later he was the seventh Captain in the Twenty-First Regiment of Foot, Colonel Jonathan Ward, commanding under Washington, at Cambridge, and third Captain of the same regiment, at the close of the campaign, in 1776. Later he was promoted to the rank of Major. Amos Fowler, great-grandfather of John Wingate Weeks, was a member of Washington's Life Guard. He was in the retreat from Long Island and served throughout the war.

The farm in Lancaster, where John W. Weeks was born and where his earlier days were spent, was situated on the bank of the Connecticut River. Financial conditions were such that the family, consisting of parents, two brothers, and one sister, was obliged to practice the strictest economy. At the age of eight or nine years, John went to the district school, about half a mile from home, where, with the other boys, he took his turn in building a fire in the big box stove to make the room comfortable for the morning session. We can imagine the little fellow, trudging along the road, in all kinds of weather, carrying from home a bundle of kindling wood under his arm, with which to start the fire at school.

In addition, of course, were the necessary chores, incident to a New England farm, to be performed before and after school hours. Many years later, when Mr. Weeks was in Congress, he said of his early life:

'I have never been thankful enough that I was born on a farm; that I commenced to work as soon as I could toddle about, and that the hard work I did at home, when I was not at school, was the real foundation which has enabled me to accomplish what I have, because it gave me habits of industry and prepared to give me physical health.'

A farmer's boy in those days did not need any artificial stimulant to exercise such as that furnished by a gymnasium. However, John and his brother rigged up a horizontal bar over the hay in the barn, which was very popular in the neighborhood.

About forty days in March and April is the time when maple sugar is made in New Hampshire, and for several years John took charge of one of his Uncle James's 'sugar places,' as they were and are called. This made it necessary not only properly to make the sugar, but to gather the sap from the trees, with a sap yoke and buckets. One man could not, as a rule, do this work alone, but John was able to do it without any help. He taught one term in the district school and was well fitted intellectually and physically for the task. Brawn as well as brains was, at times, necessary to preserve the respect of scholars, some of whom were inclined to be turbulent.

When he was about sixteen years old, Dr. Harrington, the Congregational minister of the town, asked John if he would like an appointment to the Naval Academy at Annapolis. The matter was carefully considered by the family. John's only doubt seemed to be as to whether his father could spare him from the farm; finally, however, it was decided that he should go.

He entered the Naval Academy in 1877 and graduated in 1881. I think I cannot do better than to consolidate what his classmates have written about his life there.

I get the impression of a good-natured, rather easy-going boy, perhaps somewhat immature when he entered, but who steadily developed, manifesting many of the qualities which were so conspicuous in his later life. He was physically the largest boy in his class and perhaps in the Academy, and also the strongest. He could lift a heavier dumb-bell than any one else, was the key man in class scrimmages, in tugs of war, and like tests of strength and endurance. He was a fun-loving boy. A classmate who had a room on a lower floor than his, having hit John with an improvised water bomb, upon returning to his room after drill rather incautiously opened his window and, leaning out, received on the back of his head a bucket of cold water from John's room above. He was fond of all social pleasures and his friends were devoted to him; not conspicuously brilliant as a student, but a plodder who worked hard for what he got, but each year occupied a relatively higher position and highest at the time of his graduation.

He was regarded by the Midshipmen and by the Academy officials as the 'best-balanced' man in the class.

He was Sergeant-Major of the Battalion during the first class year, and when some trouble arose between the Midshipmen and the town police, in which John was himself involved, was made Chairman of the Committee to adjust the matter, which he did successfully. Indeed he was always a peacemaker, an adjuster of differences between his fellow men throughout his life. In his student days at the Academy, his interest in National politics became evident. A classmate has told me that on one occasion he went to John to make some inquiry about a newly appointed Cabinet officer and that in the course of the conversation John named to him all of the Senators in every State of the Union.

He was very fond of his classmates, and after he left the service in 1883, was prominent in arranging for the publication of a class report and for periodical class reunions. It was one of the most cherished associations of his life.

His most conspicuous trait in the Academy continued to be throughout his life, and that was 'character.'

After graduating, he served in the Navy as a Midshipman until 1883, when, there being a surplus of officers, he and others were legislated out of the service under the terms of an act passed August 5, 1882, in the First Session of the Forty-Seventh Congress, entitled 'AN ACT making appropriations for the Naval Service for the fiscal year ending June 30, 1883, and for other purposes,' and running as follows:

'And if there be a surplus of graduates, those who do

DISTRICT SCHOOL, LANCASTER, N.H.
Where John W. Weeks taught school

not receive such appointment [to fill vacancies in the lower grades of the line and Engineer Corps of the Navy and of the Marine Corps] shall be given a certificate of graduation, an honorable discharge, and one year's sea pay, as now provided by law for Cadet Midshipmen.'

Regarding the cruise he made to China, after his graduation, in the U.S.S. Richmond, one of his shipmates says:

'The cruise from Panama to Yokohama on the old U.S.S. Richmond, flagship of the Asiatic Station, was a long and rather tedious one, lasting one hundred and thirty-five days, though our stops at Papeete, Pango Pango, and Apia did much to break the monotony of the voyage. John was the oracle, on most occasions, in the mess, and old Lauch was about the only one who used to take issue with him, which he did regularly nearly every evening after dinner, with the full knowledge that notwithstanding his struggles he was going to be picked up bodily by John and rolled under the table, from which point he was not allowed to emerge until the criticisms were retracted or a call to "stand watch" relieved him from his uncomfortable position. What joyous days those were when one thinks of them now! No matter how rough the weather, how disagreeable the orders we sometimes received, nor how meager our rations on that long cruise, one could always depend upon the mess to find something to raise hilarity and dispel gloom and pessimism; something that youth always has stored away for rainy days, an optimism that will not down.

'As a matter of fact, I remember very little peculiar to John Weeks while on our cruise. We visited the same ports, ransacked the curio shops and searched out the interesting and historical spots together. I think the one outstanding characteristic of Weeks during our cruise was the fact that he had so impressed himself upon us by his fairness and broadmindedness that we came to rely upon him more than upon any other of our shipmates for a safe and sane opinion upon the many differences that were liable to arise among a lot of youngsters thrown together so intimately and for so long a time.'

U.S.F.S. Richmond, 2nd Rate
Hong Kong, China
April 5, 1883

Captain J. G. Walker, U.S.N.
  Chief of Bureau of Navigation, etc.

Sir:

Cadet Midshipman J. W. Weeks has served under my command since September 30, 1881, discharging the duties devolving on him with credit, and to my satisfaction. He has performed duty on deck, and in the engine room; and, as a subordinate divisional officer, he has discharged his duties in a manner to command my respect, and esteem. I take pleasure in commending him to the favorable consideration of the Department. His bearing is gentlemanly and officer-like.

Very respectfully
Your obedient servant
(Signed)   J. S. Skerrett
Captain, Commanding

Navy Department
Bureau of Navigation
Washington, *Mar.* 24, 1915

A true copy from the records of the Bureau.
(Signed)   Victor Blue
(Copy)   *Chief of Bureau*

After leaving the Navy, the important question for John to decide was what he should do.

Mr. Ossian Ray, the member of Congress from his District, offered him a position as his secretary, and he also considered going into the firm of Ray, Drew & Jordan to study law, but on the advice of an old friend of his father's, who said, 'You never would make a good lawyer, John: your hands are too big,' he decided to go to Florida with an ex-Navy friend where he got the position of land surveyor for Orange County with headquarters in Orlando. It was there that he met his future wife whose father had large orange groves near Orlando. In the autumn of 1886, he was offered the position of Land Commissioner for the Florida Southern Railroad, and went to Jacksonville, where he remained a year and a half; in the meantime surveying most of southern Florida. He was fond of telling his friends of the fortune he just missed making at that time. It seems that he bought a tract of phosphate land for two dollars an acre, afterwards selling it for four dollars, being well satisfied with the profit, until a few years later when the same land sold for a good many hundred dollars an acre, proving to be some of the richest in the phosphate section. He was also much tempted to buy a large tract of land on Biscayne Bay, where Miami is now situated, which, at the time he surveyed it, could all be had for a dollar and a quarter an acre. Very likely it was lack of money which deterred him from doing so.

Years afterwards, when he became Secretary of War, General Summerall, just home from his distinguished service in France, went to pay his respects to his Chief, whom he had never met. In the course of conversation it developed that the General was born in Florida, and that when John Weeks was surveying the little town, consisting of six houses, where the General was born, the latter was painting the hotel in which Weeks lived.

The question may occur, Where did John Weeks get his education as a surveyor? I think that he probably picked up the rudiments of the profession when he was a boy in Lancaster. Several of his near relatives had practiced it quite extensively, and, besides, it was not uncommon for boys in the country to acquire at least some knowledge of it, which was no doubt supplemented by his study of mathematics at the Naval Academy.

On October 7, 1885, he married, in Haverhill, Massachusetts, Martha A. Sinclair, whom he had previously met in Florida. She was the daughter of John G. Sinclair, Esq., of Littleton, New Hampshire.

They had two children: Katherine Sinclair Weeks, now Mrs. John Washington Davidge of Washington, D.C., and Charles Sinclair Weeks.

As the climate of Florida did not agree with Mrs. Weeks, a change was sought. About this time Mr. Weeks was introduced by a mutual friend to Mr. Henry Hornblower, who was then associated with his father in carrying on a banking and brokerage business in Boston under the name of Hornblower & Page. Mr. Page had recently died and Mr. Hornblower, Sr., felt obliged to retire because of failing eyesight. Whereupon these two young men, taking over the business of Hornblower and Page, formed a copartnership under the name of Hornblower & Weeks, which is now nation-wide in its extent.

The partnership papers of Hornblower and Weeks were dated August 6, 1888. Mr. Hornblower represented the firm on the floor of the Stock Exchange, Mr.

MIDSHIPMAN JOHN W. WEEKS
At the United States Naval Academy, 1881

Weeks in the office; they, together with one bookkeeper and the office boy, James J. Phelan, who has since become a prominent member of the firm, made up the staff.

The business, originally located in one room of the old Merchants' Exchange Building in Boston, torn down to make room for the Exchange Building, was at that time, 1889, moved into quarters in the Merchants' Bank Building on Devonshire Street. In 1894 the firm occupied a suite of offices on the second floor of the Exchange Building and on August 6, 1908, moved into their own building at 60 Congress Street.

In 1901 an office was opened in New York; in 1907, in Chicago, and Providence; in 1908, Detroit; in 1915, Portland, Maine; in 1924, Cleveland, Ohio; in 1927, Pittsburgh, Pennsylvania.

The personnel of the firm has increased from two partners and three employees in 1888 to thirteen partners and six hundred and sixty-four employees in 1927.

Mr. Weeks did not give close personal attention to the business after he took his seat in the Fifty-Ninth Congress in December, 1905, and withdrew entirely from the firm when he was elected to the Senate in 1913, to succeed Winthrop Murray Crane.

He also had an important part in establishing upon a firm foundation the First National Bank of Boston.

The Massachusetts Bank was the first in Boston, the oldest in New England, and the third in the country, its original charter dating back to 1784. It later became the Massachusetts National Bank.

The first building occupied by the Massachusetts State Bank was located on Long Acre (Tremont) Street, opposite the Granary Burying Ground, where Hamilton

Place now is. It was known as the Manufactory House, and, while designed for carrying on the manufacture of linen, was occupied by the bank for a long time, owned by it in 1794, and torn down in 1806. Mr. Weeks was elected a director in January, 1895.

In 1898 and 1899 the Massachusetts National Bank passed through the most depressed period in its history. In January, 1900, Mr. Weeks became President to serve until such time as the bank's affairs could be put in a satisfactory condition and a suitable person found to succeed him. Great credit is due for his successful efforts, which resulted in increasing the deposits, which had fallen to $1,172,000 in January, 1900, to $6,674,000 in November, 1902.

At the annual meeting in January, 1903, he declined reëlection, believing that his work was done and that his successor, Daniel G. Wing, would be abundantly competent to manage successfully the business. Mr. Weeks was elected Vice-President at this meeting.

On June 27, 1903, the Massachusetts National Bank was merged with the First National Bank of Boston. Mr. Wing continued as President, Mr. Weeks as Vice-President and Director of the consolidated institutions which became the First National Bank of Boston.

Mr. Weeks remained a Vice-President and Director of the First National Bank for ten years, resigning on April 23, 1913, because of his election to the United States Senate. The following extract is from the records of a meeting of the Board of Directors held on that day:

'A letter from John W. Weeks, tendering his resignation as a Director and Vice-President of the bank, was presented to the Board by the President. In presenting this resignation, Mr. Wing expressed his personal regret that the election of Mr. Weeks to the United States Senate made necessary and proper the severance of his official connection with the bank, and made a brief statement in appreciation of Mr. Weeks's services to the bank during the past fourteen years.

'"In 1898–99 the Massachusetts National Bank, the oldest bank in New England, became involved in the general distrust aroused by the failures of the Globe and Broadway National Banks, and suffered a very material decrease in its deposits. Mr. Weeks was at this time a Director and a small stockholder in the bank. He and his associates decided that they would not allow the Massachusetts Bank to fail and placed their private resources behind its deposits. For a number of weeks, through the most trying period, the Clearing House losses of the bank were made good by Hornblower & Weeks.

'"Mr. Weeks assumed the Presidency of the bank in January, 1900, and with the return of confidence began building up its deposits. For three years Mr. Weeks devoted a considerable part of his time to the upbuilding of the bank, strengthening its directorate, and increasing its importance among the financial institutions of Boston. Having accomplished his purpose, he retired from the Presidency and active management and was elected Vice-President. This position he has held through the various consolidations to the present time.

'"When the stock of the First National Bank was purchased in June, 1903, it was paid for with the certified check of Hornblower & Weeks. That consolidation, and the consolidation made in 1904 with the National Bank of Redemption, were brought about with the active aid and coöperation of Mr. Weeks and his firm.

'"To remind you of Mr. Weeks's great pride in the institution which he has done so much to build, and his fine sense of personal honor, I need only recall to you how he paid and took out of the bank a certain note amounting to several hundred thousands of dollars, when the maker became insolvent. Mr. Weeks was under no legal liability whatsoever upon this note, but his pride in seeing that the bank suffered no loss through a loan made in the ordinary course of business but to a company in which his firm was interested, determined him and his partners to personally assume the loss.

'"During the panic of 1907, no Officer nor Director supported the bank with greater coolness, courage and ability than did Mr. Weeks. In building up this institution from one million dollars of deposits in the old Massachusetts Bank; through the consolidation with the old First National and with the National Bank of Redemption; during the trying times of 1907; the purchase of our present location and erection of our new building, his advice, assistance and time have been freely given. Our personal relations have been most intimate and pleasant and the severance of his official connection comes as a personal loss to every Officer and Director of this bank.

'"Few directors have served an institution as loyally, as faithfully and as disinterestedly as John W. Weeks has this bank in the fourteen years during which he has been an Officer and Director.

'"I am making this statement to the Directors in appreciation of Mr. Weeks's service to the bank and of his support and friendship to me personally."

'On motion it was

'VOTED: That with deep regret Mr. Weeks's resignation as Vice-President and Director of the bank be accepted, and that the remarks of the President, in connection with this resignation, be spread upon the Records.'

Mr. Weeks served in the Massachusetts Naval Brigade for ten years and in the Volunteer Navy during the Spanish-American War, at which time he was a member of Governor Roger Wolcott's Military Advisory Board.

On July 10, 1898, the following telegram was sent

from the Navy Department in Washington to Lieutenant John W. Weeks, U.S.N., U.S.S. Minnesota, Boston, Massachusetts.

'You will assume charge second district auxiliary naval force, relieving Commander Nelson and establish headquarters on Minnesota. Orders follow by mail. Give immediate attention to protection of mine fields. Wire what you need to perform the service.'

On July 12, 1898, a letter followed of which the following is a copy:

NAVY DEPARTMENT
WASHINGTON, *July* 12, 1898

SIR:

Report immediately, by letter, to Captain John R. Bartlett, U.S.N., Retired, Chief of the U.S. Auxiliary Naval Force, office of Naval Intelligence, Navy Department, Washington, D.C., for the Command of the U.S.S. Minnesota, and for duty as Assistant Chief in charge of the Second District of the United States Auxiliary Naval Forces, Boston, Mass.

This employment on shore duty is required by the public interests.

Respectfully

JOHN D. LONG
Secretary

Lieutenant JOHN W. WEEKS
  U.S.S. Minnesota
  Chf. Aux. Force

The following letters belong to this period:

September 28*th*, 1898

SIR:

I have to-day received your report dated September

10th, and have read the same with much interest. I thank you for the care and thoroughness with which you have gone into the matters connected with the Auxiliary Naval Force in your District, and for the full information contained in the various appendices to your report.

Since you wrote the report, the Catskill has gone out of commission, and I can get the information I wish about the crew, as well as the Prairie, from the Bureau of Navigation. I can also get from the same source the date of the honorable discharges of the officers, the data for which you did not have at hand.

I congratulate you personally on the splendid showing made by the Massachusetts Naval Brigade, and the number of efficient officers which it furnished to the Service. Its record is one of the conclusive proofs of the value of the Naval Militia, and I realize how much of its efficiency is due to your own example and untiring efforts.

Respectfully

(Signed)   JOHN R. BARTLETT

Chief of U.S. Auxiliary Naval Force

Lieut. JOHN W. WEEKS, U.S.N.
   Asst. to Chief U.S. Auxiliary Naval Force, 2nd Dist.,
   U.S.S. Minnesota, Boston, Mass.

April 13th, 1900

Captain John W. Weeks
   53 *State St. City*

CAPTAIN:

I am directed to inform you that the following endorsement was placed on your application for retirement on the day you were retired.

CAPTAIN WEEKS WITH THE MASSACHUSETTS NAVAL BRIGADE AFTER THE DEWEY PARADE,

OCTOBER 14, 1899

COMMONWEALTH OF MASSACHUSETTS
ADJUTANT-GENERAL'S OFFICE
BOSTON, APR. 10TH, 1900

In accepting the retirement of Capt. John W. Weeks as Chief of the Naval Brigade of the Militia of the Commonwealth, with which he has been connected for more than ten years as a commissioned officer, the Commander-in-Chief seeks the opportunity to express his appreciation and thanks for the earnest endeavor and faithful service rendered by Captain Weeks during his term of service.

The Commander-in-Chief accepts the retirement of Captain Weeks with regret.

(Signed) SAMUEL DALTON
Adjutant-General

The Navy was Captain Weeks's first love and to the Navy he gave a lifelong and enthusiastic loyalty. Forced by circumstances out of the service, he retained as close a connection with it as possible. When the Naval Militia was organized, Weeks was among the first to join. In this experiment, first tried in Massachusetts, he foresaw great possibilities. Its originator, John C. Soley, who was Weeks's predecessor in command of the Naval Brigade, was a man of extraordinary personal magnetism and gathered about him a number of graduates of the Naval Academy and young professional and business men who had a love for the service, among whom were some of exceptionally brilliant and interesting personality. To these associates, Weeks, whose chief characteristic was a genius for friendship, extended the same affectionate loyalty that he gave to his classmates at the Academy.

Shortly before the Spanish War, the old frigate Minnesota had been assigned to the Naval Brigade as its training ship and headquarters. It was the scene of

much hard work, for real efficiency was Weeks's aim
and goal, but it also served for the officers as one of the
most unique and delightful clubs imaginable. Former
officers were most hospitably welcomed at its wardroom mess, where the Captain always presided.

After the Spanish War, some of the officers of the old
Naval Militia foregathered for a reunion dinner which
was held at the picturesque quarters of the Wharf Rats,
and it was decided to form an organization, with quarters on the water-front, to keep alive, through the medium of monthly dinners, memories of the old intimate
days of association in the Naval Brigade and in the war,
and perhaps to be of some service to the Navy.

The result was the formation of the Wardroom Club.
It originated with Weeks, it was gathered around him,
centered in him, and existed through him and for him.
The song with which for many years every dinner began,
that asserted that 'John, John, John W. Weeks is a man
we all adore,' was literally true, and he knew it. He was
an amazingly simple and modest man, but the devotion of the members of the Club to him seemed perfectly natural, for he fully reciprocated their affection and to each one of them he gave a personal, loyal
and most helpful friendship. He was too wise a man,
and possessed of too keen a sense of humor, not to know
their individual foibles and weaknesses, but he also knew
and instinctively called out from each his best. Simplicity and loyalty are qualities that he greatly prized
and these he found in the Wardroom Club.

A few old officers who had been unable to get into the
war were asked to join in the formation of the club, and
it was thought that it might afford opportunities for the
exchange of views and of friendships between officers in

the regular establishment and those in the volunteer organizations, and bring the hopes and needs of the service home to men in active civil life.

The qualification for membership is a present or past commission carrying the privileges of the wardroom on a ship of the United States Navy. This, of course, included the Marine Corps. There is also a small associate membership of men peculiarly interested in the Navy, and one President (Harding) and several Secretaries of the Navy have become honorary members.

As former classmates and shipmates of active members came to Boston on duty, they were brought to the Club and many became interested and enthusiastic members. The Navy list outnumbers the active list by four to one.

The most successful men in active service have evinced a keen interest in the problem of how best to use the volunteer and the civilian for the good of the service. This problem appealed particularly to Weeks. In his own service, as a volunteer officer, as a Senate member of the Committee on Military Affairs, and as Secretary of War, he did more than any other man to solve it. He stimulated all discussion of this and kindred topics at the Wardroom Club. At its dinners in the midst of the fun there has almost invariably been one serious talk on some professional subject. To aid the Navy has been the dominant purpose of the Club. Weeks attended its meetings whenever possible. When distance or duty prevented, he usually sent some message or word of greeting.

Song and story, wit and nonsense, came on with the canapé and lasted throughout the evening. Weeks was essentially a good fellow. Dullness could not live in his

company. But he never parted with the essential simple
dignity that characterized his bearing.

The first quarters of the Club were on Otis Wharf,
with many windows looking down the harbor and a
messroom fitted up to resemble, as nearly as possible,
the wardroom of an old-time ship. The sideboard and
other furniture of the wardroom of the old Minnesota
were acquired, and with its simulated mainmast, its
frieze of flags spelling, in the international code, amus-
ing and hospitable signals, and its walls covered with
pictures and mementoes of service on all seas, it afforded an unusual and appropriate setting for the dinners. Some of the members had served on sailing ships
of the old Navy, others had brought back to the Club
souvenirs of the Spanish War and of the World War,
and to insure the safe-keeping of these memorials of
the past the Club was incorporated. Captain Weeks
was its first and only President.

At a dinner of the Wardroom Club, given on October
20, 1914, the following verses were sung. On the reverse
side of the card, on which they were inscribed, was the
photograph of 'Captain John,' as a cadet at the Naval
Academy.

CAPTAIN JOHN

While winter winds are blowing across a sea of snow
The Wardroom lights are glowing, and we all are snug below!
Then welcome! to a sailor bold, who steers the Ship of State!
Thrice welcome! to a comrade old, whose fame we celebrate!
To-night let's slip our cable, and drift off down the stream —
Where Villa is a fable, and Huerta but a dream!
Where rates are fair, and trusts unknown —
Where tariff-bills are barred —
Where public censors dare condone
And times are never hard!

So fill your glasses to the brim
With good old blood-red wine —
Then stand and give a health to him
For days of Auld Lang Syne!

And when the loyal draught you drain,
Till ev'ry drop is gone —
Your voices raise with might and main
To cheer for Captain John.

Since Weeks's death the Club goes on, mostly through younger men to whom he is only a splendid tradition, but it goes on in his spirit. He created it, he loved it, and it filled a very warm and unique place in his heart and in his life.

CHAPTER II

Alderman and Mayor of Newton, Massachusetts — The 'Faithful Ten' —
Election to the Fifty-Ninth Congress — New era in American politics.

PRIOR to the nineties, Newton consisted of a dozen or
more villages, each with its independent community
life and interests, and with little in common save political association as parts of one city. The only important public improvement, that had been undertaken
which concerned all parts of the city, was the water
supply. The recent completion of the so-called 'Newton
Circuit' of the Boston & Albany Railroad had given the
different villages of the north and south sections some
means of intercommunication, but this was hardly sufficient to arouse any sense of solidarity. No doubt the
pleasant intimacies of this village life were among the
reasons which moved Captain Weeks to select West
Newton for his home.

But in the decade which followed, a definite change
took place. The construction of the Metropolitan
Sewer provided long-needed sewage disposal for the
city. Commonwealth Avenue was projected from Lake
Street near the Chestnut Hill Reservoir across the city
to the Weston Bridge with a reservation for a double-
track street railway. The grade crossings on the main
line of the Boston & Albany Railroad were abolished
and in connection therewith Washington Street was
widened with provision for a double-track street railway location from Nonantum Square to West Newton.
Tremont and Park Streets were widened to provide for
a double-track street railway location from Nonantum

Square to Boston, and Centre Street was widened for like access to Cambridge. A new high school was erected. The Metropolitan Park System was created.

The discussion of such important and costly public improvements stimulated interest in civic affairs. The burdens they imposed created new problems which concerned the entire city. Newton had long been overwhelmingly Republican in National and State politics. But its voters were by no means blindly partisan and it was a period of revolt against machine politics. Under these circumstances coincident with a change in the city charter a definite effort was made to elevate and broaden the local political life by persuading business men of large affairs, through an appeal to their sense of duty, to participate actively in administering the government of the city. It is not surprising that Captain Weeks, with characteristic public spirit, should respond to such an appeal. Nor is it surprising that, although relatively a newcomer, he was chosen as Alderman-at-large without opposition. The 'easy' Republican boss in local affairs, which that period developed, Charles E. Hatfield, became from that time on one of Captain Weeks's staunchest and most loyal supporters and in many a campaign one of the leaders of his hosts. From that time on, also, Captain Weeks's readiness to serve was taken for granted by his neighbors and friends.

It is difficult for most men trained in an atmosphere where orders are obeyed and not discussed, or accustomed to the administration of large business affairs in which decisions must be made and executed with promptness, to adapt themselves to the routine of a legislative assembly in which persuasion rather than command prevails and where the vote of the weakest member counts as much in the result as that of the strongest. But Captain Weeks brought to this new task not only a generous spirit but great practical wisdom, tolerance of the views of others, and strength of character — the strength of one who knows his own opinion, asserts it frankly when — and only when — the occasion requires, and accepts the decision of the majority without elation or bitterness.

For three years he served the city as an Alderman with a record for faithful attendance at board and committee meetings equaled by few of his colleagues. In the third year he was Vice-President of the Board, and throughout his service a member of the important committees on Finance and Street Railways. Street railway expansion was then at its height. Washington Street and Commonwealth Avenue were occupied by street railway lines. Two other lines went north and south from Newtonville to Watertown, to Newton Upper Falls, and to Needham, respectively. Promoters had their eyes on the Worcester Turnpike, while other promoters were submitting attractive plans for lines crossing Newton from north to south. Moreover, still other promoters were projecting competing telephone service. In addition, the school buildings, which for a generation or more had served the several villages of the city well, were outgrown, and an extensive rebuilding programme had to be considered and settled. It is unusual when such questions do not provoke controversy, and this was particularly true of a city made up of so many communities; each urgent of its own needs and armed with an improvement society to give them expression. In the perplexing problems which arose, Captain Weeks's cool, calm judgment was soon recognized by his colleagues and his views were listened to not only with respect but were eagerly sought. The Clerk of Committees of that period says:

'I distinctly recall Mr. Weeks's influence at Committee meetings. The Street Railway Committee was particularly busy at that period on account of the many applications for locations to reach all parts of the City. Mr. Weeks would listen to the remarks and opinions of the other members, but not until he was asked directly by the Chairman would he enter the discussion. He would then leave his chair and, walking up and down the Committee room, would give his reason for the action he proposed in such fashion that when he had finished he would have the entire Committee with him.'

Time has dealt rather cruelly with these street railway projects. That there were not more victims is due in no small measure to the foresight and understanding of the problem by Captain Weeks and his influence with his fellow Aldermen.

One of the memories which will linger long with those who served with him during his first year was the dinner held at its close, by his invitation, on board the old ship Minnesota. The animosities and verbal strifes of the year were forgotten, and under the leadership of one of the little band of 'irreconcilables' of that year no one's idiosyncrasies escaped attention. But the prize was won by the lawyers in a limerick which ran —

> Now, here's to the man from Ward Seven,
> Who talks law from eight to eleven.
>   He fights so with Ivy
>   And makes things so lively
> We thank God they can't argue in Heaven.

In the fall of 1901 the need arose for selecting a new

mayor. The finger of destiny pointed to Captain Weeks. He was not merely a logical candidate, but the inevitable candidate. He met with opposition at the hands of an independent candidate projected into the situation by the Democrats, who were never loath to put a fly in the Republican ointment. However, the contest served only to bring out a record vote, almost as large as that cast in a presidential year, and the Captain won handsomely. This was his first experience in political campaigning. He was wont to tell with some glee that one of his fellow Aldermen, who had arranged a rally in an industrial section of the city and desired the Captain's presence, said, 'I told them you ain't much of a speaker, but they want to see you just the same.' A veteran of many a hard-fought contest in a neighboring city asked the Captain about his campaign during its progress. The Captain told him and asked the veteran's advice. The latter asked, 'What salary does the office carry?' The Captain replied, '$2500.' The veteran asked, 'Well, you don't need that, do you?' The Captain replied, 'No.' And the veteran said, 'Well, then, spend it.'

In the city charter of 1897, to which allusion has already been made, the executive powers were vested solely in the Mayor, to be exercised by him either personally or through the several officers or boards under his supervision and control. This provision was in sharp contrast with the city's first charter in which the executive powers were vested in the Mayor and Aldermen, and in fact were exercised in large measure by committees. It took several years to live down the old tradition, and Captain Weeks was the first Mayor who caught the full significance of the change. With characteristic directness he said in his first inaugural:

'The most important duty of the Mayor, as I understand it, is to insure through the proper officers an
honest, wise, and economical administration of city
affairs. The City of Newton is entitled to adequate returns for the liberal salaries and wages paid, and I will
endeavor to obtain a return for the City as nearly commensurate with that obtained by private corporations
as possible, and I will especially try to see that equally
favorable results are obtained in purchasing supplies.'

To the task thus set himself, he devoted the two following years faithfully and with a marked degree of success. He followed closely the administrative details of
the several departments, and his training and business
experience made him quick to detect and improve inefficient methods and to readjust and reorganize where
old methods had outlived their usefulness. Naturally
the financial problems of the city made a primary appeal to him and by intelligent oversight and prompt
interference when necessary, he caused the city's revenues to be collected more promptly and temporary
loans to be limited to the needs of the current fiscal year,
thus saving substantial payments of interest. He exercised a close supervision and control over departmental
expenditures and insisted upon keeping expenses within
appropriations. Incidentally he caused the collection of
all monies due the city to be concentrated in the City
Collector and Treasurer's office; thereby ending the
existing loose and somewhat irresponsible method long
followed in handling monies other than taxes due the
city, and especially the considerable revenues of the
Water Department. He also inaugurated the policy of
issuing serial rather than sinking fund bonds for the
city's permanent debt, a step which time has amply

justified, a policy which later he urged be adopted by the National Government.

Certain marked inequalities in valuations made by the assessors had been for a number of years a source of widespread complaint. Mayor Weeks reorganized the department, introduced new blood into its personnel, and provided for systematic and periodic revaluations of real estate; at the same time treating those who had served the city long and honestly in that department with such consideration that there was no resulting bitterness among them or their friends. With the same close attention to detail, he secured an increase in the number of permanent men in the Fire Department and so improved its effectiveness; he standardized the pay of the police officers and the rules for sick-pay for all city employees; improved the distribution of poor relief; investigated the city printing; caused the vital statistics of the town up to 1850 to be printed; greatly improved the street lighting without increasing cost to the city; and arranged with the telephone and electric lighting companies to buy a certain number of units of their lines yearly for a period of years.

Some measures which he advocated failed for the moment, but later he had the satisfaction of knowing that his suggestions had not fallen on sterile soil. He was the first to suggest that the Boston & Albany Railroad should stop its trains at Newtonville, a policy which was adopted some ten years later. He urged that interest on damages for land-takings be computed at four rather than six per cent, but the legislature waited for over fifteen years before adopting this suggestion.

His official activities were by no means confined to administrative details. There were more important measures to claim his attention. The separation of the grade crossings on the Newton Highlands branch of the Boston & Albany Railroad, which had been initiated by his predecessor, had aroused the opposition of the railroad and needed and received Captain Weeks's vigorous and successful support. The widening of Boylston Street to provide a reservation for the tracks of the Boston & Worcester Street Railway, and to secure this important improvement at the expense of the street railway company rather than of the city, involved delicate negotiations. Most careful consideration of the Charles River Basin improvement was necessary in order to protect the city's interests.

Throughout the two years great harmony prevailed between the Mayor and the Board of Aldermen. Only once did Mayor Weeks have occasion to exercise the veto power, and we have since moved so fast and so far in shortening hours in all lines of work that the mere existence of such a controversy now seems strange. The Board voted to grant to the permanent members of the Fire Department one day off in ten, the practice then prevailing being one day off in fourteen. The Mayor in a vigorous and well-reasoned veto demonstrated the lack of any necessity for such action and its substantial cost to the city. But too many members of the Board were already pledged to their first position and, notwithstanding their regret at any difference with the Mayor, the veto was not sustained.

In 1902 Newton, in common with all New England, was confronted with an unexpected shortage of coal due to the strike of the miners in the anthracite region. The experience was novel and the resultant hardships and suffering were serious and at times acute. Captain

Weeks met this emergency with characteristic energy and vision. After making ample provision for the fuel needs of the city's buildings and pumping station, he set himself to the task of relieving private citizens who were without fuel. Finding that by a recent decision of the Supreme Court he could not employ public funds for this purpose, he organized a syndicate of his neighbors, purchased six hundred tons of soft coal and two hundred cords of wood, involving an expenditure of over eighty-five hundred dollars, and arranged for their distribution at cost to those in greatest need, with the result that there was no serious suffering in Newton that winter for lack of fuel even among the very poor.

The matter which perhaps aroused at the time more widespread interest than any event of his administration was the so-called 'Tarbox' case. Chief of Police Tarbox had been brought to Newton from Fitchburg several years before. A growing spirit of hostility to the Chief, among the rank and file of the police force, culminated, during Mayor Weeks's second term, in definite charges by certain of its members against their Chief. The charter provided that the Mayor might suspend an executive officer, and in that event was bound to report his action and his reasons therefor to the Board of Aldermen. In fifteen days such suspension amounted to a removal unless within that period such executive officer asked for a hearing before the Board. At the conclusion of the hearing, if the Mayor's suspension was not sustained, the officer was reinstated. Having these provisions in mind and these charges having been made public at the time of their submission, Mayor Weeks deemed it fair that he should give both parties to this controversy a public hearing before determining whether or not he should exercise his power under the charter to suspend the Chief. This hearing lasted several days and was given wide publicity. Many of the charges were of themselves trivial and based on personal grievances and petty jealousies so common in police forces and they seemed even more trivial in evidence. The more serious charges were not sustained and Mayor Weeks reached the only conclusion warranted, that they were not proved and that he was not justified in suspending the Chief — a conclusion receiving the approval of all save the immediate friends of the complaining officers.

The two terms which Captain Weeks was willing to accept passed quickly. He himself had stipulated at the outset that two years must be the limit, and due to his advocacy the term of his successor was made two years instead of one. This brief account of his administration gives but an imperfect idea of his official activities. Aside from keeping in daily touch with the work of the several departments, public works and public buildings had to be visited frequently and the city's legislative and external interests cared for. There was the constant stream of visits from those with projects or grievances, not merely at the City Hall but at his Boston office as well, and often the call to appear at public functions. No man could have been more accessible to those who wished an interview, or more patient and courteous to the humble and the importunate. He was asked once, after he had met and listened to the several stories of an unusually long line of visitors, if such a crowd did not make him nervous, and he replied in his calm fashion, 'I don't know what nerves are.' His fellow Alderman may have been right in his comment on him as a speaker. Eloquence he certainly would have been the last to claim, but he had what is often more effective — an engaging personality that invited confidence and a simplicity and directness of speech which commanded attention. Throughout his official life as Mayor, he preached the gospel of good citizenship with an earnestness which carried conviction and aroused in many an indifferent citizen a new interest in public affairs. In his own fashion he was an idealist accepting as part of the day's work his share of responsibility for the common welfare. To him an essential of the Christian life was that a man should so live that his particular corner of the world should be the better for his living in it.

Mayor Weeks was noted for his disregard of form and precedent. Once convinced that an object was desirable and the means for securing it proper, he was little concerned over any objection that it was novel and untried or that it was of doubtful constitutionality. The coal strike resulted in a serious public emergency to be met with as such, and perhaps it is not to be wondered at that he was restive over the constitutional obstacle to any use of the power of the government to protect the individual citizen. With equal disregard of a narrow legal construction of public rights, he insisted that the Boston & Worcester Street Railway Company light its location, knowing full well that it must light the street as well. He also urged compensation for the use of the public streets by the various public utilities and the construction of public conduits for fire alarm wires with spare ducts to be rented for telephone and electric light wires as well. It was also characteristic and prophetic of his future career that in concluding his term as

Mayor he urged strengthening the executive power, while at the same time showing his faith in democracy by advocating that the Board of Aldermen, with its important legislative function of appropriating money, should be as representative as possible.

Captain Weeks left the City Hall with many evidences of the affection and respect of those with whom for five years he had been so closely associated and with the confidence of the whole community. He took a lasting satisfaction in his first experience in public office.

John Weeks's friendships were so large a part of his life that reference to them should be made, revealing as they do the devotion of his friends to his fortunes and their unbounded confidence in him.

He was intimately associated with many different groups, organized for widely divergent purposes, in each of which he was the dominant personality and natural leader. One such, known as 'The Faithful Ten,' was organized in the spring of 1904 for the particular purpose of assisting in the political campaign of that year when Mr. Weeks was for the first time a candidate for Congress. The relations among the members proved so congenial that they have continued, severed during the last twenty-four years by the deaths of five members.

Although the need of any political activity in his behalf ceased after Mr. Weeks became a member of the President's Cabinet, the group has met one or more times annually and at every such reunion the 'Captain,' whether the host or not, was always of those present, and to the others the recollection of them will always be most delightful.

During the winter of 1903–04, the Honorable Samuel L. Powers, who was serving his second term as Congressman from the then Twelfth District, made it known to some of his political intimates that he would not be a candidate for reëlection. It became a matter of interest to them to agree upon his successor, some one who not only possessed the necessary qualifications, but who could be brought to consent to become a candidate.

This was before the days of the direct primary, when the candidate was nominated in a district convention.

John W. Weeks had just ended his service as Mayor of Newton, and was naturally thought of as a most desirable successor to Mr. Powers. Mr. Weeks, rather grudgingly, yielded to the persuasions of his friends and consented to be a candidate.

Immediately a small group of three or four gathered others and conferences were held. The first meetings were held in late January, 1904, attended by five Newton men. The district then embraced parts of Middlesex, Worcester, and Norfolk Counties. A representative from Worcester County was next brought in, followed, almost at once, by three from Norfolk. Thus an active working group of nine was created which, with one more, who lived in Boston, became known subsequently as 'The Faithful Ten.'

Meetings were held intermittently during February and March and regularly on Fridays in May, June, and July at luncheon at Young's Hotel. Soon there was an enthusiastic team of willing workers pulling together as only a team in love with its leader can. Each did all he could for the benefit of the cause. The sagacity and good sense of the candidate guided all their deliberations.

'When this campaign is over, I want to look at myself in the glass without any loss of self-respect,' was a remark, in substance, made by Mr. Weeks not once, but very frequently, during the campaign.

To celebrate the successful outcome of the convention, at which Mr. Weeks was nominated by an overwhelming majority, he entertained, at a dinner at his house, the ten members of the group who had been so closely associated. It was a most happy affair, but the guests were not satisfied. They wanted to be hosts to their 'Captain,' and so, soon after the following election, another dinner was arranged at the Newton Club. On that evening the group was named and christened 'The Faithful Ten,' a more appropriate designation than 'The John W. Weeks Campaign Lunch Club,' which some were tempted to say was a more descriptive title.

At that dinner, one of the group was assigned 'to bring in something entertaining.'

Perhaps a description of the purpose of their meeting and the personnel of the gathering can best be given by a quotation from 'what was brought in':

> Listen, my friends, and I'll tell you what's true,
> But you must not repeat it — that never would do:
> Let our good friends believe we met only to dine,
> They must not know how ten of us, in a combine,
> Controlled the election; though the Twelfth District speaks
> Of only the man we elected — John Weeks.

> There was Garcelon, Jones, and Hatfield — Charles E. —
> Flanders and Bullard and Baker — that's me;
> Bancroft and Wiley and Shaw — known as Jim;
> And Sweet, of course — we'd have starved without him.
> These are the ten whom history seeks
> To learn just how they elected John Weeks.

The organization of the group has always been: Seward W. Jones, Chairman; Charles E. Hatfield, Treasurer; Edward W. Baker, Secretary.

The Chairman

Jones was our Chairman, as gray and as stern
As an old granite tombstone — either tablet or urn;
A friend of the Captain, loyal and tried,
With an itch for the Councillorship on the side;
That honor escaped him, but how he does thrive
On an honor far greater — 'The Boss of Ward Five.'

The Treasurer

Hatfield, Charles E., paid the bills for 'The Ten' —
We don't know how and we don't care when;
But he paid them all as we knew he could
And as any good treasurer always should;
Whenever he likes he may pay them again
By unanimous vote of 'The Faithful Ten.'

The Secretary

Baker, the scribe of 'The Faithful Ten,'
Was always busy with pencil or pen;
In the little black book he wrote all we knew
And carefully checked the false from the true;
He told us the balance looked good in his sight
And at the election 'twas proved he was right.

The five from Newton who formed the nucleus for what later became 'The Faithful Ten' were: George B. Bullard, William M. Flanders, William F. Garcelon, Charles E. Hatfield, and Seward W. Jones. Each represented different elements in Republican political activities in Newton as well as different sections geographically.

Those from other parts of the Congressional District were: Eben D. Bancroft, of Hopedale; Edward W. Baker, of Brookline; Jesse S. Wiley, of Brookline; James

THE 'FAITHFUL TEN,' 1904

Standing: William F. Garcelon, Jesse S. Wiley, George S. Bullard, Eben D. Bancroft,
William M. Flanders, Henry N. Sweet. Seated: Seward W. Jones, Edward W. Baker,
John W. Weeks, Charles E. Hatfield, James F. Shaw

F. Shaw; Henry N. Sweet, a boyhood friend of Mr. Weeks, a member of the firm of Hornblower & Weeks.

There were two others who worked closely with 'The Ten' and contributed valuable assistance. Captain Weeks styled them 'By-products.' They were: Howard A. Crossman, of Needham, and Charles C. Pierce, of Dover.

The work of 'The Ten' in the first campaign of 1904 is recorded in a scrapbook, still carefully preserved, containing all kinds of information contributed by the individual members, clippings from the Congressional District newspapers, lists of committees and delegates, copies of correspondence, and memoranda of interviews with representatives from different parts of the District. To one at all familiar with the Congressional District as it then existed, this old scrapbook is a political catalogue of great value.

At the election of November 8, 1904, John W. Weeks, of Newton, was elected to the Fifty-Ninth Congress, from the Twelfth Congressional District. He received 19,312 votes against 10,813 votes for Augustus Hemenway, of Canton, the Democratic candidate, and 1372 votes for the Socialist, George Elmer Littlefield, of Westwood. The District at that time consisted of the following cities and towns: Braintree, Brookline, Canton, Dedham, Dover, Foxborough, Franklin, Holbrook, Holliston, Hopedale, Hopkinton, Hyde Park, Medfield, Medway, Mendon, Milford, Millis, Needham, Newton, Norfolk, North Attleborough, Norwood, Randolph, Sharon, Sherborn, Stoughton, Upton, Walpole, Watertown, Wellesley, Westwood, Weymouth, Wrentham.

In that year Theodore Roosevelt was elected President of the United States and William L. Douglas, of

Brockton, Governor of Massachusetts. An evidence of the unstable character of the electorate is seen in the fact that while Roosevelt, Republican, carried the State by a plurality of over 89,000 votes, Douglas, Democrat, received a plurality of nearly 37,000.

It may be appropriate to say here that with the succession of Roosevelt to the Presidency in 1901, a new era in American politics began. Not only were the political problems very different in 1900 from those in 1865, but the electorate had experienced a complete transformation. New generations had been born and our population had been greatly increased by immigration from foreign countries, first from the north and then from the south of Europe. The Civil War had a far greater influence upon the political history of the country subsequent to 1865 than is generally realized. When the men were mustered out of service, young in years but hardened veterans in the sternest of experiences and prematurely matured, they were scattered North and South among our thirty-two millions of people.

At the North, through the Grand Army of the Republic, and at the South, through a similar organization, the war spirit was kept active in every community in the country, with all the convictions and prejudices inseparable therefrom. The experience on the field of battle by the men, and at home by the men and women who waited anxiously, was one never to be forgotten by that generation. The rank and file of those great armies was speedily absorbed in civil life. Many of the soldiers entered public life and were members of our State Legislatures and of both houses of Congress. In the Fifty-Fourth Congress, veterans were a majority of the Judiciary, Military Affairs, Appropriations, and Ways and Means Committees. It is a fair statement that our industrial and political life was dominated by the opinions that had been formed and hardened during the war, and even our best men, or some of them, took into the field of business and politics the rule of conduct of the battle-field, that might makes right, that the end justifies the means. Burke says somewhere: 'Wars suspend the rules of moral obligation and what is long suspended is in danger of being totally abrogated. Civil wars strike deepest of all into the manners of the people; they vitiate their politics, they pervert their natural taste and relish of equity and justice.'

Democrats and Republicans fought shoulder to shoulder in the Northern armies. Nevertheless, the North looked upon the war as a Republican war and upon the great war measures as Republican measures, and so it happened that the same spirit that animated the army in the field dominated the party in politics. An election must be carried — why? to save the country, and in that holy cause all means were justifiable that were necessary to attain that end. The Republican Party that had fought the war through was the dominating party; its politics were carried into execution with the determination and precision which characterized the movements of an army. The government which had been saved at a fearful cost was to be administered by those who had saved it as they thought best.

It was a great generation of men that the war developed. Every President from Grant to McKinley, save Arthur and Cleveland, had served in it, and Arthur was, I believe, prominent in the administration of the New York Militia, and was trained in the same school with the other Republican leaders. Is it any cause of surprise, then, that the purpose, the discipline, the determination which dominated the Union army on the battle-field should have dominated the Republican Party in politics? Thus animated, it accomplished much and also afforded much just ground for criticism, for the very reason that some of its leaders carried the ethics of war into political strife, and, with their experience, could hardly have been expected to do anything else. While that generation lived, there was nothing of doubt or uncertainty in the policies or management of the party. When that generation passed off the stage — as it did with the death of McKinley and Hanna — a new generation succeeded to the management of the affairs of state; a generation to which the war was a matter of history, rather than of experience; a generation that had not passed through that awful trial; in some ways, perhaps, a better generation, in others not so well disciplined; certainly a different one.

It was by men of this later generation that our political and social questions were to be discussed and settled. The men of the former generation could not do more than save the Nation; that certainly was a service that entitles them to our gratitude for all time: to them, other questions, by comparison, naturally seemed insignificant. Thus it happened that the men of the new generation, secure in their citizenship and threatened by no great calamity, were engaged in building a superstructure upon foundations which were laid under conditions of extreme difficulty. Meantime, the spirit of grim determination of those who, in sweat and blood, preserved the Union was succeeded by a spirit of unrest, of doubt, and of inquiry. That feeling was increasing when Roosevelt became President and was more clearly accentuated when he was nominated in 1904 and became the dominant force in our political life.

If, then, we may assume that the war spirit, as I will call it for lack of a better name, pervaded the Republican Party and the North and insured unity of action for so many years, what happened to weaken it and to make discord where, in spite of temporary lapses, comparative harmony had so long prevailed? I have suggested that the war spirit had not only grown weaker because the generation inspired by it had passed on, but also because the weakening influence was being spread over a constantly increasing number of people through the growth in our population, through the birth of new generations, and by immigration. A very potent influence in the apparent lack of unity in the Republican Party in these latter days, and one to which too little importance has been attached, has been the weakening of the war spirit accompanied by a large increase in our population, a considerable portion of which is uninfluenced by our traditions. The question might naturally be asked, if what I say about the northern section of the country be true, why is it that there has been no disintegration of the solid South? The answer is that the animosity engendered by the war was naturally very much more intense in the South than in the North and that the population in the South has not been increased by immigration to the extent that it has been in the North.

Almost all the battles were fought in the South, sections of the country were stripped bare by both armies, the fortunes of many great families were entirely destroyed, and very naturally, when the war was over, a feeling of great bitterness remained, a feeling that has been transmitted from one generation to another. For this reason we have had in the South what we would naturally expect to find under these conditions, a solid support of the Democratic Party, representing not so much allegiance to that party as an undying hostility to the Republican Party, which the Southern people hold responsible for the war, for the equally cruel experiences of the reconstruction period, and for the negro problem.

It may be added that in the South the descendants of those who lived through the Civil War feel, at least some of them, even more bitterly than their elders, because, as a result of the losses incident upon the war, they have been denied opportunities for education and a position which by inheritance is theirs, and have been compelled to turn for a bare livelihood to occupations which in the early days would have been considered ill suited to them.

That feeling of bitterness is, of course, growing weaker as new generations enter upon the duties of citizenship, but it has remained a very potent influence much longer than the corresponding influence in the North.

CHAPTER III

MR. WEEKS took his seat on December 4, 1905, upon the assembling of the first session of the Fifty-Ninth Congress. A banker by profession, it was most natural that he should have been appointed to the Committee on Banking and Currency. He was also made a member of the Committee on Expenditures in the State Department, one of the minor committees of the House.

His first appearance in debate was in the discussion of the Philippine Tariff on January 11, 1906, from which I quote, to make clear Mr. Weeks's position, at that time, in regard to our acquisition of the Philippines and his attitude upon the tariff question:

'Mr. Chairman, I should not venture to take part in this discussion if it had been confined to the bill before the committee, for I am well aware that those who have spoken and others who may speak have had opportunities to give the subject a personal scrutiny which entitles them to speak with authority. I propose to very briefly refer to another phase of the tariff which has been injected into this debate, but before doing so, as I intend to vote for this bill, I wish to put on record my reasons for favoring its adoption.

'We frequently hear repeated the statement that if Admiral Dewey, having found and destroyed the Spanish fleet, as he was ordered to do, had then sailed away, the Philippine question would have been settled then

and there, but such a suggestion, made as an after-
thought, does not do justice to the situation which we
had to face. In time of war it is a duty to damage the
resources of the enemy as well as the enemy himself, and
I believe that it would have been bad tactics to have
turned our backs on a captured dependency of the enemy which was a source of revenue and which might
have been used as a base in future operations before
the end of the war, and we should remember that the
Spanish fleet was destroyed and Manila captured
months before peace was made. Moreover, there was
another vital reason why this course was not practicable. Admiral Dewey had been ordered to leave Hong-
kong, a neutral port, within forty-eight hours, so he
could not have returned there or have gone to any other
neutral port without being either warned away or in-
terned; his only resource would have been to go to
Hawaii, which, if our Democratic friends had prevailed,
would not have been available, or to return to an
American port, leaving Manila and all of the foreign
interests there liable to pillage and destruction. I doubt
if there is a Member of this House who, if he had
had the responsibility of acting at that time, whatever
might have been his judgment or wishes as to the future of the islands, would have taken any other course.
There was then and is now a great diversity of opinion
among the people of this country as to the advisability
of retaining these islands, and while I would welcome
any honorable and practical suggestion to get them off
our hands, I see no such way at present, and I doubt if
there has been a day since that eventful May morning
in 1898 when we could have turned them over to others
with honor or credit to ourselves or to the advantage

of the Filipinos; furthermore, such policy as we have
formulated indicates that we are likely to hold the
islands for years, if not perpetually; therefore, whether
we like them or not, whether they are a desirable acquisition or not, I believe that we have reached a stage
in the development of this question when we should
cease treating them as half American and half foreign,
and, being in complete control, with peace prevailing
throughout the islands, I cannot see why they should
not be treated as have been Alaska, Hawaii, and Porto
Rico.'

In order that Mr. Weeks's ultimate position upon our
relations with the Philippine Islands may be known, it
may be well to interpolate here that when in 1924 he
was Secretary of War and had an official responsibility
in the matter, he said to a Congressional Committee
that 'the present advantage of the Filipinos in their relations was reason enough for our retaining them,' and
called attention to the fact that they would suffer very
much if, as an independent nation, they were compelled
to pay duties on imports of sugar and tobacco into this
country, and to market their bonds without our moral
guaranty that they would be paid. He added that business in the Philippines was largely in the hands of for-
eigners; that capital was needed to develop the resources of the islands which would not be forthcoming
unless we should make it understood that we intend to
hold them for twenty-five or thirty years to come. Secretary Weeks also opposed any action excepting, when
the time should come, complete independence and complete divorce from any responsibility, of the United
States.

Returning now to that part of his speech that dealt with the tariff, Mr. Weeks said:

'... We believe that tariffs should be changed from time to time to meet conditions and we believe this is one of those times, so we are going to continue to call this fact to the attention of our fellow Republicans until action is taken.

'But the fear of Democratic attempts to revise the tariff were only incidents among the reasons which prompted this action. It was taken notwithstanding a firm belief that the Dingley Tariff was the most scientific and has proven the best tariff ever adopted by Congress, added to the knowledge that in many respects at least it is still, as a revenue producer and protector of labor, difficult to improve upon; but it is apparent to any one in touch with the business affairs of this country that never in its history have there been such radical changes in the manner of conducting the public corporation or great transportation companies as have taken place in the last eight years, and that many of these changes have produced conditions which prevent the necessity for the continuance of the present schedules.

'I shall be glad to take up this subject in detail at some more opportune time, but for the moment I will instance one example, the duty on hides, to illustrate the point which I wish to make. For twenty-five years there was no duty on hides, and if there were any necessity for it when the Dingley Bill was enacted, I believe that necessity has passed; the control of the hide market has passed from the producer to the packer. I am doubtful whether the producer receives any benefit whatever from the duty, but in any case the tanners and manufacturers of shoes in Massachusetts believe that a removal of the duty will assist them to increase the exportation of shoes; and to remove any lurking fear that this is an entirely selfish move from which the consumer is to receive no benefit, I believe I am stating the substantially unanimous willingness of the shoemakers of Massachusetts in making the suggestion that they will gladly agree to a reduction of the duty on shoes equivalent to the amount removed from hides. In many cases the whole duty could be removed; in others, in the cheaper grades of shoes, less reduction should be made. This suggestion is not made in a haphazard way, but as the result of a canvass, and further it is believed that if the duty were entirely removed from hides and an equivalent amount from shoes that the shoemaker could easily continue to control this market and increase exportations in the next ten years from $8,000,000 exported last year, to $50,000,000, and as the labor item is about 25 per cent of the cost of shoes it follows that $10,000,000 from this source alone would be added to the wages of the laboring men of this country.

'We have become, under the provisions of the Dingley Bill, a great manufacturing nation, and such changes as the one I have mentioned will, in my judgment, secure what we have and provide an opening for a large increase.

'The people of Massachusetts are not unmindful of the fact that there are now in this House, in the full strength of their capacity and possessing an experience which is invaluable, many of those men who were active, indeed vital factors, in framing the Dingley Bill, and they want the benefit of the ripe experience of these men in the revised edition which would come from their hands.

'The minority leader of this House stated on this floor the other day that the trouble with the people of this country was that they were tired of the Republican Party and afraid of the Democratic Party. I subscribe to the last part of that statement without hesitation or reservation, and I have a lurking fear that the first part may come true if we do not follow common business procedure and adopt ordinary business foresight in making repairs while they can be made safely and economically. The wise owner of a mill never delays replacing a doubtful piece of his machinery while his force is intact and competent to do the work, even though the necessary shut down may cause a temporary loss. He would be a fool to wait until his boiler had exploded, killing or crippling his engineer force and compelling him to resort to the inexperienced and inefficient to make his repairs and renewals.'

On February 8, 1906, a vote was taken on a bill to amend an act entitled 'AN ACT to regulate commerce, approved Feb. 4, 1887, and all acts amendatory thereof; and to enlarge the powers of the Interstate Commerce Commission.' This was the so-called 'Rate Bill' of that day. It passed the House by a vote of 346 to 7. Mr. Weeks voted against the bill. I mention this fact as an indication of his courage. Legislation on this subject had been progressive in its character, and the first act of importance was passed in 1866, forty years before the above act became a law and three years before the completion of the Union Pacific Railroad. It established the principle of continuous lines of traffic in interstate commerce.

In 1868 the House Committee on Roads and Canals,

as it was then called, submitted a report in which was favored a liberal interpretation of the powers of Congress over interstate commerce. Meanwhile the movement got some popular support in the organization of the Patrons of Husbandry. In 1872 the State Grange of Iowa was founded, and by the close of that year thirteen hundred granges, more or less, had been organized in various parts of the country. In two years more the order had spread over the whole country, with an aggregate of over twenty thousand lodges. In 1874 the Grand Master, alluding in his address to the exorbitant and varying rates, discrimination, and uncertainties then existing in railroad rates, said: 'When we plant a crop we can only guess what it will cost to send it to market, for we are the slaves of those whom we created.'

A recommendation in the President's Message of December, 1872, led to the appointment of a Senate committee of seven, known as the Windom Committee. The report of this committee contains the first presentation of a comprehensive plan of regulation of the whole subject of commerce between the States as conducted since the introduction of railroads.

In the President's Message of 1872 and in the report of the Windom Committee, the fundamental measure recommended included publicity of rates, prohibition of combinations and of stock-watering, and the inhibition of a greater charge for a shorter than a longer haul over the same line, and reforms in the shipment of grain and in the operation of freight.

In 1876 the doctrine was enunciated by the Supreme Court in the so-called 'Granger Cases,' declaratory, in part at least, of the common law that railroad companies were carriers for hire and as such were engaged in a public employment affecting the public interests and were subject to legislative control, as to their rates of fare and freight, unless protected by their own charters therefrom, and that as carriers they must carry when called upon to do so and can charge only a reasonable sum for the carriage.

In 1878 the Reagan Bill, which appeared in the process of evolution, was introduced. Discussion in and outside of Congress resulted in the appointment of the Cullom Committee, whose report in 1886 was, in a sense, the corner-stone of the act to regulate interstate commerce. The chief ground of contention was not so much as to rates as to discriminations in their various forms.

Prior to the enactment of the interstate commerce law in 1887, the Government exercised no supervision over interstate railway rates. Under the act, the Interstate Commerce Commission assumed that the power to pass upon the reasonableness of a rate carried with it the right to fix a rate to take its place, until the Supreme Court held in the Maximum-Rate Case in 1896, that 'the power to prescribe rates or fix any tariff is not among the powers granted to the Commission.' This practically withheld from the Commission any effective control over rates.

On February 19, 1903, the Elkins Bill was passed, making the published rates conclusive against the carrier and every deviation from such rates punishable. The scope of the act was extended as to parties subject to its provisions and fine was substituted for imprisonment in the penal provisions of the act. This act was very effective in stopping rebating.

For the purpose of remedying the defects found to

exist in the original interstate commerce act, and after prolonged discussion, the Hepburn Bill was passed in June, 1906, against which Mr. Weeks voted, as above stated.

Perhaps the most important change in the law was that conferring upon the Commission power to fix the maximum rate to be charged. The absence of this right had destroyed the effectiveness of the rate-making power of the Commission. Its presence made the Interstate Commerce Commission a very much more authoritative body. It had been urged by President Roosevelt and was emphatically an administration measure. To oppose it was to invite the adverse judgment of its proponents, but Mr. Weeks thought that it was open to objections among which was that the bill did not give an affirmative right of appeal to the courts, and so he voted against it.

After the bill had been debated and discussed in conference between the two houses, and the defects, as Mr. Weeks thought, removed, he voted in favor of the final conference report and the bill became a law on June 30, 1906.

On March 24, 1906, the House began the consideration of a bill granting authority to the Secretary of the Navy, in his discretion, to dismiss midshipmen from the United States Naval Academy and regulating the procedure and punishment in trials for hazing at the said Academy. This was a subject with which Mr. Weeks was very familiar and the House was ready and anxious to hear from any one who could speak with authority.

He once told me that this was his first utterance which brought him into prominence in the House. The speech was a short one, but it was most effective, and the bill passed. Mr. Weeks spoke as follows:

'Mr. Speaker, under ordinary circumstances, when a committee of this House has given careful and intelligent attention to a matter such as has been given to this bill by the Committee on Naval Affairs, I should not presume to take any time of the House; but having entered at Annapolis, in the Naval Academy of the United States, with four years' service there, and having been a graduate of the Academy twenty-five years ago, I therefore presume the House will be willing to listen to my own experience for a very few minutes, because that judgment may be worth having.

'Now, there has been a vast amount of hysteria on this subject of hazing which has been going on at the Naval Academy all the time for the last thirty years, and, each time there has been a violent outbreak, it has been responded to by Congress by enacting some law. In 1874 a law was passed, which was referred to. It was practically the result of an outbreak of hazing in the Naval Academy, and was one of the most drastic and unjust laws, in my opinion, ever enacted by anybody, without care and without investigation, which has been given to this country. There was no distinction in hazing made, and there was no option to the court-martial which tried any man.

'Now, as a matter of fact, hazing differs as widely as a West Indian hurricane does from a gentle summer zephyr. Ninety-five per cent of the hazing practiced at the Naval Academy and at West Point is simply a collection of boyish pranks. Five per cent of it may be violent. I do not know any man in the Navy or out of the Navy who is not in favor of punishing violent hazing by dismissal from the Naval Academy or by any other severe punishment. But I wish to say to you that to punish the ordinary hazing by dismissal, to permit to remain on the statute books a law which provides that in any case where a cadet is found guilty there shall be no less punishment than dismissal, is unjust and unfair. It is only in cases in the Navy of a deserter where, in case the man is found guilty, the court-martial is compelled to dismiss him from the service.

'In 1903 Congress enacted another hasty law in regard to hazing; passed it so hastily that it forgot to repeal the previous legislation, with the result that the Secretary of the Navy, when this outbreak which has recently taken place at Annapolis occurred and he was looking to see what course he should take, referred these two laws to the Attorney-General, who decided that the law of 1874 was in force and the one which was passed in 1903 was not, and that any action that was taken must be taken under that. Now, the result has been the court-martials, which we have read about, in the Naval Academy.

'Now, the point that I have in my mind is this: That the law prepared by the Naval Committee is an infinitely superior law to those now on the statute books. Those laws ought to be repealed and this law enacted. It is not such a law as I would offer myself, exactly, because I believe in limiting the authority to one person, and if I had the drawing of this bill, I would have made it so that the Superintendent of the Naval Academy, who is the responsible discipline officer of the Naval Academy, should have had full authority to punish cadets and to dismiss them. But I expect to vote for a great many laws which are not in exactly the form that

I would make them if I drew them myself. For that reason I wish to say to this House that, in my judgment, this bill, prepared after careful investigation by the Naval Committee, should be passed.'

During this session, Mr. Weeks spoke upon the following subjects: Acquirement of land at Deer Island, the District of Columbia police force, the Geological Survey, hazing at the Naval Academy, National Bank loans, the Naval Appropriation Bill, and the Philippine Tariff Bill.

The following letter, written in 1906 to the Secretary of the Unity Club of Lancaster, New Hampshire, explains itself:

'I have received your letter of March 27, enclosing a copy of the resolution adopted by the Unity Club, March 26, referring to my proposed gift of a library building to the Town of Lancaster in memory of my Father. I wish to assure you that I appreciate not only the resolution of the Club, but also your own personal sentiments, both of which I am sure are sincere.

'It is a great satisfaction to me to be able to do what I propose to do, not only for the Town of Lancaster but in memory of my Father, whose example and advice are largely responsible for whatever success I have had. You can imagine that it is with more than ordinary pride that I am able to say that in all my somewhat varied experiences with men since I left my home in Lancaster, twenty-nine years ago, I have never met or known a man who seemed to me to so thoroughly deserve the respect and admiration of mankind as did he, and I shall be a little short of an ingrate if I do not do whatever I can to keep his memory alive, at least among those who knew him or knew of him.'

During this first session of the Fifty-Ninth Congress there were passed the following important matters of legislation: The Rate Bill, the Meat Inspection Law, the Pure Food Law, the Immunity Bill, so-called, and the Naturalization Bill.

A characteristic expression of Mr. Weeks's attitude toward legislation is found in a letter written at about this time in answer to questions asked by a constituent:

'The first question is — "If elected a member of the Congress of the United States, will you as a member of that body use your influence and vote towards securing the passage of a law which will prevent the abuse of the power of injunction by Federal judges in labor disputes?"

'Relative to this question, I can make no distinct pledge. Generally speaking, I am opposed to limiting the power of the courts and while a bill may be so framed that it will meet the wishes of yourself and those you represent, which I could support, I cannot put myself in the position of pledging myself to support legislation of this character.

'The second question — "If elected a member of Congress of the United States will you as a member of this body use your influence and vote toward securing the passage of a law which will prevent railroad companies engaged in interstate commerce from working their employees engaged in the operation of trains an excessive number of hours?"

'Replying to this question, I wish to say that I am entirely in sympathy with the purposes of this question and I have no doubt that I shall approve of the legislation which may be proposed to correct any abuses in this direction, but as in the previous case, I do not wish to pledge myself to vote for any distinct proposition until I have seen the act itself. I am glad, however, of the opportunity to say to you and your fellow railroad men this — that while I have great hesitation to pledge myself (in fact, I never have in any single instance done so) to support any specific legislation, I do, when Congress is in session, devote my entire time to the work of Congress; that I study the details of legislation which is likely to be enacted with the greatest care and I propose to vote on all matters in such a way that the great majority of the people of this country will be benefited. I have supported labor matters and labor legislation, and doubtless shall do so in many other cases. On the other hand, I am quite sure that some form of labor legislation I shall feel called upon to oppose, as I did the matter which I am being criticized for — that is, the extension of the eight-hour law to alien labor on the Isthmus of Panama.

'My judgment was then and is now that it was entirely unjustifiable to make this extension, although I thoroughly believe in the eight-hour law for Government employees who are American citizens.'

The second session of the Fifty-Ninth Congress met on December 3, 1906, and ended on March 4, 1907. Mr. Weeks's committees were the same as in the previous session: 'Banking and Currency' and 'Expenditures in the State Department.'

A graduate of the Naval Academy, Mr. Weeks was naturally interested in and well informed upon all matters relating to the Navy. In the course of a speech he made on this subject, he said on February 15, 1907:

'Mr. Chairman, the determination of a naval policy should be based on the necessity for a navy and the possibility of being brought into contact with other countries. If there is no such possibility we are extremely foolish to expend the large amounts of money which are now being appropriated for our Navy. It could be better devoted to other purposes. But if there is any possibility of our having trouble with other nations, we might as well face that proposition and consider just exactly what our policy should be. We are seeing and are going to continue to see great industrial and military development in the East, and we should consider whether we are able to defend our commerce, our insular possessions, and our Pacific coast against every eastern country or probable combination of them. We are not in a satisfactory position in our relation with oriental countries, for we do not treat them as we do the most-favored nation, but rather as we treat the least-favored nation. It is undoubtedly true that our treatment of China, with the single exception of excluding coolie labor, has been more rational and fairer than the treatment which has been accorded China by any other first-class power, but the fact remains that even though this be true, we do not consider questions which arise with China on the same plane that we do similar questions with other countries. We may naturally expect sooner or later that they will resent such treatment, and as to Japan, we are now in the midst of a decidedly live and irritating question which may at any time cause serious trouble. It is folly to attempt to delude ourselves with the idea that this is not serious. We are trying to build up a large trade with these eastern countries, and at the same time we announce to them that we are not going to give them the same privileges which we give European countries. The people of a large section of our country are opposed to the admis-

sion of Japanese labor, and this very morning we have
read in the papers that a delegation representing these
people are urging their position to the President. Japan
has proved that it is a great military power, and the
people of Japan and the Japanese Government may
naturally be sensitive relative to any proposition which
is going to militate against the Japanese people.

'I am not for one moment considering the merits
or demerits of this live question whether we should or
should not limit Japanese labor; but if we are not going
to do it, if we are not going to treat the Japanese as we
treat the Hun and the Pole, and, in fact, every other
people of Europe, then we may expect that Japan will
resent it. They may not resent it with force now, but
it is our duty to assume that they will later, and to prepare for just that possibility. As between the Japanese
navy and our Navy to-day, I believe that we are prepared; but Japan is continuing to build. It has outlined
a building policy. It has already one ship of the Dread-
nought class, and it has recently given a contract for
another; and if we do not maintain our present relative
position we are simply flying in the face of Providence
by neglecting to perform a duty which must be apparent
to almost any one, even to a professional peacemaker.
If we do not perform that duty we shall deserve, and
very likely have to face, a national humiliation greater
than this country has ever felt.

'Again, we know that we are in active competition
with the great eastern nations for the trade of the world,
and I hope very shortly to be in active competition
with them for the world's commerce. Financial disagreements produce about nine-tenths of the differences between men, and in future commercial troubles will pro-

duce nine-tenths of the differences between civilized nations. That being the case, it is our business to consider whether we are in position to maintain our commercial rights, to protect our trade and our commerce against the great nations of Europe. If we are in that position, let us maintain it. If we are not in such a position, we should be up and doing without delay. I believe we are relatively in a good position, but every European nation of the first rank is increasing its navy. Most of them have definite building policies. I wish they would stop. I have no doubt a great majority of the Members of this House feel as I do. But until they do stop, or show some indication that they have reached the limit of their developing policy in the way of armament, we cannot afford to follow any other course than to do as they are doing. If we do stop, we shall endanger the peace. If we keep on building, we shall, in all probability, keep the peace. And it is infinitely better, and cheaper for that matter, to prepare for war and not fight, than to go unprepared and be obliged to fight, and probably be humiliated as a result of war.

'I believe the Spanish War would have been impossible if Spain had comprehended our naval strength, and it would have been wiser, and even cheaper, for us to have maintained a navy twice as strong as was ours before 1898 rather than to have fought the war and brought on ourselves the expenses and troubles which our eastern possessions have brought us and will continue to bring us until we, in some honorable manner, manage to get rid of them.'

Mr. Weeks made a very characteristic speech on February 27, 1907, upon the Merchant Marine Bill then pending and subsequently defeated, in the course of which he said:

'Mr. Chairman, it must be admitted that it is a matter of some speculation just what legislation should be adopted to give the greatest impetus to our merchant marine and to put us in more direct communication with markets which are now reached either through indirect channels or not at all. The fact is, however, and it must be apparent to every one, that our merchant marine is at its lowest possible stage and that our direct communications with various sections of the world, especially those South American countries which should be among our best markets, and for whose products we should supply a market, are extremely unsatisfactory. If any business man were managing the entire business affairs of the United States, and there were millions of people producing a billion dollars of foreign trade, as is the case in South America, with whom he had no satisfactory connections, he would be utterly lacking in enterprise if he did not at once attempt to obtain some part of that trade; and even though his first attempts might be failures, he would continue to modify his methods until he had obtained a reasonable share of it. Adopting the same reasoning, I am in favor of passing this bill reported from the Committee on the Merchant Marine, although in many respects it lacks what I believe are the good qualities contained in the bill passed by the Senate last winter. Among the objections to it there are very many which apply to the principles involved in this legislation. As these objections will be discussed by others, I do not propose to consider them; but I am specially interested in and am going to speak briefly on that part of this legislation which applied directly to the establishment of a national naval reserve. This part of the subject has not been given the consideration which it deserves, neither has it met the criticisms which have been made against other parts of the bill. In fact, in my search for reasons why a national naval reserve should not be established I am confined almost entirely to the objections which have been made by Mr. Samuel Gompers, the president of the American Federation of Labor, a gentleman well known to many Members of this House. . . .

'To summarize: If this bill passes and the steamship lines authorized by it are established, it will prevent the waste which was so evident at the beginning of the Spanish War in providing auxiliaries for our fleet; it will furnish vessels which can be transferred into scouts, or even cruisers, if it is necessary to do so, and it will supply a reserve for our permanent naval establishment without which it will be necessary to largely increase the number of men in the permanent establishment, or leave ourselves in the position of having built men-of-war which we have no means of manning. Instead of manning parts of our fleet which will be put in reserve, provided there are reserve men to man them, I believe that I have conclusively shown that a saving of about $4,000,000 annually can be made. This is more than the entire appropriation for subsidies called for by the bill, and would in itself, in my judgment, justify the passage of the bill if there were no other reasons for its passage.'

During this short session, he spoke on National Bank loans on real estate, the Navy Appropriation Bill, pension agencies, service pensions, ship subsidy, and incidental subjects.

CHAPTER IV

Elected to Sixtieth Congress — Financial legislation foreshadowed — Panic of October, 1907 — Aldrich-Vreeland Bill — Secret service and President Roosevelt — Appalachian-White Mountain forest legislation — Letter to Gifford Pinchot — Speaker Cannon's attitude — Payne-Aldrich Tariff Bill — Mr. Weeks, Chairman of the Committee on the Post Office and Post Roads — Cannonism.

MR. WEEKS was elected to the Sixtieth Congress at the election of November 6, 1906, by a vote of 18,948 against 10,591 for David W. Murray, of Hyde Park, Democrat, and 1289 for Calvin C. Jordan, Socialist, of Weymouth.

Curtis Guild, Jr., had succeeded William L. Douglas as Governor of Massachusetts.

The first session of the Sixtieth Congress met on December 2, 1907. Mr. Weeks was again a member of the Committee on Banking and Currency and on Expenditures in the Department of State, and was also made a member of the Committee on Agriculture which led to very important results.

A foreshadowing of his views of the situation regarding financial legislation is reflected in the following extract from a letter which he wrote on December 7, 1907:

'The Comptroller of the Currency is going to recommend in his annual report a Central Bank, and that idea has many friends among those who are best qualified to pass on this question, but it is pretty nearly the universal opinion here that the adoption of legislation providing for a Central Bank is impossible. There is a great amount of prejudice against it, especially from those representing the West and South, and in this period of denunciation of centralization it would be unusually difficult to get even as sane a proposition as this favorably considered. In fact, any bank or currency legislation must be obtained as a result of some serious condition, such as we have just been going through.'

He came into considerable prominence in this session by reason of the part he took in the preparation and passage of the so-called Aldrich-Vreeland Bill, which led to the creation of the Federal Reserve System. Let Mr. Weeks explain his views of conditions which made necessary the passage of the Vreeland Bill, as it was known in the House, expressed in his speech of May 14, 1908:

'Mr. Speaker, about the middle of last October rumors circulated questioning the solvency of certain national banks located in New York City, followed by the failure of a large trust company, precipitating the worst financial panic which this country has seen. It is easy to demonstrate that the reasons for this panic were similar to those which have obtained in almost every other financial crisis in which this country has been involved, and they would also apply to panics the world over. They were, generally speaking, due to overspeculation, overcapitalization, overexpenditures by the Government, States, and municipalities, as well as by individuals; the tying up of large amounts of capital in permanent fixtures instead of retaining it as liquid capital, the carrying of excessive stocks of goods, the abnormal development of business in every branch, all of which led to the credit expansion of the dollar to the breaking point. Many other reasons were assigned for this collapse; and while they may have been, in some slight degree, instrumental in bringing it about, there can be no question that the reasons just given were paramount in precipitating it, and that it would have developed sooner or later, as a result of some comparatively insignificant accident, if the bank troubles referred to had not happened.

'Credit having broken down, the natural and usual result followed. Country banks became suspicious of their reserve correspondents and commenced to draw home their reserves, continuing this policy until the reserve which most of them had on hand greatly exceeded the amount which the law requires them to carry. Individuals in all parts of the country became alarmed and drew their deposits from the banks, not to deposit them elsewhere, but to hoard the currency. This process was continued until, to prevent a total collapse, it became necessary for the banks in central reserve cities to issue clearing-house certificates, which action was followed by the clearing-house associations in every reserve city in the United States. Banks in reserve cities, and especially those in New York, have been severely criticized because they did not respond to all demands for currency. The most casual examination of consolidated bank statements would show the most ignorant person how impossible it would be to meet any such demand. . . .

'In preparing the Vreeland Bill, or at least that part of it which provides for an emergency currency, the committee has kept in mind certain phases of this question in which there has been practical unanimity, and has arrived at its conclusions after considering them, and it especially calls attention to the following:

'"1. That the volume of currency now in circulation, which is larger per capita than ever before in this country and larger per capita than that enjoyed by any nation in Europe, is quite adequate for the ordinary demands of business, and therefore there should not be any permanent additions to it.

'"2. That if additions are made in the form of emergency currency, they should take such form that the currency will not be readily distinguished from money now actually in use; for if this were done, the very appearance of the new currency might occasion alarm and defeat the purpose for which it was issued.

'"3. As panics come on suddenly, frequently without any warning whatever, this currency should be prepared for immediate use and so located that it could be used in the locality where needed without any delay whatever.

'"4. That it should be so taxed, or otherwise circumscribed, that as soon as the demand for it ceased it would be automatically retired."

'All of these conditions are provided for in the Vreeland Bill. It takes advantage of the methods of segregating assets which have been used so successfully in issuing clearing-house certificates in the past, issuing certificates against those assets, and provides for an issue of circulation, basing this circulation on the clearing-house certificates authorized in the first step....'

The bill passed the House. Some changes were made in the Senate, whereupon a conference was had. Edward B. Vreeland, Theodore E. Burton, and John W. Weeks were the conferees on the part of the House. Their report was presented to the House on May 27, 1908. One of the provisions added to the bill in the Senate was the following: 'That a commission is hereby created to be called the National Monetary Commission to be composed of nine members of the Senate and nine members of the House of Representatives ... that it shall be the duty of this commission to inquire into and report to Congress at the earliest date practicable what changes are necessary or desirable in the monetary system of the United States, or in the law relating to Banking and Currency.'

The act by its terms expired by limitation on June 30, 1914, so that it became necessary for the Commission to report within that time. Upon that point, Mr. Weeks said in a speech he made on the subject May 27, 1908:

'Again, there is one feature which the gentleman from New York did not refer to that I wish to call your attention to, and that is the time limit placed upon the life of this bill. There has been a great deal of criticism because that was not done in the Vreeland Bill. The time limit in this case is six years. A commission is provided for, which is supposed to study this question from every standpoint, and, if radical changes are necessary in our currency system, as many believe, the commission will file its report before six years — I presume in two years, and I hope within one year — whatever their findings may be. But in any case this bill provides for, and is, a temporary measure. It is not intended that it should be permanent law. Recognizing that idea, the conferees have agreed to make the time limit which it shall remain on the statute books six years.'

The conference report passed the House May 27, 1908, by a party vote of 166 to 140.

The investigations and report of the Monetary Commission, of which Mr. Weeks was a member, made possible the creation of the Federal Reserve Bank System in 1914, during a Democratic administration. The Aldrich-Vreeland Bill, the life of which was extended for that purpose, made possible also our financing during the early days of the Great War before the Federal Reserve Act became operative.

In the first session of the Sixtieth Congress, Mr. Weeks spoke on the Aldrich-Vreeland Bill, forest preservation, Navy pay increase; in favor of a naval station at Pearl Harbor, Hawaii; soil surveys, and incidental subjects.

The second session of the Sixtieth Congress began on December 7, 1908, and ended March 4, 1909.

Early in the session an incident occurred, now generally forgotten, which aroused prolonged discussion in the House and action, in which Mr. Weeks had a prominent part. It appeared that in President Roosevelt's Message, read in Congress on December 7, 1908, he said, among other things:

'Last year an amendment was incorporated in the measure providing for the Secret Service, which provided that there should be no detail from the Secret Service and no transfer therefrom. It is not too much to say that this amendment has been of benefit only, and could be of benefit only, to the criminal classes. If deliberately introduced for the purpose of diminishing the effectiveness of war against crime it could not have been better devised to this end. It forbade the practices that had been followed to a greater or less extent by the executive heads of various departments for twenty years. To these practices we owe the securing of the evidence which enabled us to drive great lotteries out of business and secure a quarter of a million of dollars in fines from their promoters. These practices have enabled us to discover some of the most outrageous frauds in connection with the theft of government land and government timber by great corporations and by in-

dividuals. These practices have enabled us to get some
of the evidence indispensable in order to secure the conviction of the wealthiest and most formidable criminals
with whom the Government has to deal, both those
operating in violation of the anti-trust law and others.
The amendment in question was of benefit to no one
excepting to these criminals, and it seriously hampers
the Government in the detection of crime and the securing of justice. Moreover, it not only affects departments outside of the Treasury, but it tends to hamper
the Secretary of the Treasury himself in the effort to
utilize the employees of his department so as to best
meet the requirements of the public service. It forbids
him from preventing frauds upon the customs service,
from investigating irregularities in branch mints and
assay offices, and has seriously crippled him. It prevents the promotion of employees in the Secret Service,
and this further discourages good effort. In its present
form the restriction operates only to the advantage of
the criminal, of the wrongdoer. The chief argument in
favor of the provision was that the Congressmen did
not themselves wish to be investigated by secret-service
men. Very little of such investigation has been done in
the past; but it is true that the work of the secret-
service agents was partly responsible for the indictment
and conviction of a Senator and a Congressman for land
frauds in Oregon. I do not believe that it is in the public
interest to protect criminals in any branch of the public
service, and exactly as we have again and again during
the past seven years prosecuted and convicted such
criminals who were in the executive branch of the
Government, so in my belief we should be given ample
means to prosecute them if found in the legislative

branch. But if this is not considered desirable a special exception could be made in the law prohibiting the use of the secret-service force in investigating members of the Congress. It would be far better to do this than to do what actually was done, and strive to prevent or at least to hamper effective action against criminals by the executive branch of the Government.'

This language gave great umbrage to many of the members of the House.

On December 11, 1908, Mr. James Breck Perkins, of New York, offered the following privileged motion:

'Whereas there was contained in the sundry civil appropriation bill, which passed Congress at its last session and became a law, a provision in reference to the employment of the Secret Service in the Treasury Department; and

'Whereas in the message of the President of the United States to the two Houses of Congress it was stated in reference to that provision:

'"It is not too much to say that this amendment has been of benefit only, and could be of benefit only, to the criminal classes," and it was further stated, "The chief argument in favor of the provision was that the Congressmen did not themselves wish to be investigated by Secret Service men," and it was further stated, "But if this is not considered desirable a special exception could be made in the law, prohibiting the use of the Secret Service force in investigating Members of Congress. It would be far better to do this than to do what actually was done, and strive to prevent or at least hamper effective action against criminals by the executive branch of the Government"; Now, therefore be it

'Resolved, That a committee of five Members of this House be appointed by the Speaker, to consider the statements contained in the message of the President and report to the House what action, if any, should be taken in reference thereto.'

The resolution was agreed to and the Speaker appointed the following committee: Mr. Perkins, Mr. Edwin Denby, later Secretary of the Navy in President Harding's Cabinet; Mr. Weeks, Republicans; Mr. John Sharp Williams, later a Senator, and Mr. Lloyd, Democrats.

This committee reported in the form of a privileged resolution introduced by Mr. Perkins on January 8, 1909, in which, after quoting the paragraph in the President's Message objected to, the resolution continued:

'Understanding this language to be a reflection on the integrity of its membership, and aware of its own constitutional duty as to its membership, the House in respectful terms called on the President for any information that would justify the language of the Message or assist it in its constitutional duty to purge itself of corruption.

'The President in his Message of January 4 denies that the paragraph of the Annual Message casts reflections on the integrity of this House; attributes to the House "an entire failure to understand my Message"; declares that he has made no charge of corruption against any Member of the House, and by implication states that he has no proof of corruption on the part of any Member of this House.

'Whether the House in its resolution of December 17, 1908, correctly interpreted the meaning of the words used by the President in his Annual Message, or whether it misunderstood that language, as the President implies, will be judged now and in the future according to the accepted interpretations of the English language. This House, charged only with its responsibility to the people of the United States and its obligation to transmit unimpaired to the future the representative institutions inherited from the past, and to preserve its own dignity, must insist on its own capacity to understand the import of the President's language. We consider the language of the President in his Message of December 8, 1908, unjustified and without basis of fact and that it constitutes a breach of the privileges of the House: Therefore be it

'Resolved, That the House, in the exercise of its constitutional prerogatives, declines to consider any communication from any source which is not in its own judgment respectful; and be it further

'Resolved, That the special committee and the Committee of the Whole House on the state of the Union be discharged from any consideration of so much of the President's Message as relates to the Secret Service, and is above set forth, and that the said portion of the Message be laid on the table; and be it further

'Resolved, That the Message of the President sent to the House on January 4, 1909, being unresponsive to the inquiry of the House and constituting an invasion of the privileges of this House by questioning the motives and intelligence of Members in the exercise of their constitutional rights and functions, be laid on the table.'

After a very extended debate, the resolution passed by a vote of 212 to 36 — 135 members not voting

A single sentence from the speech of Mr. Weeks expresses his attitude: 'I do not yield to the gentleman [an opponent of the resolution] in my admiration of the President or of his great qualities, but I occasionally take issue with certain things the President does and says, and this resolution, which is reported to the House, in my opinion, justly takes issue with his Message of December 7.'

On February 3, 1909, a bill providing for the Appalachian-White Mountain Forest Reservation was reported to the House from the Committee on Agriculture, Mr. Scott, of Iowa, the accomplished Chairman of the Committee, being one of the dissenters. On March 1 Mr. Weeks moved to suspend the rule and pass the bill. This subject had been before Congress in one form or another for several years. In 1900 it had been proposed that the Government should purchase land in the White Mountain and Appalachian Mountain watersheds. Bills passed the Senate repeatedly, but not the House, where they were referred to the Committee on Agriculture which, in accordance with Speaker Cannon's views, was so organized as to be hostile to this legislation.

The Speaker, however, had so high an opinion of Mr. Weeks that he made him a member of the Committee on Agriculture in the Sixtieth Congress, although he knew he was in favor of the principle embodied in these bills, and so it happened that Weeks took charge of the bill in the House as explained in a letter to me from Mr. Scott in which he said: 'In the matter of the White Mountain-Appalachian Bill, I remember, of course, that it was drawn by Mr. Weeks and owed its passage entirely to his activity. I was opposed to it as chairman of the Com-

mittee, but the Committee made a favorable report
upon it and when it got into the House, I naturally
turned the management of it over to Mr. Weeks.'

After a very extended debate covering fifty pages of
the 'Congressional Record,' the bill passed the House by
a vote of 157 to 147, the leaders on the Republican side
being for the most part against it. A change of five votes
would have defeated it. Mr. Weeks marshaled the
forces of the North and of the South so effectively that
this great measure of conservation was ultimately enacted into law on March 1, 1911. The title of the act
was: 'AN ACT to enable any State to coöperate with any
other State or States or with the United States for the
protection of the watersheds of navigable streams and
to appoint a commission for the acquisition of lands for
the purpose of conserving the navigability of navigable
rivers.'

As this is one of the most important matters of legislation with which Mr. Weeks's name is connected,
without whose support it could not have been enacted
into law, his own account of his relation to it is very
interesting. It is contained in a letter written by him
to Mr. Gifford Pinchot, dated June 18, 1912, which is
substantially as follows:

'Although I was born and brought up in the country,
and in the White Mountain region, I did not have any
other interest in forestry problems than that which
comes from inheritance and environment under such
conditions until I came to Washington to take my seat
in the Fifty-Ninth Congress. As you very well know,
new Members are not of the first importance here, and
very frequently they wonder, especially if they have
been busy men, employed in comparatively large under-

takings, why they are here at all, and quite as frequently
they look around for something of reasonable importance with which they can become connected and perform some kind of good public service. Almost the first
thing which attracted my attention was the Forestry
Service. I commenced to look it up along general lines
and soon ascertained the situation which obtained relating to the White Mountain and Appalachian bills,
coming to the conclusion that if any result was to be obtained it must mean coöperation between the Eastern
and Southern sections of the country. As you know, attempts have been made for nearly twenty years to get
some kind of legislation for forestry protection for these
regions, but they had not been undertaken with sufficient energy or under such conditions that any favorable
result had been secured. I regret that I have not at
hand the date of the introduction of the different bills
relating to this subject, with which I was connected, or
of the hearings which were given on those bills, although
I could have that looked up very easily if doing so would
be any particular trouble to you, and will be glad to do
so if you wish the information and will so advise me.
Generally speaking, the older Members of the House,
those recognized as the leaders on both sides, were opposed to this legislation and voted against it when final
action was taken. It was equally true in the case of Mr.
Clark, Mr. Williams, and other Democratic Members
as it was in the case of Mr. Cannon, Mr. Dalzell, Mr.
Payne, and Mr. Tawney on the Republican side, so
that it was not only necessary to get the Members
stirred up to the importance of the legislation, but also
to overcome the positive opposition of these men, and
that at a time when their influence was at its strongest.

'During the first session of the Sixtieth Congress, I was very much surprised one day to receive a request from Mr. Cannon to call at his office, on which occasion he announced that he wished to put me on the Committee on Agriculture. Upon his having made the announcement, I said to him, "I have no particular interest in the work of the Agricultural Department other than that which any other Member of Congress might have. I am on one very important Committee and Chairman of another Committee of less importance, so that I have all the Committee places to which I am entitled, and I think you would do well, not only from the Committee standpoint, but your own, if you would give this place to some one of the many who desire to be members of the Agricultural Committee." To this Mr. Cannon substantially replied that the Agricultural Committee had come to the first importance, that the Department had grown rapidly, that it was undertaking many new and somewhat unusual things, of many of which he doubtless approved, but some of which must necessarily be experimental, and such experiments should be stopped when it was determined that they were impracticable, and for that reason it was especially essential that trained business men should be on the Committee. He further stated that on looking over the House membership he had selected me as the most available man offering and he wished I would take the place, which, under the circumstances, I, of course, consented to do. Before giving this assent, however, I said to him that I thought he ought to know that I was in favor of certain legislation which the Agricultural Committee would have to consider, to which he was opposed, or reported to be opposed, and that I did not think he ought to give me the appointment without having a full understanding of my views. He immediately said, "I suppose you refer to forestry legislation." I said I did refer particularly to that. He said, "Well, now, let me tell you just what my idea is. I think forestry legislation is coming in time, but it has not seemed to me that the time has arrived yet when we ought to commence to purchase lands for forestry purposes. I may be mistaken in this proposition, but my judgment is that it is too early to undertake such a policy. I am not, however, putting you on the Agricultural Committee because I expect you to make my views yours. In fact, I would not put you there, or give you any other appointment of responsibility, if I thought you would, and I want to say this, that if you can frame a forestry bill which you, as a business man, are willing to support, I will do what I can to get an opportunity to get it consideration in the House." And although Mr. Cannon voted against the final passage of the forestry bill, he carried out the statement which he made at that time and was of material assistance in getting the bill up for consideration. In fact, if it had not been for his assistance, I should have failed in getting it through at the time we finally succeeded. As you will recall, the bill first passed the House in the Second Session of the Sixtieth Congress about a week before adjournment and was finally killed in the Senate by filibustering, so that it was necessary to take it up as a new proposition in the Sixty-First Congress. I was not during that Congress a member of the Agricultural Committee, having been made Chairman of the Post Office Committee at the beginning of the session, but after a pretty long struggle the bill was reported out of the Agricultural Committee by a vote of

To my friend Hon John M Meeks
With my Compliments
April 16th 1909   J G Cannon

ten to seven, finally passing the House and Senate in what seemed to me at the time to be workable shape, and time has demonstrated that that conclusion was correct. I think I ought to say that the Agricultural Committee, during both the Sixty-First and Sixty-Second Congresses, was made up of members, many of whom were radically opposed to this legislation. This included the Chairman of the Committee, Mr. Scott, and other influential members, all of which added to the difficulties of getting the bill reported out, and in the Sixtieth Congress it was finally reported from the Committee by a vote of nine to eight. As I have previously said, the vote in the Sixty-First Congress was ten to seven.

'There have been very few policies undertaken since I have been in Congress on which there have been given such thorough hearings as on this bill, and in behalf of which there has been such widespread interest. I think the hearing during the Sixtieth Congress was one of the most important that I have attended. At least a dozen States, and I think more, were represented by citizens of importance, three or four Governors being among this number and Governor Hoke Smith of Georgia taking charge of the hearing. Naturally, as a Congressman's work is devoted to specialties, I have not had time to give to Western forestry matters any more than the time which I can devote to other incidents of legislation as they come along, although I have always supported a reasonable conservation policy and liberal appropriations to maintain it. During the last Congress, especially, the Sixty-First, I was made Chairman of the Post Office Committee, which took practically all of my time, particularly during the first session, because I had not before been familiar with the work.

'A very interesting report has recently been made by George Otis Smith, Director of the United States Geological Survey, on the influence of forestry on stream flow as relating to the White Mountain region. You will recall that, in order to make constitutional the bill which I originally introduced, it became necessary to base the reason for the legislation on that proposition, and it was over that, that much of the contention took place during the hearings and in the debates which followed them. Even after the legislation was enacted many officers of the Army continued their opposition to it, contending that there was no connection between forestry and stream flow, and, therefore, the reasons for the legislation did not come within constitutional limitations. They even went so far as to say to Mr. Smith, the Director of the Geological Survey, that he could not certify, as the bill required, that in any particular instance there was such a connection without certifying to a false statement. This, naturally, put the Director of the Geological Survey on his guard and it was only after the most thorough investigation by that office that he was willing to attach his certificate to the principle thus involved. Within the last two weeks, however, he has reported to the Commission, established under the provisions of the Weeks Bill, that stream flow in the White Mountain region is, without question, affected by forestry conditions, coming to this conclusion after diligent and thorough investigations which seem to the Geological Survey and, after careful examination, to me, conclusive proof of the correctness of our previous theory. Purchases of land have already commenced in the Appalachian region, and last Saturday, June fifteenth, the Commission voted to buy about forty-two thousand acres in the White Mountain region. My own judgment is that the policy which the Government has now undertaken, hedged around as it is with suitable precautions and provision for care, will continue as long as the Government itself and that it will not only be a great advantage to the country along the lines covered by the purposes of the bill, that is, in promoting stream flow and protecting watersheds, but will continue the beauty of mountain regions which are visited by millions of people, which beauty, under other conditions, might be destroyed; and, in addition to all this, that it will prove to be a profitable venture for the Government, producing a revenue which will amply repay it for any expenditures made in the original purchase and which may be necessary to carry out the policy. I have not been associated with any legislation since I have been in Congress which has given me any more satisfaction than this.'

During this session of the Sixtieth Congress Mr. Weeks spoke on the following subjects: Appalachian Forest Reserve, Boston Custom House, Forest Service, purchase of ships for the Panama Canal; the Secret Service, referred to in President Roosevelt's Message, and ship subsidy.

The first session of the Sixty-First Congress continued from March 15, 1909, to August 5, 1909. Mr. Weeks was elected November 3, 1908, by a vote of 21,097 to 9069 for the Democratic candidate, Jesse C. Ivy, of Newton, and 1779 votes for Albert E. George, of Walpole, candidate of the Independence League. At this election William Howard Taft was elected President of

the United States and Eben S. Draper was elected
Governor of Massachusetts.

Mr. Weeks was made Chairman of the Committee on
the Post Office and Post Roads. He continued a member of the Committee on Banking and Currency. This
was an extra session of Congress and was called for the
purpose of passing what is known as the Payne-Aldrich
Tariff Bill which was brought into the House on March
22, 1909, and became a law on August 5, 1909. The
Committee on the Post Office and Post Roads is one
of the great committees of the House, appropriating,
at that time, over $200,000,000 annually. Mr. Weeks
was not appointed to the chairmanship because of seniority. It is very unusual to disregard the rule of
seniority in appointing a chairman of a major committee. He had not previously been a member of the
Committee, but he possessed Speaker Cannon's confidence in a very high degree.

An interesting and important incident in the early
days of this Congress was the adoption of certain amendments, liberalizing the rules of the House. It appears
that on March 15, 1909, the customary resolution was
offered that the rules of the previous Congress be
adopted as the rules of the existing Congress. This resolution was defeated by a vote of 193 to 189, due to the
combination with the Democrats of certain Republicans, known then and thereafter as 'insurgents.' This
was the first attempt to destroy the alleged 'autocratic'
power of Speaker Cannon. In the parliamentary struggle that followed, the result was, and with the acquies-
cence of the Speaker, the establishment of 'unanimous
consent day,' so-called, on which bills that had reached
a certain stage could be brought before the House in

the absence of objection. It removed from the Speaker the responsibility of deciding what bills should be considered and placed it on the Members. This was the beginning of a struggle with the Democrats and insurgents which ultimately resulted in radical changes in the rules of the House.

As this was a revolt in the House against Speaker Cannon and what was known as 'Cannonism,' a synonym in the minds of many for everything that was arbitrary and coercive in our legislative machinery, I may as well express here Mr. Weeks's attitude toward Speaker Cannon and the changes proposed in the rules of procedure in the House during this session of Congress.

Speaking of the reëlection of Speaker Cannon and the organization of the House of Representatives Mr. Weeks wrote, on March 15, 1909, to a correspondent:

'I assume that in this matter you are more or less prejudiced by the current reports which are published in certain magazines and some newspapers. Very much of this matter is entirely without warrant. The rules of the House are the result of the experience of one hundred and twenty-five years of legislative life, and they would not be changed materially by any political party, or by any men who had sufficient knowledge to entitle them to an opinion on the subject. I think myself that in some details they might be improved, and have no doubt that in one or two matters changes will be made, but the suggestion of electing committees, or any such radical move, would be, in my judgment, a piece of folly which ought not to be thought of. It would institute a practice of log rolling which would materially increase appropriations in directions which could not be justified.

'The Speaker, in my judgment, has an experience

which is extremely valuable to the Government. I have no doubt he has been the means of saving tens of millions, if not hundreds of millions, of dollars during his incumbency of the Chairmanship of the Committee on Appropriations and the Speakership, and I, therefore, consider it my duty not only to support him for re-election to the Speakership, but to aid as far as possible in preventing any vital changes in the rules which now regulate proceedings in the House. The recent passing of the Forestry Bill is a complete demonstration that the Speaker is in favor of acting on legislation when public sentiment is sufficiently educated to favor it for sound reasons. As you doubtless know, the bill was considered and passed the House, although the Speaker and many of the leaders on both sides were opposed to the measure itself and voted against it.'

And to another who had telegraphed, a little later in the month, urging Mr. Weeks to 'annihilate Cannonism' he replied: 'I have to confess that I do not know exactly what is meant by the term of "Cannonism," but, having a regard for popular government, for the public welfare, which means to me economy and wisdom in expenditures, and success based on sound principles, I voted against a change in the rules of the House, which, in my judgment, will breed extravagance and will lessen the capacity of the House to legislate wisely, and I also voted to sustain the Speaker personally, because I believe him to be the best fitted man in the House to occupy that place. This does not, of course, mean that I always agree with the Speaker in his acts and views, but I hope I am broad enough to judge a man by all of his acts and views and not by a few, and I am, therefore, forced to the above conclusion.'

CHAPTER V

Bill to protect migratory birds — Post Office Appropriation Bill — War on House Rules — Postal Savings Banks — Bonds for Panama Canal — Naval Reserve — Speakership — Opinions on various questions — Reciprocity with Canada — Elected to Sixty-Second Congress — Offers services to President in the event of war with Mexico — National highways — 1912 Campaign — Elected to Sixty-Third Congress — Payne-Aldrich Tariff Bill — House on Mount Prospect, New Hampshire — Elected to Senate.

THE origin of the legislation to protect migratory birds of the United States, with which Mr. Weeks's name is so closely associated, is decidedly interesting. Early in August, 1908, he received a letter from a constituent, of which the following is a copy:

NEEDHAM HEIGHTS, MASS., *Aug.* 2, 1908
CONGRESSMAN WEEKS:

DEAR SIR: I have a bill enclosed here that I would like to have passed through Congress, to have a national law put on all kinds of birds in every State in the country, as the gunners are shooting our birds that Nature put here to eat the grubs and worms. The grubs and worms are eating up all the foliage on our trees, and also our fruit and vegetables so we cannot get one-half the good fruit as we used to on account of grubs and worms eating them. Now, we would like to have a national law put on all kinds of birds, except crows and English sparrows, as these two kinds of birds do more harm than good. All other kinds are worm eating birds and would like to have a strict law on them to save our trees and fruit. Nature put them here for that purpose and let us keep them here to do Nature's work and not have to let each State send out men every year to do it for us at a large expense. Now, you will find bill enclosed here and do all you can to have it go through. If you would like more particulars, please let me hear from you.

Hoping you will do all in your power to have this bill go through, I am

Yours respectfully

(Signed)　　CHAS. H. HUDSON

Needham Heights, Mass.

The following is a copy of the proposed bill referred to in the letter:

'To have a strict law placed on all birds in the country the year around, against killing or robbing nests. Have the law placed on all kinds of birds except hawks, crows and English sparrows, this to be a National law — all States alike, and to impose a fine, or a term of imprisonment on any person violating such law.'

To this letter Mr. Weeks replied, under date of August 6, 1908, as follows:

'I have your letter of August 2nd, expressing your desire to have a law passed which will protect birds of all kinds, wherever they may be. I am not sure that a national law of that character would be constitutional. In any case, it is a matter which requires careful consideration, and I will keep the matter before me and see what can be done when I go to Washington next winter.'

On May 29, 1909, Mr. Weeks introduced a bill to protect migratory birds of the United States, which was referred to the Committee on Agriculture. Nothing was done with the bill at this session. In the following Congress, Senator McLean, of Connecticut, introduced a similar bill which passed the Senate and was reported favorably by the House Committee on Agriculture, but for lack of time could not be reached for a vote and therefore was incorporated in the Agricultural Appropriation Bill, which became a law on March 4, 1913, nearly four years after Mr. Weeks proposed the legislation in the House. The bill is generally known as the 'Weeks-McLean Law.' Among the provisions of the bill is the following:

'All wild geese, wild swans, brant, wild ducks, snipe, plover, woodcock, rail, wild pigeons and all other migratory game and insectivorous birds which, in their northern and southern migrations, pass through or do not remain permanently the entire year within the borders of any state or territory, shall hereafter be deemed to be within the custody and protection of the Government of the United States and shall not be destroyed or taken contrary to regulations hereinafter provided therefor.'

The Supreme Court of the United States has passed upon this act in a case entitled State of Missouri *v.* Holland, decided April 19, 1920.

It appears that the State of Missouri brought a bill in equity to prevent a game warden of the United States from attempting to enforce the Migratory Bird Treaty Act of July 3, 1918, and the regulations made by the Secretary of Agriculture in pursuance of the same, on the ground that the statute is an unconstitutional interference with the right reserved to the States by the Tenth Amendment.

The Court held that the treaty between the United States and Great Britain, proclaimed December 8, 1916, regulating the killing of migratory birds is valid and the Act of July 3, 1918, carrying the stipulations of the treaty into effect is also valid under that provision of the Constitution which gives to Congress the power to make all laws necessary and proper for carrying into effect the powers vested by the Constitution in the Government of the United States.

The Court said, among other things:

'Here a national interest of very nearly the first magnitude is involved. It can be protected only by National action in concert with that of another power. The subject matter is only transitory within the State and has no permanent habitat therein. But for the treaty and the statute there soon might be no birds for any powers to deal with.

'We see nothing in the Constitution that compels the Government to sit by while a food supply is cut off and the protectors of our forests and our crops are destroyed. It is not sufficient to rely upon the States. The reliance is vain, and were it otherwise, the question is whether the United States is forbidden to act. We are of the opinion that the treaty and statute must be upheld.'

The second session of the Sixty-First Congress began on December 6, 1909, and continued until June 25, 1910. In this session Mr. Weeks figured prominently. On February 22, 1910, he brought in his first Post Office Appropriation Bill. This is as complicated as any of the great appropriation bills. It is full of material for controversy and almost every paragraph is debated.

Mr. Weeks's management of the bill won the admiration of the House. He defended it with great skill at every point and showed great tact in dealing with complicated situations.

One of the most dramatic scenes which ever was witnessed in Congress was that which arose out of a resolution offered by Mr. Norris, of Nebraska, on Saturday, March 19, 1910, which ran as follows:

House Resolution 502

'Resolved, That the rules of the House of Representatives be amended as follows:

'1. In Rule X, paragraph 1, strike out the words "on Rules, to consist of five Members."

'2. Add new paragraph to Rule X, as follows: "Paragraph 5. There shall be a Committee on Rules, elected by the House, consisting of 10 Members, 6 of whom shall be Members of the majority party and 4 of whom shall be Members of the minority party. The Speaker shall not be a member of the committee and the committee shall elect its own chairman from its own members."

'Resolved further, That within ten days after the adoption of this resolution there shall be an election of this committee, and immediately upon its election the present Committee on Rules shall be dissolved.'

A point of order was made that the matter could not be considered at that time, for certain technical reasons. The Chair sustained the point of order, but, on appeal to the House, his decision was overruled by a vote of 183 to 160, the Democrats and so-called 'insurgents' of that day voting in the affirmative and the Republicans, as a rule, voting in the negative. Then the resolution was taken up for debate, and was adopted by the House by a vote of 191 to 156. The position of the 'insurgent' Republicans was stated by Mr. Norris, the mover of the original motion:

'... First, I want to absolutely deny that this movement to change the rules of the House is intended as any personal slap or any personal thrust at the Speaker or any other man. Those of us who favor this rule represent a principle here far beyond the personality of any man or any set of men.

'I want to say that there is no feeling against the Speaker in this matter unless it is brought into it by the Speaker or his friends. I want to deny the charge that this is anti-Republican. From every hamlet, from every fireside, and from every farm of Republican constituents to-day there are going up prayers and hopes that this resolution to change the rules of the House will be successful here to-day. (Laughter and applause.)'

The substitute was adopted, the 'insurgents' voting for it and most of the Republican regulars, including Mr. Weeks, against it.

The dramatic scene came when the Speaker, after the vote was announced, said that, as a majority of the House was opposed to him, he would entertain a motion to declare the office of Speaker vacant, whereupon Mr. Burleson of Texas, a Democrat, later Postmaster General in the Wilson Cabinet, offered the following resolution: 'Resolved that the office of the Speaker of the House of Representatives is hereby declared to be vacant and the House of Representatives shall at once proceed to the election of a Speaker'; but this was going to a more extreme position than sensible Democrats and insurgents cared to go and the resolution was defeated 192 to 155.

A legislative assembly, in its varying moods, reminds one of the ocean: now with unruffled surface, and then, almost without notice of an approaching storm, lashed to fury. In this controversy the angry waves of discussion beat upon the Speaker's rostrum through three days and nights of an almost continuous session, and then quickly subsided to the dull calm that usually follows the raging of the elements or of human emotions.

The demand for legislation permitting the Postmaster General to establish Postal Savings Banks, or depositaries in connection with post offices, had been steadily growing for several years and had been recommended by succeeding Postmasters-General.

Mr. Weeks had a large part in shaping this legislation which had warm advocates and strong opponents. The situation was so delicate that the bill was considered in a Republican caucus before it was brought into the House. Mr. Weeks had efficient aid, but he managed the bill in the caucus and in the House; he was the one to remove obstacles, to be insistent here, to yield there; in a word, to deal with a situation in which the convictions and prejudices of honest men were at variance. The bill passed the House on June 9, 1910.

In closing the debate, Mr. Weeks spoke in part as follows:

'Mr. Speaker, it is quite apparent that the House is ready to vote on this question, and I shall hardly make use of the time which I have reserved to close the debate.

'But there are a few questions relating to the whole subject which I want to call to the attention of the House, and especially to reply to some criticisms which have been made. I presume criticism, possibly legitimate criticism, can be made of any bill which is brought up for consideration in this House. But I think that the bill which the Republicans have reported from their

caucus is as far removed from ordinary criticism as any
bill with which I have been familiar since I have been a
Member. Twelve men, the Republican members of the
Committee on the Post Office and Post-Roads, devoted
many days, after hearings on the subject, in the preparation of this bill. Naturally, there was great variance of
opinion. But after long deliberation these 12 men arrived at a conclusion, the soundness of which is proven
by the fact that the Republican caucus, after spending
fifteen hours in the consideration of the bill, reported it
without making any material changes. To be sure, 19
slight changes were made; but they were not fundamental in any instance. I doubt if there has ever been a
bill considered by a caucus on either side of the House
for fifteen hours and unanimously reported as this one
was. . . .

'The reasons for this legislation have been well explained. Gentlemen speaking in support of the bill have
stated that they believe it would bring from hiding certain moneys not hitherto deposited anywhere. There
are $3,500,000,000 of circulation in the United States;
$1,500,000,000 of this amount can not be accounted for
by the Treasury officials. How much of it is actually in
hiding nobody knows. But when we read, as we did this
morning, of a woman who died in a Chicago hotel with
$26,000 in a steel box in her room, and have heard of
many instances where people have been found after
their death to have large sums in their possession, it may
naturally be inferred that those of smaller means would,
in many more instances, hoard money, especially when
we consider that those of larger means are usually better
fitted to invest their savings and would be much less
likely to hoard circulation.

'Whatever money is brought out of hiding will add to the stock in commercial use and will aid the development of those sections where it is brought to light. . . .

'This legislation has not been brought about without long and earnest consideration, as is the case in almost all important legislation. For more than thirty-five years bills have been introduced in this House providing for postal savings banks, and many of these bills have been given consideration, not only in Congress, but in the press and in other public discussion. . . .

'Mr. Speaker, just one word more. I believe that in every change the House Republicans have made in the Senate bill, a better bill has been provided. I believe that in every change that has been submitted to the House by the minority, a lessening of efficiency would be the result. If I had the time to take up in detail the changes made in the Senate bill by the Republican majority and, again, the changes made by the minority in the bill which they have submitted, I believe, with proper order, I could demonstrate to this House that the Republican measure in every respect is more workable, is fundamentally sounder, and furnishes a basis for a better system. That is really all we are doing now. We do not anticipate that this legislation will not require changes from time to time, but we do contend that this measure will form a sound nucleus, around which it will be possible to develop a perfect system.'

The third session of the Sixty-First Congress met on December 5, 1910, and continued until March 2, 1911. During this time Mr. Weeks spoke on a great variety of questions and always effectively. As Chairman of the Post Office Committee, he reported the Post Office Bill which he managed with his usual tact. Among the other subjects to which he devoted his study were two which, perhaps, should receive especial attention. He spoke of the way in which $290,000,000 of bonds for the payment of the Panama Canal should be issued, laying down some very sound principles in finance and made the following very interesting statement, in the discussion of a bill to promote the efficiency of the Naval Militia, upon the necessity for a Naval Reserve:

'Mr. Speaker, the greatest military necessity which this country has is an adequate naval reserve. Sixty thousand men would be required to man our fleet in time of war. We would have for that purpose but 45,000 men, if the quota of the Navy were filled. We have no naval reserve, except that furnished by the Naval Militia of the several States, numbering from 6500 to 7000 men.

'The record which they have made in the Spanish War is a clear demonstration that those men would be efficient and useful in case of another war, and they would be the principal source from which we could draw a supply of men with which to man the ships of the Navy not manned by the regular force; they would especially be available to man vessels for coast defense, and taking the place of men who ought to be serving actively at sea.

'Now, it is complained that we are going to spend $200,000 a year for this service. We have been spending $125,000 a year for it, but not one penny of this money goes to the men themselves. It goes to buy their uniforms and to purchase equipment, which equipment belongs to the United States, and it would be available in case of war. Not a naval militiaman has ever received one penny from the Government which has gone into his own pocket, and not one of them will receive a penny of this appropriation. I have served 10 years in the Naval Militia, and I am proud of it. I know the time men put in to make themselves effective and useful in time of need — time which would otherwise be used for personal purposes — and we owe to them as well as to the Government that we do everything possible to make them efficient.

'Now, this is a small matter in dollars and cents, but it is a very large matter from the standpoint of our military defense. It is a more useful appropriation — and I think I speak advisedly — in proportion to the dollars appropriated than any appropriation we make for the military service of this Government. It would be flying in the face of Providence not to take advantage of the opportunity which we have to make these men more efficient.

'How will this bill make them more efficient? It will make them more efficient because the Government can call on them at once in case of need. Under the old regulations they were simply State militia; they were in no way bound to United States service. Their officers and men were not examined until the need came, and then very frequently we found officers and men serving in capacities for which they were not competent. Under this bill they will be examined. The officers will be commissioned only after they have passed an examination which is approved by the Secretary of the Navy.

'The men will have to pass a technical examination, the petty officers will all have to pass examinations. They will all have to pass physical examinations, so that we may be sure when the time comes that every one of the men in this force will be fit for the position which he occupies at the time, and we will not be wasting money on men who cannot be made suitable for the service.

'More than three thousand of these naval militiamen went into the Spanish War. As has been stated by the gentleman from Michigan, they manned four large vessels and very many other small vessels used in the coast defense. Sixty of these men were on the Oregon. A great many of the Illinois naval militiamen were serving on other vessels of the fleet before Santiago, and in not a single instance which has come to my attention did these men fail to perform good service. I want to call attention to the fact that many of the gentlemen who are now crying economy when referring to this $200,000 appropriation were willing enough to vote for a pension bill, largely going to men who do not need it which carried $45,000,000 or $50,000,000. These Spanish War militiamen were patriotic as well as useful men. I shipped five hundred of them at the beginning of the Spanish War, and only one of those five hundred men has ever applied to me for a pension. Shattered in health, he died before he received the pension which was due him.'

Among Mr. Weeks's colleagues there had been many expressions favorable to his being a candidate for Speaker, to succeed Mr. Cannon. In response to a letter from one of them he wrote, under date of October 20, 1910:

'Literally speaking, I am not a candidate for Speaker of the House. It has seemed to me, however, that Mr. Cannon could not, under any circumstances, be reëlected — quite likely will not be a candidate —

and very many of my friends have suggested that I might be the man to succeed him. Having a reasonably correct appreciation of myself, I have not thought it wise to become a candidate, or make any statement about it whatever. If we succeed in electing a majority of the Sixty-Second Congress, which looks very doubtful now, I assume that will be the time to look the field over and decide what course I should take. My general principle has been that a man should be able to creep well before he attempts to walk, to say nothing of running, and that my record in the House would be a much better argument in favor of my candidacy, or against it, than any declaration I could make. All this means that I think it wise to wait until we know "where we are at" for the Sixty-Second Congress before considering the Speakership.'

The House in the Sixty-Second Congress was Democratic. On the day before Mr. Weeks was elected to this Congress, he wrote the following replies to questions asked by a constituent:

'1. "Do you believe that the Speaker of the House should hold the power of appointing Committees?"

'I do. I am opposed to any other method being adopted. The election of Committees would mean a system of log rolling which would place weak and untried men, who would promise anything, in positions of responsibility, and would inevitably mean very largely increased appropriations as a result.

'2. "Are you for or against the general policies exemplified in ship subsidy bills and White Mountain National Reservation bills?"

'I am. I prepared and had charge of the White Mountain National Reservation Bill, and I am in favor of the reëstablishment of our Merchant Marine; not by any particular method, but by some means, so that we would be carrying the major part of our three billions of foreign commerce. We are now not carrying over ten per cent of it, and we are paying foreign ship owners over two hundred millions a year for the service which they are performing for us in delivering our goods to our own customers.

'3. "Would you be inclined to favor the construction of one, two or more than two first-class battleships per year?"

'I am in favor of an adequate Navy. I wish conditions were such, however, that we could dispense with the Navy altogether, and I shall vote for the number of battleships which seem to me necessary to place our Navy on an efficient basis. This number must be determined by the conditions as they prevail at the time the matter is being considered.

'4. "Are you in favor of reduction in the present rates of tariff on wool, fuels, iron and steel and machinery?"

'I worked as hard as I could to reduce the duty on all raw materials which we use when the Payne-Aldrich Bill was formulated. We did make material reductions in iron, steel and bituminous coal, and in lumber, and put hides on the free list. As to wool, I doubt if the duty can be materially reduced without materially affecting the number of sheep produced in this country, which in turn would affect the cost of living. After the duty was reduced in the Wilson-Gorman Bill to eight cents a pound, we lost twenty millions of sheep, and that phase of any change in the wool tariff must be taken into consideration if a change is made.'

One of the most important administration measures was that relating to reciprocal trade relations with the Dominion of Canada, popularly known as 'Reciprocity with Canada.' The bill passed the House on February 14, 1911, by a vote of 221 to 93 — 67 not voting. It was supported by a minority of the Republicans, but by a large majority of the Democrats. It failed to pass the Senate at that session. President Taft called a special session of Congress, which convened on April 4, 1911, to consider the matter. The bill again passed the House, then Democratic, by a vote of 268 to 89 — 28 not voting. Mr. Weeks voted for the bill on both occasions. To a correspondent who criticized his action he wrote in May, 1911:

'It is a fact that I voted for the Canadian Reciprocity Bill, but I did so, not because I approved of all the features of the bill, but because it is a form of legislation which I have advocated very frequently; and it was a large element in bringing about my original nomination and election to Congress. Under these circumstances, it did not seem wise for me to vote against the proposition, although it was not in line with the kind of reciprocity arrangement which I should have been glad to have seen entered into. However, there is a vast difference between such an agreement with one country, and general free trade, with all countries.'

To another correspondent he wrote:

'The debate on reciprocity was a good one and the weight of the argument, it seemed to me, was entirely with those opposed to reciprocity. . . . The vote indicated that influence or argument had drawn away from the reciprocity cause some of its earlier advocates and even some of those who voted for it last winter. I think there is a good deal of feeling among those who opposed reciprocity against those who voted for it. Yesterday, I asked John Dalzell for some time on the free list bill, which I may or may not use, and which he, of course, gave me, and incidentally he asked me if I were coming back into the Republican Party.... Senator Penrose told me that he did not expect a vote on reciprocity before the first of August. As it stands to-day, there are eighteen Republicans who will vote for it, not one of whom, I think, is in favor of it.'

As a matter of fact, the Senate passed the bill on July 22, 1911, by a vote of 53 to 27 — 10 not voting. The regular and insurgent Republicans gave more votes against the bill than for it. Both Senators from Massachusetts, Mr. Lodge and Mr. Crane, voted in the affirmative.

Without considering the economic aspects of the question, upon which there may well be a divergence of opinion, viewed politically it must be regarded as an unfortunate incident. It split the Republican membership of Congress and placed the Republican administration in the position of having to defend a measure which could not have been enacted into law with Republican votes. This embarrassment, however, did not long continue because Canada refused to become a party to the proposed arrangement in a general election in September, 1911, which resulted in the defeat of Sir Wilfrid Laurier and the advent to power of the Conservative Party. This result was attributed, in some degree, at least, to the fear on the part of Canadian voters that this reciprocity relationship would be the first step in the absorption of Canada by the United States. Some foundation for this fear is found in the declaration of

Speaker Champ Clark, often more flamboyant than wise in his utterances, who said, in a speech advocating reciprocity, that he was in favor of it because he hoped 'to see the day when the American flag will float over every square foot of the British North American possessions clear to the North Pole.'

There were, of course, other influences which affected the Canadian vote, but this was one of them.

The first session of the Sixty-Second Congress convened on April 4, 1911, and continued until August 22, 1911.

On November 8, 1910, Mr. Weeks was elected by a vote of 19,037 to 14,696 for Daniel J. Daley, of Brookline, Democratic candidate. Eugene Foss, the Democratic candidate, was elected Governor over Eben S. Draper. This being a Democratic House, Champ Clark, of Missouri, was elected Speaker to succeed Joseph G. Cannon. Mr. Weeks naturally lost his chairmanship of the Post Office Committee and was succeeded by Mr. John A. Moon, of Tennessee, the ranking Democratic member in the previous Congress. Mr. Weeks became the ranking member on the Republican side. This was Mr. Weeks's only committee in this Congress. Mr. Cannon became the ranking Republican on the Appropriations Committee.

When trouble was threatening with Mexico in March, 1911, Mr. Weeks wrote the President as follows:

'In case there develops any serious trouble with Mexico, I wish to volunteer for assignment to any position where my services may be of value, without regard to pay or other conditions. I am a graduate of the Naval

Academy, commanded the Massachusetts Naval Brigade for many years and served as a Lieutenant in the Spanish War.'

To this President Taft replied:

'I have yours of March 14th, in which you say that in case there develops any serious trouble with Mexico you wish to volunteer for assignment to any position where your services may be valuable, without any regard to pay or other conditions; that you are a graduate of the Naval Academy, commanded the Massachusetts Naval Brigade for many years and served as a Lieutenant in the Spanish War.

'In reply I beg to say that I have every hope that there will be no war with Mexico and no intervention in that country of a military character necessary, but I assure you, Mr. Weeks, that, should occasion arise, it will gratify me as President to avail myself of your valuable services in connection with the Navy of the United States.'

On April 13, 1911, the proposed amendment to the Constitution of the United States, which became the Seventeenth Amendment, providing that Senators should be elected by the people and not by the legislatures, passed the House by a vote of 296 to 16 — 77, among whom was Mr. Weeks, not voting. It became effective on May 31, 1913. The discussion of a Democratic tariff bill, in which Mr. Weeks took a prominent part, occupied much of the time of this session.

As early as 1911 the subject of involving the National Government in a plan for building highways and post-roads within and between the States was under discussion. Mr. Weeks was opposed to this because he regarded road-building as a local project to be cared for by the States, counties, and towns, for reasons which he gives in the following extract from a letter of that year:

'... Without going into details, I think I ought to say that I am opposed to the National Government taking any other part in good road construction than the work which it is now doing, — that is, furnishing expert advice as to the manner of road building and the character of construction which may be used to the best advantage in any particular locality. Road building by the National Government would involve us in enormous expenditures, much of which, in my opinion, would be wasted and no sooner would the roads be built than we would commence another enormous expenditure to keep them in repair. Highways are essentially local and it should be the business of the people whose interests are directly involved, to maintain good roads in any community. This is being done to my knowledge in New England, New York, New Jersey and Pennsylvania, — all of which states will very soon be equipped with well-constructed highways, — the expense being divided generally between the local communities and the states directly interested, which seems to me far and away the best way to handle this question.'

This matter was taken up by the Government in 1912 in the passage of an act creating a General Joint Committee on Federal Aid for Roads. This resulted in legislation in 1916, which was amended in 1921. An attempt, in which Mr. Weeks joined, was made to restrict the participation of the Government to loaning its credit to the several States which were to assume the ultimate burden. This attempt failed and the National Government is committed to a plan on which it has al-

ready expended $400,000,000. It is not surprising that
this legislation should be popular in Congress. Under the
present plan thirty-five States receive more than they
pay in taxes and thirteen less; for example, when the
National Government appropriates $75,000,000 for
good roads, Massachusetts receives about $1,100,000,
but contributes in direct taxes in excess of $5,000,000 to
get it.

In the second session of the Sixty-Second Congress
which began on December 4, 1911, and extended through
August 26, 1912, Mr. Weeks, still in the minority party
as he had been in the previous session, spoke on a
number of widely different subjects. This session covered part of the period of perhaps the most exciting and
bitter Presidential campaign in our history, in which
Mr. Weeks took an active part. Early in 1912, there was
much speculation whether Roosevelt would be a candidate. He finally decided to be and announced his intention on February 24, 1912. Three days previously
he made a speech at Columbus, Ohio, on 'A Charter
of Democracy,' in which, among other things, he advocated the recall, in certain cases, of judicial decisions.
This speech alienated hundreds of thousands of Republican votes. Had that speech not been made, Roosevelt would have been nominated in 1912, and, had he
been elected President, the history of the world would
have been changed. Roosevelt and his followers believed that the action of the Convention did not represent the wishes of a great majority of the Republicans
of the country; and, furthermore, that a majority of the
delegates entitled to seats in the Convention were in his
favor. This led him to repudiate the action of the Con-

vention and to the organization of the Progressive
Party which held a Convention in Chicago on August
5, 1912, at which Roosevelt was nominated for the
Presidency. That Convention had about it a distinctly
religious atmosphere. The delegates sang 'Onward,
Christian Soldiers,' which became the hymn of the
Progressive Party, and their battle-cry was, 'We stand
at Armageddon and we battle for the Lord.' The campaign that followed was one of extreme bitterness.
Roosevelt was imbued with the spirit of the crusader;
he believed that he was leading a great cause and that in
doing so he was serving the best interests of his country-
men. A leader on the field of battle sees nothing but his
goal and in his progress tramples alike on friend and foe.
Such was his relation to the conflict which became almost a tragedy when Roosevelt was shot at Milwaukee
in October, 1912, as the campaign was at its height. The
Republican Party was hopelessly divided in this fierce
conflict and Mr. Wilson was elected President. When
Roosevelt was charged with having disrupted the party,
his reply and defense were that those who forced the
nomination of Mr. Taft upon the Convention against
the wishes of a majority of the Republican voters were
the ones responsible for the catastrophe. Mr. Weeks,
of course, stood with the regulars, and was a warm supporter of Mr. Taft.

On November 5, 1912, Mr. Weeks was reëlected by
a vote of 15,934. The Democratic candidate, John J.
Mitchell, of Marlborough, received 13,583 votes and
the candidate of the Progressive Party 5853. This, his
last election to the House for the Sixty-Third Congress,
was from a new district, the Thirteenth, the old
Twelfth District having become too large by about

27,000. The new district consisted of the towns of Ashland, Bellingham; Boston, Ward 25; Brookline, Dover, Framingham, Franklin, Holliston, Marlborough, Medfield, Medway, Millis, Natick, Needham, Newton, Norfolk, Plainville, Sherborn, Southborough, Sudbury, Walpole, Waltham, Wayland, Wellesley, Weston, Wrentham. The new district was Republican under old conditions by from 2000 to 2500 votes, yet with nearly 6000 votes cast for the Progressive candidate, most of which were cast by Republicans, Mr. Weeks won with the nominal Republican majority and ran ahead of every other candidate on the ticket.

At this election Woodrow Wilson was elected President of the United States and Eugene N. Foss was elected Governor of Massachusetts.

In reply to a correspondent who had criticized the policy of the Republican Party and also Mr. Weeks, the latter wrote in August, 1912:

'. . . I did not write before with the intention of attempting to divert what may be your conscientious views as to your political duty. I did attempt to call to your attention the fact that you were entirely influenced in this matter by your own personal interest, and I see no reason to change that opinion. I am not going to take the time to defend or to discuss the Payne-Aldrich Bill. It contained many good provisions, it was a revision downward and was the best result that could be obtained from that Congress. For that reason I voted for it and I should probably do a similar thing again, for I am constantly voting for measures which do not meet my full approval, but which are an improvement over those in force, and, therefore, I take the best I can get. Of course the wool tariff is not the most important public measure before the country. It is only a part of one of the many important public questions, and, even from your own viewpoint, it seems to me that you should give some credit to my service in Congress other than describing the acts with which I have been connected as minor. I do not need to make a list of them other than to call your attention to forestry legislation, for which I am almost entirely responsible, to framing a Post Office Bill which practically meant a saving of ten millions of dollars and which, for the first time in the history of the Government, was approved by the Senate without the change of a word, and to the fact that I was the author of, and had in charge, Postal Savings Bank legislation. If those are minor matters I do not know what major subjects have been considered by Congress since I have been here.'

In 1912 Mr. Weeks carried out a plan he had long had in mind — one might almost say a dream of his youth, and built a house on Mount Prospect, in the town of Lancaster, an eminence over two thousand feet in height, thickly wooded, which he had often visited in his childhood days. His grandfather, James B. Weeks, was the original owner of Prospect Farm which lay on the south slope of the mountain. The house was opened in September, 1913, and thereafter was the scene of a most generous hospitality. The members of 'The Faithful Ten' were frequently entertained here and many others of Mr. Weeks's friends, including President Harding. There was a good deal of innocent horseplay on these occasions. One visitor who evidently had been admitted to honorary membership in 'The Faithful Ten,' wrote in the guest book:

Most glad am I to join the 'faithful ten'
As loyal to their gallant chief, as when,
In earlier days, he started in the race
Which we all hope will land him in first place,
And we will constant be and never turn
While he has grub to eat, good cheer to burn.

The view from Mount Prospect is superb in every direction. To the south the majestic Presidential and Franconia Ranges; to the northwest, the broad interval land, through which the course of the Connecticut may be traced. The whole visible area of country, dotted with villages, farms, and ponds, is surrounded by a mountain wall several hundred miles in length. It was here that John Weeks best loved to live, and it was to this spot, in response to his most earnest wish, that he was permitted to return to die.

Winthrop Murray Crane, who had succeeded the late George Frisbie Hoar in the Senate by appointment of Governor John L. Bates, on October 12, 1904, and who had been elected for the term ending on March 4, 1913, had made it understood that he would not be a candidate to succeed himself. As they were very close friends, it was natural that Senator Crane should desire that Mr. Weeks should succeed to the seat in the Senate.

The election was made by the Legislature, the last to be made in that body, as the Seventeenth Amendment to the Constitution of the United States, providing for the election of Senators by the people, did not become effective until May 31, 1913. The balloting began on January 8, 1913. On the thirty-first and final ballot, Mr. Weeks received 97 votes; Mr. McCall, his principal competitor, 57, and Curtis Guild, 5.

SUMMER HOUSE ON MOUNT PROSPECT, LANCASTER, N.H.

With view to the north

On January 16, 1913, Senator Crane presented the credentials of John W. Weeks, chosen by the Legislature of the State of Massachusetts, a Senator of that State for the term beginning March 4, 1913.

CHAPTER VI

IN commenting on 'Progressivism' and Republicanism, a subject which had been earnestly discussed in the 1912 Campaign, Mr. Weeks wrote in January, 1913:

'... I am especially mindful of the comments which you make about Progressivism and Republicanism. It is, of course, true that many honest and sincere men have become dissatisfied with Republican leadership and accomplishments, and yet I feel convinced that the Republican Party has very generally responded promptly to the real demands of the public needs, but even if that is not the case, and some leaders in the Republican Party are properly criticized for their positions, it is not an altogether bad thing in our government to have a force which is holding back action until it may be demonstrated that it is absolutely necessary. If this is not the case, there would be much ill-advised legislation put on the statute books. Speaking for myself, however, I think a reasonably impartial view of my course would indicate that I have been very ready to act when I have been convinced that action was necessary and in the new position to which I have been elected, I shall, with great pleasure, coöperate with all those who believe that advanced legislation in any direction is of importance. I cannot avoid the responsibility of being one of those to whom Republican citizens, generally, in Massachusetts are to look for leadership, and in that position I want to have your assistance and friendship as well as that of all other right-thinking citizens.'

The first session of the Sixty-Third Congress began on March 4, 1913, and continued through December 1, 1913. Mr. Weeks, now in the minority party, the Democrats being in control of the executive and legislative branches of the Government, was appointed to the following committees in the Senate: Banking and Currency, Coast Defenses, Conservation of National Resources, Forest Reservations and the Protection of Game, Indian Depredations, Philippines, Public Health and National Quarantine.

Speaking of the organization of the Senate, Mr. Weeks wrote, under date of March 8, 1913:

'The Democrats are squabbling over offices and the disappointed ones are already commencing to fill the air with their lamentations. . . . The Democratic caucus yesterday voted to replace all Senate officers, probably including the veterans, who have heretofore been excluded in such changes, and they have commenced with the Chaplain, who is to be among the first to go. They are also having many difficulties in arranging their committees, but the insurgents are in the saddle, so the old-timers have to take their medicine whether they like it or not. As the Republicans are nearly equal in number to the Democrats and have the minority place, it is difficult to get new and good committee assignments. In fact, on most of the committees there are no vacancies, and on some of them, like Finance and the Judiciary, it will either be necessary to enlarge them or some old member will have to get off. On Finance it will be La Follette and on the Judiciary Root, so an attempt will be made to enlarge these two committees. I am told that I am to go on the Committee on Post Offices, the Philippines, Conservation, and something else, I have forgotten what. I don't think I fancy any of them very much, but as our senior Senator is the Chairman of the Committee on Committees, I am not in a position to complain, and even if I did complain I could not get on either Foreign Relations, Finance, or Naval Affairs, on all of which committees he is now a member, and those are particularly the committees which would appeal to me. The Democrats are going to be more liberal with their new members, although I think they are not going to break down the seniority rule as far as chairmanships are concerned.'

The assignment to so many committees, inevitable in the Senate, led to an intimate acquaintance with so large a variety of subjects, coupled with the fact that the Senate is the great debating body of Congress, that Mr. Weeks spoke more frequently than when he was a member of the House. Of the eleven subjects on which he spoke in this session, I will quote from only two to make clear his views upon the tariff and income tax, prominent parts of the financial system favored by the Administration.

On July 24, 1913, he made an elaborate speech in opposition to the so-called Underwood Tariff Bill which had come up from the Democratic House, and was entitled a bill 'to reduce tariff duties and to provide revenue for the Government and for other purposes.' It passed the Senate in September of that year.

'Mr. President, it is not my purpose to discuss at this time the details of any particular schedule; that should be done later during the reading of the bill; but there are some general observations which I wish to submit, having a direct bearing on this legislation and the policies and principles involved, including the reasons for the proposed changes.

'As far as our fiscal policy is concerned, the country has come to the parting of the ways, and when the pending bill is passed we shall have an opportunity to determine whether such radical changes can be made without greatly impairing business activity and the general prosperity. If the results are like those which have followed previous changes along similar lines, there will be no question about the verdict of the country when it again has an opportunity to pass on this action. If, on the other hand, it is found that the changes have demonstrated their soundness, then the question of a tariff policy will have been settled for a long term of years. It is undoubtedly true that the Democratic Party is doing what a large minority of the people of the country understands it promised to do, the reasons given for these promises being sufficient to persuade this minority of the voters — many of whom have had no experience with hard times — to support radical changes in the tariff. Whether this is being done wisely, as to details or not is quite another question. The chairman of the Ways and Means Committee of the House in discussing the so-called Underwood bills of last year, on being challenged on the floor of the House of Representatives at different times, stated that as far as he knew, and as far as it could be done, protection had been eliminated from the, at that time, pending legislation. As the bill which we are now considering is much more drastic than they were, from a protection standpoint, undoubtedly he and all others who agree with him would make the same answer now. It is not of any particular importance to try to determine whether this leading Democrat or that leading Democrat is in favor of free trade, for the Democratic Party has at different times advocated all shades of tariff principles, from declaring protection is robbery, to advocating a tariff for revenue with incidental protection. What we are concerned with is the fact that the Republican Party believes in placing a duty on articles of home production, raising sufficient revenue by so doing, and at the same time protecting the labor and capital engaged in the industry from unequal competition. This bill provides, as far as it can be done, for raising the required tariff revenue from those articles which our people are not large factors in producing, a glaring example of this being the putting of many food products on the free list, the assigned purpose being to reduce the cost of living, and at the same time making up the loss in revenue by putting a duty on bananas, another food product which we do not produce. . . .

'How easy it is to use popular phrases in political resolutions, to make statements if they do not have to be proven, to constantly repeat clattertrap until people think it may be true and even those who indulge in it become convinced from repeated repetition, especially as it may not have been denied, that there must be something in it. That is the position in which we find the Democratic Party, the tariff, and the people. The former has constantly repeated statements relative to the tariff and its relations to certain elements in our life, and the latter, always wishing to improve their condition, and properly so, skeptical, no doubt, of the result of this experiment, have concluded to give the Democratic

Party a chance to do what it has stated could be done, if the tariff were reduced; that is, reduce the cost of living, strangle the trusts, make the rich poorer and the poor richer, and to develop competition, giving every man an equal chance with every other, and this Congress is trying to carry out these promises. I wish it were possible to do these things, but if there is any merit in what I have stated, the people will find that their net income is not increased, but will probably be decreased; that there will be rich and poor, dependent on the brains, industry, and thrift of the individual; that the large corporation is here to stay, under proper control, because it is in many cases the economical way in which to do business; that there is, as there always has been, a chance for every man, which is dependent on himself and his own power of initiative; and that there never has been a greater demand for skillful, honest, industrious men than now. And I believe that the people will find that an attempt to change conditions in this way has injured all classes of citizens, who will at the first opportunity proceed to depose those who have been humbugging them and will restore to power the party which has, on the whole, managed the country's affairs with intelligence and honesty.'

This prophecy was abundantly fulfilled, as all will remember, in the great business depression of the winter of 1913–14 and consequent unemployment — a condition which remained until the war conditions, beginning in August, 1914, practically prevented the importation of foreign-made goods into this country.

On June 23, 1913, Mr. Weeks wrote:

'The new currency bill is born, as you have of course

noticed. Most of the machinery proposed in it has been taken bodily from the Monetary Commission Bill and, roughly speaking, it seems to me that what is good in it has come from that source and what is bad in it has been prepared to conform to the Democratic platform adopted at Baltimore. The especially bad features are the methods of issuing additional circulation and the intensely political character of the Central Board which is to be authorized to direct the banking, currency and credit affairs of the country. In its latest form, the bill provides for seven members, only one of whom need be a banker and all to be appointed by the President. This includes, of course, the Secretary of the Treasury, the Secretary of Agriculture and the Comptroller of the Currency. I am to have, at the President's request, an interview with him on next Wednesday night regarding the bill and of course I shall try to point out to him the bill's weakness.

'I really want to support the proposed legislation if it can be gotten into reasonable shape, but apparently Mr. Bryan's political hand has been at work in the last draft of the bill which not only makes the Central Board entirely political but eliminates the refunding of the two per cent bonds and the other wise features of the first proposition. I expect to give the papers Thursday, after I have had an interview with the President, my criticism of the bill.'

At the White House interview above referred to, as Mr. Weeks told a friend, the President said in substance, that Senator Weeks was more familiar with financial affairs than any one in the Senate, and he wanted the benefit of his judgment on the various clauses of the bill. The President then read the bill asking

Mr. Weeks to comment on each paragraph giving his reasons for approval or otherwise.

In going through the bill, Mr. Weeks noticed that as to the paragraphs which he regarded as bad, after stating his reasons, the President, after some thought, said, 'Well, I can't yield on that,' and then passed on to the next paragraph.

Mr. Weeks, however, decided to favor rather than oppose an amended bill. The President had enough influence to pass it just as it came from the House. In the Senate, to the surprise of a good many Republicans, Mr. Weeks stated that he was in favor of the measure, but that, naturally, some changes ought to be made which he would discuss at length later; which he did, and as a result over four hundred amendments were adopted which greatly improved the bill.

At a somewhat later date he wrote: 'We are having interesting hearings before the Banking and Currency Committee, and as things stand now, those who are determined to give suitable consideration to the bill have full control of the Committee, so you need not expect to see legislation until we have thoroughly thrashed out the whole subject.'

On August 27, 1913, Senator Weeks made the following comment upon the tendencies of some of the advocates of an income tax:

'During my service in the House, at a time when an income tax was being considered, a prominent Member of the House was discussing the question of a minimum amount to be taxed. At that time it was proposed to make the minimum $5000, and he said he would make the minimum higher than that. When interrogated as to where he would place the limit, he finally said that if he had his way when a man had $100,000 income he would take a quarter of it; "yes," he said, "I would take half of it"; and added that the citizen would have enough left even if that were done.

'Now, I would like to ask the Senator from Nebraska where we are likely to stop in the unequal taxation which is proposed in this income tax provision, and I think the country would like to know where the limit is to be placed. Are we to adopt the suggestion of the gentleman to whom I refer, that eventually if a man has $100,000 income we will take half of it, on the theory that he will have enough left, or are we to approach this subject in moderation and determine where we can get the most income with the least danger of unduly sacrificing reasonable equality in our system of taxation? Now, where is the limit at which we are to stop?'

In the second session of the Sixty-Third Congress, which ran from December 1, 1913, to October 24, 1914, Mr. Weeks spoke on fifty subjects, more or less. By far the most important was that bill which, on its passage, was entitled 'An Act to provide for the establishment of Federal Reserve Banks, to furnish an elastic currency, to afford means of rediscounting commercial paper, to establish more effective supervision of banking in the United States, and for other purposes.' Mr. Weeks, as has been stated, was an advocate of the Aldrich-Vreeland Bill in the House, he was a member of the Conference Committee to adjust differences between the two houses, he was a member of the Monetary Commission, and, in consequence, was deeply interested in, and well informed upon, all of the intricacies of this most complex subject. When the bill reached the Senate, he devoted his energies to perfecting it.

Writing on the progress of the legislation October 11, 1913, he said:

'We have worked out the currency situation so that, in all probability, there will not be any more effort to bring about undue haste. The President has had some exceedingly poor advice on this subject and had gotten pretty clearly in his mind the idea that he could pass a currency bill under exactly the same conditions that he could pass a tariff bill. As you can judge from the fragments in the papers, we have been, as diplomatically as possible, controverting this position, having insisted on investigations and hearings and have conducted the whole question so that we have not united the Democrats in the Senate, but have on the contrary Messrs. Hitchcock, O'Gorman, and Reed committed to our side of the question. My impression is that it is a victory of real importance because it will demonstrate to the Administration that the possibility of passing general legislation must depend somewhat on the information furnished and the quality of the legislation rather than the dictum of the powers that be. We have reached a point when the President recommends legislation, recommends what the legislation shall be, in fact, insists on it, and, a third stage which is now, when the legislation should pass. I am glad to say that there has been sufficient balking on this last proposition to prevent his policy prevailing. I do not know that we can get a good bill. There is a great variation of views and it will be pretty difficult to get them together, but we are in much better shape to do this than a month ago.

'I have in mind, if it seems to me I ought to support the bill which the committee reports, to make a speech outlining my ideas of what the correct legislation should be and my reasons for being willing to support the legislation notwithstanding the failure to come up to that particular standpoint.'

The bill passed the Senate on December 19, 1913, by a vote of 54 to 34 — 7 not voting, among whom was Mr. Lodge. Mr. Weeks and five other Republicans with one Progressive voted for it; thirty-four Republicans voted against it.

Conferees were appointed to adjust the differences between the two houses, and the conference report was agreed to in the Senate on December 23, 1913, by a vote of 43 to 25 — 27 not voting, among whom was Senator Lodge. The bill was signed and became a law on December 23, 1913.

It is not possible to consider at any length the extended discussion, in the Senate, of this currency bill. Perhaps as distinctive a quotation from the frequent comments made by Mr. Weeks is the following on December 5, 1913:

'I am not disposed to take from the House Committee on Banking and Currency, or from the House itself, or others who had to do with the banking and currency bill as it came to the Senate, such credit as is due them for having gotten together a measure which contains many sound and wise provisions, and yet the bill, at that time, was far from what it should be, and a majority, at least of the Senate committee, believed that this was the time when we should get the best legislation possible. It is an intricate and to many an uninteresting study, and it cannot be expected that when men, who have devoted their lives to it are uncertain about the course which should be followed, in some particulars, that men who have given the subject no study should hesitate about taking the time to inform themselves. Therefore it is not any reflection on the House to say that in the time that that body had the Glass Bill before it, considering the amount of discussion which took place, it was simply impossible for Members to have understood the merits of many of the provisions of the bill or that it should have passed, under a species of pressure, a bill, many features of which should be wisely studied and properly amended.

'That is exactly what the Senate Committee on Banking and Currency has been doing, has insisted on doing, in fact, notwithstanding the unwise pressure and insistence which has been brought from time to time to urge early legislation. No member of the Senate Banking and Currency Committee would vote for the House bill as it came to the Senate without material amendment, and I believe there is not a Member of the Senate who will not admit that much benefit and knowledge has been obtained by that committee, which is reflected in the two propositions offered for consideration. Either one of them, in my judgment, is materially better than the bill as it came from the House. I think the one to which my name is attached has many features which are superior to those in the other, and yet I can frankly and honestly say to Senators that, in my judgment, there is enough good in this legislation, however much one may dissent from some of its provisions, to warrant its being supported. If this conclusion is sound, the insistence of the Senate Committee on Banking and Currency has not only been justified in getting wiser and better legislation, but there has been no public condition which would have warranted or which necessitated earlier action; indeed, in my judgment, this bill should now be thoroughly and carefully scrutinized, every phase of it should be debated, every doubt in the minds of Senators should be removed, every Senator should listen to the discussion, should ask questions, and should come to a conclusion on the merits of the many propositions involved, independent of any fealty for any particular party or loyalty to any provision presented by either of the two factions of the Senate committee, for this legislation may be the basis of our banking and currency system for hundreds of years.

'You will hear complaints that business is falling off, that banks are husbanding their resources, that there is a demand for early legislation; and yet I can say to you that I have not had, during the past three months, a single communication of any kind, from any source, urging hasty action or criticizing me because I have been one of those who have insisted on the fullest deliberation and consideration. On the other hand, I have received or have seen a large number of indications in the press and in personal letters commending the action which the Senate committee was taking. Business is falling off. It is natural that it should. We have been putting into operation a tariff law which, whatever may be its final effect, is sure to be disturbing to some degree. We have an unusually complicated and delicate foreign question, in which the country is vitally interested. We have before us prospective corporation legislation which must necessarily be a disturbing feature in our business affairs. Any of these would be sufficient, operating singly, to affect business; operating together, they have been enough to bring about a marked diminution in the volume of trade, and it should not be charged that any delay in passing this bill has been the cause of its falling off, because there is little or no connection between the two.

'It is not necessary to attack what has been proposed in the past, in the way of banking and currency legislation in order to bring to bear sufficient arguments to warrant action at this time. Everybody whose opinion is of much value admits that we could have a better system than we have at present, and our energies should be used to get the best system obtainable; not to decry any other. I refer to this, because in his opening statement the Chairman of the Committee on Banking and Currency took occasion to refer to the plan proposed by the Monetary Commission for the readjustment of our banking and currency system, at which time he repeated a statement which he has frequently made, that the bill was reported to Congress but no attempt was made to get action, although Congress was controlled by the political party which had had a majority of the Commission. It is true that the measure was reported in January, 1912, but the Senator from Oklahoma knows perfectly well that it could not have been passed by the Senate at that time, even though there was a nominal Republican majority in this body, and he knows equally well that, even if it could have been passed by the Senate, the House was controlled by the Democratic Party and that no bill of that character, which was based on a report made by a commission controlled by the opposite party, could have been gotten through the House of Representatives. Therefore it is idle to talk about no effort having been made to adopt this legislation. None was made because it would have been futile to have undertaken it.

'Even now it will be difficult to find a thoroughly

posted financial expert in the United States, and certainly not many in Europe, who will not agree that the plan proposed by the Monetary Commission was, in most respects, much superior to any legislation that we are likely to get at this time. I for one believe that to be the case, and yet I have not attempted to inject that particular plan into this consideration, have scrupulously avoided doing so, because I knew it would be without avail; that it would add another complication to a sufficiently trying situation. I am so strongly in favor of doing some of the things which are going to be done by the pending legislation, that I do not want to inject any element which is likely to retard or prevent early action.

'It should not be forgotten, however, that six of the sixteen members of the National Monetary Commission were among the leading Democrats in Congress at the time its report was made, including Senator Teller, of Colorado, who was then closing an unusually long and distinguished public career, and who stated in signing this report that he considered it one of the most, if not the most, important act he had performed. The conclusions reached were the result of four years' study, and one of the greatest compliments to their soundness is the action of the House Banking and Currency Committee in taking bodily many sections and ideas from this report and incorporating them in the bill which we are considering. Too much reliance should not be placed on its having been condemned by the Baltimore Convention of last year, for probably not one in a hundred of those who voted to sustain the resolutions adopted there had ever read the report of the Monetary Commission, and it is well known that all Democratic platforms in recent years have been dominated by one whose financial theories have been unqualifiedly condemned, whenever the people have had a chance to pass on them at the polls. Neither was it necessary to inject into this debate any charges against the action of the New York banks in 1907. There is sufficient reason for this legislation without drifting into the realms of fancy for others. In all probability the slurs against the big banks of New York are without a scintilla of reason, for men do not attempt to deliberately injure themselves or their finances unless they are fit subjects for an insane asylum, and they would have been such if they had been responsible for bringing on the conditions that existed in 1907.

'Senators are sufficiently familiar with what transpired at that time to know that the panic of that year came about, very largely, from natural causes which had been accumulating for years and certainly had been apparent to most careful critics for months before the collapse took place. To attack bankers, and especially large bankers, and attempt to create prejudice against them and against their methods, by such statements as the chairman of the committee has made is, in my judgment, both unwise and unfair. He will admit, as will every member of the Banking and Currency Committee, that those bankers who appeared before the committee, at the hearings which have been terminated, presented their evidence with all the fairness and frankness that characterized other witnesses; that, in a sense, their testimony was invaluable to the committee; and there was not a syllable of evidence that they were trying to protect themselves or to protect the banking community against the best interests of the country at large.

'Let us be fair and sane about these things. Stop this talk tending to prejudice class against class. There are probably just as many patriotic men in one class, in proportion to their numbers, as in another. When men are wrong or do wrong as individuals they should be punished without regard to their place in society, but to condemn a class or try to create prejudice against a class by making statements which cannot be substantiated, is fundamentally wrong and does not add anything to the cause which he who makes them is advocating.'

Vice-President Charles G. Dawes, in writing of Mr. Weeks's services in connection with the earlier attempts to reform our financial system, has said: 'The debt which the Nation owed him for his splendid contest for the principles of sound finance in the House Committee on Banking and Currency, in the formative period of our present financial system, has never been fully realized. Almost alone on that Committee he never faltered and he was vindicated later by the adoption of his views by the House of Representatives over its head. Through it all he was quiet, serene, friendly and affable in all his Committee contacts, notwithstanding the bitterness felt by most of those involved in the conflict.'

Secretary of the Treasury Andrew W. Mellon, a colleague of Mr. Weeks in the Cabinets of Presidents Harding and Coolidge, has expressed the following opinion of Mr. Weeks's part in the reform of our financial system:

'I have always felt that the public at large was not sufficiently aware of the contribution which he made towards better banking and currency laws. He served for many years as a member of the Banking and Currency Committee of the House of Representatives. He was also a member of the National Monetary Commission, which did so much hard and useful work in preparation for the reform of the banking and currency system that came later with the passage of the Federal Reserve Act. When that Act was before Congress, Mr. Weeks gave it his active support and offered many valuable suggestions for its improvement. Although he did not agree with all of its provisions, he voted for the bill on its final passage through the Senate, for he tried on all occasions to be helpful and constructive and in this instance he believed the establishment of the Federal Reserve System to be of the first importance, because of the steadying influence which it would have on the finances of the country.'

Former Senator Theodore E. Burton, of Ohio, now a highly respected member of the House, a member with Mr. Weeks of the Monetary Commission, has written: 'He [Mr. Weeks] was prominent in the passage of the Vreeland-Aldrich bill of May 30, 1908, which gave us a new plan for the avoidance of panics, and, although it was superseded by the Federal Reserve System, it was very effective in the year 1914. I am glad to have had his very efficient coöperation in defeating certain objectionable propositions which were under consideration when this bill was framed. His opinion on monetary questions was highly prized when he was a member of the Monetary Commission.'

It is well known that there was a sharp difference between Mr. Weeks and most of his Republican colleagues in their action upon this question. Senator Lodge was opposed to the bill and Senator Weeks voted for it. Mr. Lodge gives his reasons for his action in a letter to Mr. Weeks:

New York, *December* 17, 1913

My dear Senator Weeks:

I am, as you know, unable to be in Washington before the holidays. I cannot, therefore, be present and give my vote in person upon the final passage of the currency bill. This I greatly regret; so much, indeed, that I am unwilling to have the bill acted upon in the Senate without making public record of the reasons which would govern my vote, were I able to give it, upon the passage of the bill.

The many details of this most important law, I have had no opportunity to master as they should be mastered by any one who presumes to discuss them. Fortunately for me, however, there is no one who has a more thorough knowledge, not only of every feature of this particular bill but also of the far-reaching and difficult questions which must be involved in any bill of this character, than you. This mastery of the subject you have demonstrated in debate, and therefore with the most absolute confidence I authorize you to pair me upon all amendments, as you yourself voted, without any statement or explanation on my part.

When, however, the Senate comes to a final vote upon the bill, as a whole, there are certain general principles involved, upon which I have very strong convictions. By these convictions my vote, could I be present and give it in person, would be decided.

I quite agree that there are provisions covering the details of the system proposed which would effect marked improvements in the system, or lack of system, of our banking laws as they now exist. This could hardly be otherwise, as many of these details are taken from the report of the Monetary Commission. But these improvements, which are not only most desirable, but which are very necessary, are not sufficient, in my opinion, to command my vote for the bill if they are linked with general principles which are both perilous and unsound.

Let me briefly state the objections which seem to me so grave, as to make the adoption of the beneficial provisions of the bill impossible without a sacrifice of the fundamental principles upon which, as I believe, all sound and enduring banking laws must rest.

Throughout my public life I have supported all measures designed to take the Government out of the banking business. I voted for the withdrawal of the Treasury notes and hoped that I should live to see the legal tenders also withdrawn — the Government confined to coining gold, silver, and copper, and wholly free from responsibility for note issues. I believe very strongly that banking should be done and bank notes issued by banks rigidly supervised by the Government, but that the Government itself should have no part in either function. This bill puts the Government into the banking business as never before in our history, and makes, as I understand it, all notes Government notes when they should be bank notes.

This bill as it stands seems to me to open the way to a vast inflation of the currency. There is no necessity of dwelling upon this point after the remarkable and most powerful argument of the senior Senator from New York (Mr. Root). I can be content here to follow the example of the English candidate for Parliament who thought it enough 'to say ditto to Mr. Burke.' I will merely add that I do not like to think that any law can be passed which will make it possible to submerge the gold standard in a flood of irredeemable paper currency.

The guaranty of bank deposits seems to me a direct encouragement to bad and reckless banking. I cannot but think that it may have results like those which followed Jackson's deposit of the surplus in the State banks.

The powers vested in the Federal board seem to me highly dangerous, especially where there is political control of the board. I should be very sorry to hold stock in a bank subject to such domination.

I will not attempt to enumerate any other objections. Still less shall I undertake to argue upon those which I have mentioned, for that would be impossible in a letter.

I merely desire, as I have already said, to make public record of the reasons which lead me to ask you to pair me against the passage of this bill. I had hoped to support this bill, but I could not vote for it as it stands, because it seems to me to contain features and to rest upon principles in the highest degree menacing to our prosperity, to stability in business, and to the general welfare of the people of the United States.

I am, as always

Very sincerely yours
(Signed)   H. C. Lodge

In his letter Senator Lodge states that he agrees that there are provisions covering details of the proposed system which would effect marked improvements in the banking system, or lack of system, then existing. He says that this could hardly be otherwise, as many of the details were taken from the report of the Monetary Commission, but he believed that these most desirable and necessary improvements were not sufficient to command his vote for the bill, if they were linked with general principles which were both perilous and unsound. He then goes on to state what those unsound principles are, saying that throughout his public life he has supported all measures designed to take the Government out of the banking business. I do not believe that Senator Weeks was of the opinion that the Federal Reserve Act would put the Government in the banking business. Certainly the Government has no stock in the Federal Reserve banks and bore no expense in connection with their organization further than the amount of about $83,000 which was expended by the Federal Reserve Bank Organization Committee. Against this can be set up more than 140 million dollars which the Federal Reserve banks have paid to the Government as franchise taxes. Senator Lodge expressed the hope that he might live to see the withdrawal of legal tender notes. The Federal Reserve Act made no mandatory provision for such withdrawal, although in Section 7 it is provided — 'That the net earnings derived by the United States from Federal Reserve banks may, in the discretion of the Secretary of the Treasury, be used to supplement the gold reserve held against outstanding United States notes.' Had it done more, there would have been raised a controversial question which would probably have defeated the bill. The total volume of legal tender notes outstanding, however, is only little more than 346 million dollars, and as the law stands, this amount cannot be increased or diminished. The greater part of the legal tender notes are in the form of small bills which are used to make change, and when the large volume of currency in circulation is taken into consideration, it is clear that the presence of the legal tender notes, as a part of the circulation, involves no serious consequences. As a matter of fact, the legal tender notes could be retired at any time by an act of Congress without any disturbance of the Federal Reserve Act. I think that Senator Weeks himself and all sound economists, as well as the most intelligent students of finance, agreed with Senator Lodge that it was unfortunate that Federal Reserve notes should have been made a direct obligation of the Government of the United States. Senator Lodge's view that banking should be practiced and bank notes issued by banks under the rigid supervision of the Government, without any liability to the Government itself, is entirely sound. It should be remembered, however, that Republican support of the Federal Reserve Bill was generally lacking and in order to secure its passage, it was necessary to placate the Bryan Democrats who demanded, as a price of their support, that the Federal Reserve notes be made an obligation of the Government. It was the view of Senator Weeks, as well as of many of the Democratic Senators who supported the bill, that while this was unsound in principle, no serious results would grow out of it, because of the security and gold reserve required. In the fourteen years which have elapsed since the Federal Reserve Act became a law, some of which have been very critical years, the Government has been put to no expense or inconvenience in connection with the issue of Federal Reserve notes, and there is no reason to believe that, with prudent management of the system, any loss will ever accrue to the Government in connection with these notes. Senator Weeks took the view that, while he did not approve of this particular feature of the bill, it provided in other respects for so many improvements over the old system that he would support it.

Another objection raised by Senator Lodge was, that the bill opened the way for a vast inflation of the currency. There was, of course, a great expansion of the volume of currency in circulation during the War, but this was essentially a gold inflation and was made possible by the enormous increase in the gold holdings of the country as a result of purchases in this country made by European belligerents. All forms of United States paper money have been maintained, since the passage of the Federal Reserve Act, on an absolute parity with gold. This would not have been possible had there been a real inflation of the currency. The gold standard was not submerged 'in a flood of irredeemable paper currency' as Senator Lodge feared might be the case.

Senator Lodge goes on to say, 'The guaranty of bank deposits seems to me a direct encouragement to bad and reckless banking.' Senator Weeks was strongly of that opinion. He spoke against it and the Federal Reserve Act did not contain the provision.

Another objection raised by Senator Lodge was as follows: 'The powers vested in the Federal Reserve Board seem to me highly dangerous, especially where there is political control of the Board.' There are many checks and balances in the Federal Reserve Act and, while the Federal Reserve Board does have powers which at times have been used in such a way as to be rather annoying to directors of Federal Reserve banks, the experience of fourteen years shows that in all vitally important matters, the Federal Reserve banks have been their own masters. As a regulatory and reviewing body, the Federal Reserve Board exercises powers which are negative rather than positive. Initiative is taken by the Federal Reserve banks and not by the Board. The

loans and advances made by the Federal Reserve banks
are made by officers or agents appointed by their directors. The three Class C directors who are appointed by
the Federal Reserve Board have, generally speaking,
coöperated with the six directors chosen by the member
banks. No Federal Reserve notes have been issued except upon the application of the Federal Reserve banks.
The Federal Reserve Board has no power to make loans
nor to force a Federal Reserve bank to discount undesirable paper for member banks, nor to issue notes
except upon the application of a Federal Reserve bank.

Thus far the operations of the Federal Reserve System would seem to justify the conclusion of Senator
Weeks rather than that of Senators Root and Lodge and
others who agreed with them.

I have dwelt on this matter at considerable length
not only because of its importance but because it so
well illustrates Mr. Weeks's independence of judgment.
He carefully investigated a question, and when he
reached a conclusion, the opinions and actions of others
had no influence upon him. This is a great virtue in a
legislator who, as a rule, hesitates, particularly if he is a
good party man, to break away from his colleagues.

I was in Washington at about the time the Democrats were discussing their policy on banking and currency and asked a friend of mine — a Democrat —
what they were proposing to do. He replied substantially as follows: 'We are going to come as near the plan
of the Monetary Commission as we dare to.' That this
was the opinion of other intelligent Democrats is
evidenced by the following quotation from David F.
Houston's book, published in 1926, and entitled 'Eight
Years with Wilson's Cabinet, 1913–1920.' Mr. Houston

was Secretary of Agriculture and later Secretary of the Treasury.

In repeating a conversation with the President, he says (Vol. I, p. 20):

'He [Mr. Wilson] said: "I am not an expert in economic or financial matters. In these things I shall have to get much advice. What would you do?"

'I [Mr. Houston] answered: "To make a long story short, I would take the Monetary Commission Bill, which had many good points, and decentralize the system it sought to provide. I would modify it to make its machinery simpler and more acceptable in the matter of control; it is too complex and not sufficiently popularly or governmentally controlled." ' Mr. Houston was a member of the Committee which located the twelve Reserve districts and the twelve Reserve cities. As a matter of economic efficiency, it makes little difference whether there be one central reservoir of credit or twelve reservoirs so piped together that the entire supply of credit may at any time be available.

It is literally true that where the Monetary Commission, a Republican creation, had sown, the Democratic Administration had reaped. I believe it is also true that had it not been for President Wilson's hypnotic influence over his party, it is extremely unlikely that so good a bill could have been enacted in a Democratic Congress. Mr. Weeks, in commenting upon his own support of the bill, said in a letter dated January 5, 1914:

'It was a pretty doubtful question with me for some time, but I made up my mind that I could not do otherwise than carry out what I maintained from the beginning, that there should be no partisanship in the legislation, so I did what appeared to me, from a business standpoint, should be done — that is, support something that had more real value in it than the reverse. My correspondence and the people I saw in Boston as well as press comments lead me to the conclusion that my action meets the approval of most of the people in Massachusetts. In fact, I have not seen a word of criticism in the papers and naturally those who have communicated with me have been most friendly in their comments. In fact, I have never had as many friendly and complimentary letters on any one subject as I have had since the currency bill passed.'

CHAPTER VII

Mexico — Offers services in case of war — Panama Canal Bill — Hay-Pauncefote Treaty — Regulation of trade — European war — European situation — Red Cross — Emergency revenue legislation.

It will be recalled that early in 1914 sailors in the uniform of the United States, upon a boat flying the flag of the United States, landed at a wharf in Tampico and were arrested by an officer in charge of a guard, taken through the streets and then returned to the boat and set free. This, of course, was an insult to the Government of the United States.

It appears that immediate amends were made, the action of the officer who made the arrest was disavowed by the Government under which he served, which was the *de facto* Government of Mexico under the *de facto* Presidency of General Huerta. The offending officer was arrested, the Commandant at Tampico apologized for the act, and General Huerta also apologized. This was not deemed sufficient by the officer in command of the American fleet at Tampico, who demanded a formal salute to the American flag.

At this juncture, Mr. Weeks, in a letter dated April 14, 1914, made the same proffer to President Wilson that under somewhat similar conditions he made to President Taft in 1911: 'As I am a graduate of the United States Naval Academy I have always felt it my duty to volunteer for active service whenever our country has seemed likely to be involved in war. In 1898 my services were accepted and I served as a volunteer during the Spanish-American War for six months. I am not sure that my services at this time will be of any particular value to the Government, but I tender them, not in a perfunctory way, but with a desire to serve, if they are needed, wherever and whenever they may be required.'

President Wilson replied as follows:

April 17, 1914

Your letter of April fourteenth is of the sort that it is very gratifying to receive. I profoundly hope that it will not be necessary to call on you for services in any war, but I none the less appreciate your offer to volunteer.

The Senate on April 21, 1914, discussed the joint resolution justifying the employment by the President of the armed forces of the United States in enforcing certain demands against Victoriano Huerta.

In the course of the discussion, Mr. Weeks said:

'. . . I am only taking the time of the Senate to say a few words, because it has been, and it is now, my intention, unless the resolution which is pending and which is likely to be adopted to-night is materially modified, to vote against it.

'I am embarrassed, however, by a change in conditions which existed at the time we met this morning and those which exist to-night. A citizen and a Senator is justified in criticizing the Administration even in an important international affair before war is undertaken, but it is the duty of every citizen, and every Senator especially, to support the Administration to the utmost limits when war has been undertaken. This morning war had not been undertaken; we had been asked to consider an important justification of the President's purposes, involved in which, in my judgment, was a justification of the President's acts in Mexico during the last thirteen months; and while we are engaged in discussing that subject we are informed that four of our men in Mexico have been killed; that twenty-one have been wounded; and we know not what other movements are on foot.

'I need not say to Senators that that means war. The President may say to us that we cannot make war against the Mexican people; that we are making war against a man and the supporters of that man; but we need not delude ourselves with any such specious plea as that, for our men have been killed and wounded in action. We have commenced an undertaking which will cost the Government hundreds of millions of dollars and thousands of lives and years of time. Let us not delude ourselves with minimizing or lessening the importance and the solemnity of this occasion and of this undertaking in which we are embarked.

'If we were not engaged in war, I had intended to call the attention of the Senate to some of the reasons why, it seemed to me, we should not indulge in haste in so important a matter, and to compare the present action with what has been done, on similar occasions in the past. For example, I wanted to call attention to what is known as the "Virginius case." Forty years ago an American ship, flying the American flag, was captured by a Spanish man-of-war; her people were taken ashore, were tried by a drumhead court-martial, and more than fifty subjects of Great Britain and America were summarily shot. That was an occasion that tried the temper and the forbearance of this country and of the people of this country, and yet did we demand the kind of reparation which some Senators would ask us to demand on this occasion? We did ask for reparation. The Spanish authorities informed our Government that they believed the ship was not an American ship; that the use of the American flag was not justified; and we gave thirty days to investigate that condition. The result proved the correctness of the position of the Spanish Government, and we never at any time demanded that our flag should be saluted as a result of this incident.

.   .   .   .

'Twenty years ago, in Chile, many of the sailors of the U.S.S. Baltimore were ashore in the port of Valparaiso, where they were attacked by the soldiers and the police of that city, and several men were killed. There was great public excitement as a result of this incident, and yet we find, ninety days after the incident itself, the President of the United States giving to Congress the facts which applied to the case, and during the intervening time the local courts of Chile had been occupied in investigating the case. There were at that time unsettled conditions in Chile not dissimilar to those which now exist in Mexico. During this interval our Government abstained from making unreasonable demands, and in the end Chile apologized for the attacks which had been made.

.   .   .   .

'During that insurrection which took place in Chile at about that time the fleet of that country rebelled and five ships put to sea under the leader of the rebellion. They were met on the high seas by our Pacific Fleet. The rebel fleet, flying the Chilean flag, saluted our flag as the fleets were passing, outside the three-mile limit, and the salute was returned gun for gun, as is always done when a salute is fired under such conditions. I point that out because the point has been so frequently made in this discussion that the provisional president of Mexico has demanded that we return a salute in kind. That is nothing but a matter of custom; it cannot be returned in any other way, and never has been done in any other way when a salute has been demanded and the demand has been acceded to. Therefore, we ought not to make a point, in my judgment, against General Huerta because he has, presumably, requested that the salute be returned gun for gun.

.   .   .   .

'Mr. President, I do not know. I wish I did know. I wish I had more information on which to form my own decision, as to what should be done in this matter. It is possible the Senator from New Jersey is right, but, in any event, if a national salute is fired on a demand from us by the Mexican authorities or any other authority, it should be returned gun for gun, because that is the customary proceeding, and if General Huerta has asked that this course be followed he has been within his rights.

'But why discuss these questions? We have passed the stage of resolutions. We are at this moment in a state of war, and under such conditions, after I have voted against this resolution — which I am going to do, because I cannot justify the course that has been followed by the Administration in Mexican affairs for the past thirteen months — in fact, I am unalterably opposed to what has been done. I am a supporter of the Administration in the prosecution of the war; we have reached the point where action must be taken, and I hope that every Senator, as well as every citizen of this country, under these conditions, is going to do his very best to support the Government. I certainly am, and after my vote has been cast on the resolution I expect to do what I can do as a citizen and a Senator to uphold the hands of the Government, much as I regret the situation in which we now find ourselves.'

On May 15, 1914, Mr. Weeks wrote: 'I am going to vote against the Canal Repeal Bill and am preparing a brief talk, giving my reasons for so doing. I do not intend to make a long argument; in fact I want to make it brief enough so that those people in Massachusetts who may feel that I am not doing an entirely honorable act will take the trouble to read why I have concluded to take the course which I am going to follow.'

On May 29, 1914, the Senate resumed its discussion of a bill to amend section five of the act to provide for the opening, maintenance, protection, and operation of the Panama Canal and the sanitation of the Panama Canal Zone, approved August 24, 1912. Under the terms of the Hay-Pauncefote Treaty it was provided that

'The canal shall be free and open to the vessels of commerce and of war of all nations observing these rules on terms of entire equality, so that there shall be no discrimination against any such nation or its citizens or subjects in respect of the conditions or charges of traffic. Such conditions and charges of traffic shall be just and equitable.'

A question arose, upon which there was a decided difference of opinion, as to whether the exemption from tolls of American ships, engaged in the coastwise trade through the Panama Canal, was in violation of the above provision in the Hay-Pauncefote Treaty.

President Wilson originally believed that it was not,

but on March 5, 1914, he had addressed Congress in the following words: 'I have come to ask you for the repeal of that provision of the Panama Canal Act of August 24, 1912, which exempts vessels engaged in the coastwise trade of the United States from payment of tolls, and to urge upon you the justice, the wisdom, and the large policy of such a repeal with the utmost urgency of which I am capable.'

In the course of a discussion of this question on May 29, 1914, Mr. Weeks said, in opposition to the President's recommendation:

'I am, as briefly as possible, going to point out my reasons for believing that (1) the Hay-Pauncefote Treaty does not necessitate our compelling our coastwise shipping to pay tolls; (2) that there is no moral reason for our following such a course; (3) that the custom of all nations has been, and is now, to exempt coastwise shipping from laws, rules, and regulations applying to other shipping; (4) that equitable conditions would not obtain, whether we charged our coastwise shipping or not, because of subsidies granted to the ships of other countries; and (5) that this contention is undoubtedly advanced for the express purpose of adding another handicap to the development of our merchant marine which would result in an equivalent benefit to our commercial rivals.

'When this question was originally considered, in 1850, Great Britain was our equal partner, and while, at that time the building of the canal by the Government was not given consideration, undoubtedly the necessary costs of fortification and maintenance, if there were such, were to be borne equally by the two countries. Under present conditions what has Great Britain done to justify our doing an unjustifiable act; that is, to show generosity to that country by giving up a form of sovereignty over what actually belongs to us as much as does the territory of the District of Columbia? The answer must be, Nothing whatever. On the other hand, she will be the most greatly benefited from a commercial standpoint of any nation by the construction of the canal; in fact, it is probably true that ships flying the British flag will make as much use of the canal as those belonging to all other nations combined. In addition to that, Great Britain will have available the $400,000,000 which we have expended in the canal's construction to develop her various industries, including her shipbuilding and shipping itself, so that in effect we will have used our capital to provide a means to enable our commercial rivals to increase the preponderance of advantage which they now hold over us, and this advantage will be increased from year to year, because still more of our capital will be necessary in order to maintain this great international development, for the cost of maintaining and protecting the canal and a reasonable interest on the investment will be at least twice any amount of money which can be received from tolls in the near future. The only possible harm that can come to Great Britain from our adopting the policy of granting free tolls to our coastwise and other shipping will come to the Tehuantepec Railroad Company — this is more or less problematical — and the possible harm which may come to the shipping of the Dominion of Canada. But the shipping of the Dominion of Canada, at least all of any considerable moment. is controlled by the subsidized Canadian Pacific, Canadian Northern, and Grand Trunk Railroad Companies.

'The total expenditure made by the Canadian Government last year for the encouragement of commerce was $2,703,200, and this stipulated that the lines of steamers receiving this subsidy shall not call at the ports of the United States.

'What a travesty on justice and fairness it would be to forbid the use of the canal to ships owned by our own railroads and then make this enormous sacrifice to open the canal to the ships of the subsidized railroads of our commercial rival to the north! It cannot do them any harm if we allow our shipping to go through free, because there is a certainty that a handicap exists equal to the tolls charged against American ships owing to the difference in the cost of construction and operation. But even if this were not so, there should not be an American who would be in favor of granting to the ships of a foreign country privileges which we refuse to grant to ships flying the American flag, owned and controlled by American capital. No contention of the kind which has been raised by Sir Edward Grey should have been thought of by that Government; they should have recognized the splendid privileges and opportunities which we were giving their shipping and the shipping of the world, and even if they had believed that they had a technically sound contention in the three points which have been raised by the English Government, reasonable fairness on its part should have led it to waive these objections and permitted us to manage our own canal and our own shipping without question or objection.

'Quoting once more from section 1 of article 3 of the Hay-Pauncefote treaty this language: ". . . so that there shall be no discrimination against any such nation or its citizens or subjects in respect of the conditions of charges of traffic or otherwise."

'Just what is meant by the expression "or otherwise" I am unable to determine, but it is a fact that our shipping of all kinds is conducted under a serious handicap, due largely to the excessive cost of construction in this country and the excessive cost of operation, so that we are not on equal terms with the shipping of the world, and probably never can be. But, in addition to these handicaps all other nations in the world in some form grant assistance to their shipping, so that it may compete successfully with that of other countries.

'In this respect we are the trustees of the American people. It is our duty to build up our shipping industry, and especially our duty to see that no action is taken which is going to militate against it in favor of that of other nations; and the very course which we are now asked to take would be another instance of the aggressiveness and industry of another nation in trying to place further handicaps on our shipping. This policy is well illustrated in the action of European Governments in the use of the Suez Canal. It is true that rates through the canal are equitable, but in order that the shipping of the individual country shall not suffer by payment of such rates it has become the fixed policy of most European nations to pay subsidies, so that to-day if we had any shipping in that part of the world it would not as an industry be receiving just and equitable treatment, because it would have the handicap of these subventions paid by European countries. It seems to me desirable to show just how comprehensively this course has been followed by our commercial rivals, and I submit herewith in detail the subsidies now paid for using the Suez Canal.'

The President's bill passed by a vote of 50 to 35.

Among Republicans voting in the affirmative were Mr. Root. Mr. Lodge was absent and did not vote, but had he been present would have voted for the bill and for the following reason: 'I think on the face of the words either view can fairly be taken. I do not wish anything done by which this government could ever be exposed to the suggestion even of not acting in good faith under a treaty.'

Mr. Weeks, differing with his colleague, voted in the negative.

Mr. Weeks has something to say in speeches which follow, about the statutes which are designed to prevent combinations among competing industries and for other kindred purposes. The first is the so-called Sherman Anti-Trust Act which became a law on July 2, 1890. The purpose of this act is expressed in the first section, in part, as follows: 'Every contract, combination in the form of trust or otherwise, or conspiracy, in restraint of trade or commerce among the several states, or with foreign nations, is hereby declared to be illegal.' This statute has led to much litigation during the past thirty-five years and has brought much confusion into the business world, which still remains, arising out of the varying interpretations of the statute by the courts.

The second statute to which Mr. Weeks refers is the so-called Federal Trade Commission Act approved on September 26, 1914, during the first Administration of President Wilson. It creates a Federal Trade Commission charged with the duty of ferreting out alleged 'unfair methods of competition in business,' and, if found to exist, to require their discontinuance, with the right to appeal to the courts for the enforcement of the order; also to gather and compile information concerning, and to investigate, from time to time, the organization, business, conduct, practices, and management of any corporation, except banks and common carriers.

The third statute is known as the Clayton Act of October 15, 1914, entitled 'An Act to supplement existing laws against unlawful restraints and monopolies and for other purposes.' This act is designed to put further shackles on business, but relieves 'labor' and 'agricultural organizations' from the taint of being construed to be illegal combinations or conspiracies in restraint of trade under the anti-trust laws, and softens the alleged asperities of the restraining order or injunction in labor disputes.

In this connection I might add that an act of March 3, 1915, forbids the use of any part of the appropriation for the enforcement of the anti-trust laws in the prosecution of labor combinations or for the prosecution of farmers who organize for the purpose of obtaining fair and reasonable prices for their products.

When on July 24, 1914, the Senate had under discussion a bill to 'create an interstate trade commission, to define its powers and duties, and for other purposes,' Mr. Weeks made a very elaborate speech, in which he considered the attitude the Government should take toward corporations and great combinations of capital.

His fundamental views of the question are expressed in the following quotation:

'The whole question of what should be the Government's connection with corporations and combinations of capital should be the result of a most thorough, painstaking, and exhaustive examination. We do not legislate, in such matters at least, with the same care and prudence exhibited by our commercial rivals, and especially by the German Nation. It is well known that before adopting their present tariff law a commission studied the subject for several years, taking up every phase of the question, so that its report contained a substantially clear course to be followed. We should do the same in this case. I do not wish to unduly criticize the committees which have been engaged in framing this legislation, but what we are doing now is done without the aid of technical knowledge. Business men themselves are not agreed as to the proper solution of the question at issue. Presumably they have only looked at the question from their own important and perhaps selfish standpoint. They may be influenced to advocate a trade commission with limited powers, believing that that would, practically, break down the operation of the Sherman Anti-Trust Act or they may be opposed to a trade commission because they think it would hamper and restrict their business operations. They do not know any better than the legislators who are engaged in farming this legislation what the result of its enactment will be.

'During the past eighteen months I have been a member of a commission to study the rates which the Government should pay railroads for the transportation of mail. Without going into that question in any detail, I can state with propriety and positiveness that when this question was undertaken, neither the railroads nor the Post Office Department had information which would have been even a reasonable basis for the construction of a law; in fact, both the railroads and the department have been studying this question through hearings, interrogatories, and investigations during these months, and both department and railroads have modified, in fact radically changed, their views, the department at least, several times during that period.

'If legislation had been adopted without the careful investigation which has been made during these months, I am justified in saying that it would have been unfair and unreasonable either to the Government or to the railroads themselves, or both; but as a result of this investigation I believe it will be demonstrated that a plan has been developed which will be fair to both Government and railroads and which will settle this question for many years to come.

'We have on the statute books the Sherman Anti-Trust Act, which is praised by those who have approved of the results of its operation, and condemned by those who believe that the results obtained are not commensurate with the damage they feel it has done. Now we are proposing to take further action relating to similar businesses in an entirely different way, so that corporations hereafter will be materially limited in the manner in which they may conduct their operations.

'There are those — and they are not confined to those who have the so-called conservative habit of thought — who believe that any legislation which restricts business operations is in the end detrimental to the best interests of the country.

'We are always passing legislation which is made necessary by the "joy rider," and by making it general it applies to every one else. There are comparatively few people owning and operating automobiles who do not observe and believe in observing reasonable regulations, but a few operate their machines in a manner which endangers public interest and personal safety, and therefore it becomes necessary to pass legislation which will punish these irresponsible people; this legislation is very frequently much more drastic than is necessary or desirable but it must be applied to all those who are using machines. This illustration is equally true of general business and business operations.

'Daniel Webster, in 1838, recognized the sentiment with which we are familiar, a general criticism of things as they are — a complaint that things are not right; and every complainant has a remedy at hand which, he believes, if put on the statute books, will right these wrongs. Mr. Webster said at that time: "There are persons who constantly clamor. They complain of oppression, speculation, and the pernicious influence of accumulated wealth. They cry loudly against all banks and corporations and all means by which small capitals become united in order to produce important and beneficial results. They carry on mad hostility against all established institutions. They would choke the fountain of industry and dry all the streams. In a country of unbounded liberty they clamor against oppression. In a country of perfect equality they would move heaven and earth against privilege and monopoly. In a country where property is more evenly divided than anywhere else, they rend the air shouting agrarian doctrines. In a country where the wages of labor are high beyond parallel they would teach the laborer that he is but an oppressed slave."

'It seems to me there are many things in common in the conditions as described by Mr. Webster and those of the present time. I do not refer entirely, in making that suggestion, to this pending legislation, but to the general trend of the public mind.

'We sometimes get the impression, from those who are condemning the management of large business affairs, that the men who are conducting important corporations are endeavoring to find some way to circumvent the law. Such assertions, in my judgment, are generally without foundation. Nine hundred and ninety-nine business men out of every thousand are law-abiding citizens who wish to observe and respect the law in spirit and letter and are frequently put to great expense and trouble in determining what they can do and obey the law, but not to avoid its provisions. Every corporation of relative importance, which has been conducting a large part of any special line of activity in the last twenty years, has found it necessary to employ trained and expert lawyers, not to tell its managers how they could avoid obeying the Sherman Anti-Trust Law, but to tell its managers what they could do and keep within its provisions. Very frequently the decisions of the courts have demonstrated that the opinion of the lawyers, in such cases, has not been sound, and that has brought fines and humiliation to many men who never intended to do any act which the law forbade.'

Mr. Weeks voted against the bill which became a law September 26, 1914. This bill and the so-called Clayton Bill of October 15, 1914, made up the Administration programme, in this session of Congress, relating to the restraint of unfair business methods.

Of the Clayton Bill Mr. Weeks said to a correspondent: 'I have your letter of June 25th requesting me to vote for the Clayton Anti-Trust Bill, as it passed the House of Representatives, especially for that part which exempts labor organizations and farmers' alliances from the provisions of the bill. I regret that I cannot give you a favorable reply to this request. I am opposed to the Clayton Anti-Trust Bill, in any case, because I believe it will harm rather than benefit business conditions and I am opposed to the proposition in which you are particularly interested because I think it unwise to pass any legislation which exempts from its provisions any class of our citizens.'

Commenting on the great war which had recently broken out, Mr. Weeks said in a letter dated August 18, 1914: 'I cannot yet appreciate the dreadful European situation. It almost seems like a dream, but I am hopeful that some real good will come out of it. It seems to me that the German Emperor and the German Nation have been since 1870 extremely bumptious, not only in military but in industrial matters. It is undoubtedly true that they have made wonderful developments and, as you say, it seems incredible that a nation which has organized its industrial system on a scientific basis should be willing to take the chances of the enormous waste which will come from this war. I believe the result must be the humiliation of the Germans and if it can be diverted so that in the future we can reduce the expenditures for naval maintenance, then I think that the sacrifice may be worth having. What we ought to do, in my opinion, is, as far as possible, to coöperate with England in bringing about this result and taking the general position that the building of battleships beyond some very moderate limit will be considered an unfriendly act. The world might save by following such a policy three or four hundred millions of dollars a year and be immeasurably better off as a result of the saving. That may be the outcome of the war.'

Mr. Weeks made the following comment on the economic situation in September, 1914: 'The truth of the matter is that if the Democrats had not increased appropriations as they have, a hundred millions of dollars, there would not be any necessity for additional taxes of any kind and I suspect they will have a merry time among themselves and otherwise before they get a bill through giving them the additional money, which they think they will need. This war is a God-send to them. If it had not been for the war they could not have covered up their reckless appropriations as they may be able to do now.'

Impressed with the sad conditions in Europe, Mr. Weeks addressed the following letter to President Wilson under date of October 12, 1914:

'The reports of great distress, which are already coming from Europe, relating to people who are driven from their homes and the burden which is going to be put on those who are in safe zones, suggests the certainty that there is going to be a tremendous amount of actual want during the winter months, if the war continues as it seems likely to do. Of course the Red Cross is doing everything it can with its comparatively limited resources but as they are limited, it occurs to me that possibly our Government should make some appropriation to be put in the hands of the Red Cross for expenditure, to be applied strictly along neutrality lines and only in cases where actual non-combatants are suffering for the actual necessities of life.

'Quite likely you have given the matter consideration and possibly have some plans, if you think it prudent to undertake to give assistance, but the early adjournment of Congress leads me to call the matter to your attention, thinking that if it is wise to take any action, as far as Congress is concerned, it should be done without delay.'

When the emergency revenue legislation was under discussion on October 13, 1914, in the form of a bill to increase the internal revenue, Mr. Weeks spoke in part as follows:

'The chairman of the Committee on Finance, in presenting the bill, suggested that the Republicans were opposing it for political rather than for financial reasons, stating that it was necessary to pass legislation of this character or of some character which would produce additional revenue, and that, in his opinion, no Republican really wished to have the legislation fail, but was opposing it, hoping to obtain some political advantage from so doing. There may be some basis of fact in that statement, and yet, Mr. President, I assume that no Republican would wish to have the Government insufficiently financed. I am one of those Republicans who believe that foreign conditions are such that the Government should not only be financed as it would be in ordinary times, but that it should even be stronger than in ordinary times, so that it might, if necessary, come to the relief of necessary matters which are within the provisions of law. The Treasury, in my judgment, Mr. President, is not now in good condition; in fact, relatively speaking, I think it is in weaker condition than ordinary demands justify.

'The suggestion has been made by some of those discussing the bill that if the Government would withdraw from the national banks the moneys which are deposited in them it would carry the Administration along for a few months at least, and that such moneys should be used before additional taxes are laid. There is some basis of truth in that statement, and yet, if the Government withdrew from the national banks the money now on deposit in them and paid it out without having additional revenue to offset such expenditures, the Treasury would be in a deplorable condition.

'I find on examination of the daily statement of the United States Treasury for August 1 that the net balance in the general fund was $142,741,000. That means that, including all gold, silver, and other moneys in the Treasury, all deposits in national banks, and all credits of postmasters and other officers on the asset side of the account, and assuming that all indebtedness which was current has been paid, there would be a balance left of the amount which I have stated.

'On the 2d day of September, one month later, I find that the net balance in the general fund had decreased from $142,741,000 to $122,843,000, or about $20,000,000 in one month. That means, of course, that the expenditures for that month exceeded the receipts by about $20,000,000.

'On the 8th day of October the daily statement shows that the net balance in the general fund was $103,496,-000, or about $19,000,000 less than it was on the 2d day of September. Therefore since the outbreak of the European war the Government's expenditures have exceeded the Government's receipts by substantially $18,000,000 a month.

'It stands to reason that that condition cannot continue for an indefinite time, so Congress must, at some time, make provision to take care of the appropriations which have been made. Up to that point I am quite in agreement with my Democratic friends, fearful though they are, I know, of the political effect which will result from the passage of a revenue bill of any kind at this time.

'But what I object to, Mr. President, in their programme is the reasons which are assigned for its necessity and the manner of raising the revenue. The latter objection is perhaps fundamental as between the Demo-

'Naturally we are a seafaring people. In the early days a large portion of the people of this country were engaged in seafaring pursuits. Many of the immigrants who had come to this country had come from those parts of the world which, even now, are active in everything pertaining to seafaring life, and yet we have not developed, but have constantly, in proportion to our foreign trade, decreased our merchant marine.

'We pay for the transportation of the products of American soil more than $200,000,000 a year. This is one of the great items which enter into making up the balance of trade which stands against this country or which may stand in favor of this country at the end of the fiscal year. There has never been a year, for a generation, during which there would not have been a large balance of trade in favor of the United States if it had not been necessary for us to pay to foreign shipowners and foreign nations this very large amount of money, which is required for the transportation of our products.

'There seem to me, Mr. President, to be three possible ways of bringing about a rehabilitation of our merchant marine. I am not going to discuss them in detail, but simply to mention them. We might repeal everything pertaining to the navigation laws of the country. That would mean reducing the pay of seamen, reducing the cost of ships, and lessening every safeguard which we have placed upon men engaged in seafaring pursuits. I very much doubt if there is any real sentiment in this country in favor of adopting such a course. Indeed, there is a bill now pending in conference which has to do with increasing the safeguards of not only those who are traveling at sea but increasing the insurance of every quality which surrounds those who follow the sea for a livelihood. If we are to adopt that bill, or anything like it, it will be little short of ridiculous for us to consider lowering the standard, which we have already set as desirable to surround those who follow the sea.

'As I have said, we may either remove these handicaps placed against us by our navigation laws, most of which have been removed, and the balance of which I doubt if there is any sentiment in favor of removing — I certainly am not in favor of it — or we may take one of two other courses. One alternative is to provide a mail subvention, as has been done in the Act of March, 1891, to which I have referred. Such a measure has very nearly passed Congress two or three times. Once such a bill passed the Senate and came within two or three votes of passing the House of Representatives. In my judgment, if that bill had passed, it would have provided for a large number of ships coming under the provisions of the act, so that quite likely there would not be the demand, which exists to-day, to do something for our merchant marine under the emergency conditions which exist. Senators on the other side of the aisle must take very largely the responsibility for the condition which exists to-day. While it is true that they have not been in power, yet they have unitedly and unanimously, as far as I know, voted against every attempt to do anything for our shipping during all these years, when it has been perfectly apparent that it was losing, comparatively, year after year. As the Senator from Utah suggests, they filibustered against legislation of that kind. I think I recall at least one instance, since I have been in Congress when a filibuster was carried on for that reason.

him known personally to a large number of people, upon whom he made a very favorable impression; for example, in Kansas, the *Iola Register* said under date of April 6, 1915:

'John W. Weeks is of national size and he is sure to be of national reputation. That was demonstrated by the reception that was given to him and to his message last week at Kansas City and at Topeka. In both these places he spoke to several hundred representative business men, and the impression he made upon them was one which any man may well be proud to have made — the impression that he is a clean, capable, courageous, BIG man. He practiced none of the arts of oratory, he did not utter a sentence that bore the mark of careful polishing, but he SAID something every minute he talked, and, when he finished, every man who heard him felt that he had been listening to one who knew what he was talking about and who was not only informed but sincere.

'And that is the kind of a man John W. Weeks is. The writer of this was intimately associated with him in the public service for six years and he never knew a man who more fully measured up to the highest standards of such service. He mastered every subject to which his duty assigned him, he stayed by every task, however irksome, until it was finished, he followed public opinion when he thought it was right and he combated it when he thought it was wrong, and so he came by the divine right of the capable and honest and the strong to a position of leadership in the House of Representatives. His best work in the House, perhaps, was done as chairman of the Committee on Post Offices and Post Roads, where his knowledge of the subject and his business judgment enabled him to bring in an appropriation bill carrying

$300,000,000 which passed the Senate without the change of a figure or a word — an achievement never before attained. But he also did great work on the Committee on Banking and Currency and on the Committee on Agriculture. He was a member of the Monetary Commission, and he was recognized in the Senate, although he entered that body only two years ago, as one of the highest authorities on the subject, when the new banking bill was under consideration. It was his influence, perhaps, more than that of any other senator, that was felt in the 480 changes that were made in that bill as it came from the House—changes that converted it from a bungled, impossible proposition to a measure that is at least worth a fair trial.

'Mr. Weeks was born in New Hampshire on a farm. He was educated at the Naval Academy, intending to make the navy his profession. At the time of his graduation, however, there were no battleships in need of officers, so with the rest of his class he was discharged and found himself thus unexpectedly thrown back into civil life with neither trade, profession nor fortune. He began at the bottom, therefore, and it is wholly through his own efforts that while yet in middle life he has amassed a comfortable fortune. When he entered public life he was actively engaged in banking and in a number of other enterprises, and it is characteristic of him that, when elected to the Senate, he disposed of all his business interests so that he might give his whole time to the public service and be free from even the suspicion of being influenced, by any private consideration, in any official act.

'Being schooled in the history of his country and well grounded in sound principles of government, it follows

that Senator Weeks has never followed off after any
of the political vagaries that have been so prevalent
throughout the country during these past few years. He
has been just a Republican, a typical Republican, conservative as to principles, constructive as to measures,
a statesman, not an agitator nor an experimenter. He
has been in entire sympathy with the sentiment that
has resulted in the proper regulation and control of 'Big
Business,' and he has no sympathy at all with the nag-
ging and narrow propaganda which would apply the
strait-jacket to all business.

'The mention of the name of Senator Weeks in connection with the presidency is due to no hint or suggestion of his own, and he refuses, with modesty that is
characteristic of him, to discuss it. His friends are under
no such restrictions, however, and they are responsible
for the fact that it has already become a matter of wide
and favorable comment. And the better the country
becomes acquainted with him, the wider and the more
favorable is that comment sure to become.'

The *Seattle Post-Intelligencer*, heading its article, 'A
Man of the Hour,' said:

'John Wingate Weeks, junior Senator from Massachusetts, impressed his strong personality upon this section of the coast during his recent visit. He is a fine type
of the business man in politics — the business man who
entered politics via the front door, who has full faith in
the integrity and patriotism of the business world in
general and who would see no continued estrangement
between the Government and business, but mutual
helpfulness and confidence, and unselfish coöperation
to conserve and promote the material interests of this
great country.

'His convictions, sincerely entertained and courageously expressed, are not reactionary, but truly progressive, and his statesmanship is all the broader and more inspiring because practical and possessing the dominant quality of common sense.

'Trained for the Navy, a graduate of Annapolis academy; schooled in finance in conservative Boston; a student in municipal affairs, with a record of good service as alderman; and a national lawmaker for years at Washington devoted to the public weal — his career has been full of usefulness, marked by initiative and crowned with merited success. He is a sturdy New-Englander.

'Higher honor may be in store for him. His Republican colleagues in Congress, to a man, esteem him for his demonstrated worth. His section has ambition for him. On his own part he is dreaming no dreams. But this much is most apparent and involves no hazard of the future: The country has tired of the mouthings of political demagogues and the antics of adventurers, opportunists and blatherskites, and is now demanding constructive service at the hands of honest, capable and practical men. Among these John Wingate Weeks at this moment stands forth conspicuously and honorably, and bears the limelight test.'

Newspaper comment of this sort could be multiplied indefinitely.

Mr. Weeks received promises of support from many quarters, sufficient to make a very substantial basis for a campaign.

Upon the assembling of the Convention, on June 6, 1916, it was apparent that Mr. Weeks's cause was suffering from the fact that the Massachusetts delegation was not a unit in his favor.

Senator Lodge made the nominating speech for Mr. Weeks:

'Mr. Chairman and my fellow delegates: Born and bred in New Hampshire, adopted by Massachusetts, the candidate whose name I am about to present, commands the confidence and the high respect of these two old States, whose names stand together on the Declaration of Independence and on the Constitution of the United States. (Applause.) Admitted to the Naval Academy in 1877, he received not only the thorough education which is there always given but he also learned those lessons of patriotism, of honor and of devotion to the country and to the flag, which are never forgotten by the graduates of Annapolis and West Point. After leaving the Navy he attained in civil life to a large and well-earned success in the business world, whose trust he never failed to command. In that practical school he acquired a wide knowledge of all the great economic policies and of the problems of finance, upon which the prosperity of the country so largely depends. In 1898, when war came to us, he returned at once to the profession of his youth and served his country in naval command during the conflict with Spain. He was chosen to be Mayor of Newton, the city where he lives, in 1903, and after an administration of great success he was elected a Member of Congress. In the House he rose to the front rank and to high distinction not only as a debater but as a master of economic questions and a legislator of marked constructive ability. After eight years' service in the House he was elected to the Senate, where he has not only continued but has added to the distinction which he had won in the other branch of Congress and where his standing and

reputation are known to all men. A better training for
the highest and most responsible of public offices could
not be devised, and this training rests on the firm foundation of distinguished abilities, strong and upright
character and a reputation without blemish or reproach.

'The first duty of the Republican Party in the coming
campaign is to drive from power the Administration and
the party which have so gravely injured us at home and
so deeply discredited us abroad. (Applause.) In this
great task we invite the coöperation of all citizens who
share our views in regard to the present Administration
and urge them to join with us in the work of bringing
the country back to the sound economic policies, under
which the material prosperity of the Republic has been
built up during the last half-century, and in restoring
the influence and position beyond our own borders
which the United States once held but which have been
lost in the last three years. To do this we must have a
candidate who will command support beyond the strict
limits of the party and receive it from all men who sym-
pathize with our purposes. We must have a man who is
in thorough accord with Republican principles. (Applause, and a voice, 'That's right.') Our candidate must
be a man who believes in the protection of American
rights by land and sea and who will maintain an honest
and a real neutrality; who loves peace, the peace of
justice and right, and who at the same time thoroughly
believes in a preparation both in the Army and Navy
which will absolutely defend and secure, not only our
peace but our rights and our honor. We must have a
man who believes in American policies and the protection of American interests, who is American through
and through. Most of all we must have a man who be-

lieves that this great nation is one — one in ideals, in hopes, in aspirations. (Applause.) A man who believes that all Americans should be loyal to American traditions, who represents the conscience and the soul of the American people; a man who will not only use the power of his great office to advance wise policies and protect American rights but who believes that it is his duty, above all things to keep the faith — the faith of the men who followed Washington at Trenton and of those who fell at Gettysburg. (Prolonged applause.)

'Such a man, in every fiber of his being, is the candidate I am now to present to you, and I name to you as a candidate for the nomination for President of the United States the Honorable John W. Weeks, of Massachusetts. (Loud and prolonged applause.)'

Votes were cast for eighteen names on the first ballot and seventeen on the second.

On the first ballot Hughes received 253½, Weeks 105, Root 103, Cummins 85, Fairbanks 74½, Roosevelt 65.

On the second ballot Hughes received 328½, Root 98½, Fairbanks 88½, Cummins 85, Roosevelt 81, and Weeks 79. The trend to Hughes was so marked that the fight was really over on this ballot.

On the first ballot, Massachusetts gave Weeks 28 votes, Hughes 4, and Roosevelt 4.

On the second ballot, Weeks 19, Hughes 12, and Roosevelt 5.

On the third ballot, Mr. Hughes was nominated, receiving 949½ votes out of 987.

Before the third ballot, on Saturday, June 10, Mr. Weeks, who came to the Convention with the greatest number of instructed delegates and who was of all the favorite sons considered the foremost possibility, took the platform. He was received with great applause by the delegates, and made the following statement:

'I ask the indulgence of the Convention for one moment only.

'I have been a candidate before this Convention for the nomination for the Presidency. It is quite apparent to me that the Convention prefers another, and, not wishing to delay the proceedings of the Convention, I desire to withdraw my name with the request that those who have supported me shall follow the dictates of their own judgment as to whom they shall support hereafter. I want to say to this Convention that there are no political scars on me and in thanking those who have supported me, I believe I can say with confidence that they will join me in doing their utmost to promote the success of the candidates of this Convention at the ensuing election this fall.'

I was a delegate at this Convention and think that no candidate other than Mr. Hughes could have been nominated. This result had become a foregone conclusion. Theodore Roosevelt could not have been nominated. He was much stronger in the country than he was in the Convention. The feeling toward him was kindly, the desire for his support very strong, a disposition to respect his wishes very general, but that was all.

It is a striking illustration of the violent changes in public opinion that Roosevelt, who by a large number of Republicans was held responsible for disrupting the party in 1912, who could not possibly have been nominated in 1916, would, in the opinion of competent judges, had he lived, been nominated and triumphantly elected in 1920.

His recovery of his great prestige before his death is, I think, the greatest tribute ever paid to a public man in our political history.

The great fact to be remembered of Mr. Weeks in connection with the 1916 Convention is that it made him a national figure.

Returning to Mr. Weeks's activities in the Senate takes us back to the first session of the Sixty-Fourth Congress which, covering the period from December 6, 1915, to September 8, 1916, spans the June Convention and the last months of the Presidential campaign and runs into the early autumn. In this Congress Mr. Weeks served on the following committees: Banking and Currency, Coast Defenses, Conservation of National Resources, Forest Reservations and the Protection of Game, Indian Depredations, Military Affairs, Post Offices and Post Roads, Public Health and National Quarantine.

On March 20, 1916, the Senate had under consideration a bill to erect a mill for the manufacture of armor plate. In the course of the debate, on March 21, Mr. Weeks expressed his views, which were, in brief, that there was already sufficient machinery in the country to produce all the armor plate that was needed and he did not believe in putting the Government into business in competition with its own citizens and investing in the industry an unnecessary amount of capital. The bill, however, passed the Senate.

On July 17, 1916, he spoke at great length on the Navy:

'... We are now proposing to build up a great military power in this country which may or may not result in a military oligarchy that will control the affairs of the country and place the civil authorities in subordination to its power. That is what I am afraid of. That is my principal reason for opposing the passage of the bill.

'The Republic of Mexico has as liberal a constitution and one that is as much intended and calculated to preserve the liberties of its people as our own, but Mexico and her people came under the power of the military. The civil authority has lost all power. The constitution of Mexico has meant nothing to its people for the past five years and longer; and that unfortunate country today is — and has been for five years — in a state of revolution and anarchy. The people are being robbed and murdered, the civil authorities are put in defiance, and there is in fact no government in that country, upon which the people can rely for the protection of their lives and their liberties.

'I know it is said that nothing of that kind can befall this country, that there is no danger of this country falling under such influences. But, sir, human nature is very much the same the world over, and we know enough now of the arrogance of the military in our own country to know that, if the opportunity should offer they may become just as arrogant as the military powers of other countries, if they become great and strong enough.

'Mr. President, I have not been opposed to the gradual increase of our Navy. I have never opposed such measures. I recognize the fact that it is necessary for us to have a Navy of reasonable size for our protection. But why should we now, at one bound, place ourselves in the position of one of the great military powers of the world? Is there any danger confronting us that makes it necessary that we should take this step now and at once?

'It is the effect that this sort of legislation is going to have upon the thoughts of the people that concerns me more than anything else. We are beginning already to rely upon the military power of the country and not the civil power. We are teaching the people, by this kind of legislation, that they cannot depend upon the civil authorities for their protection, but that they must be protected by armed force. This is militarism, plain and simple. If it be true, we are no longer a free and independent Republic, governed and protected by constituted civil authority.

'Mr. President, I do not believe it. I see no indication at the present time that can justify any such enormous increase of the Navy as we are now proposing to make. I think it bad policy. I think it is an expenditure of a large sum of money that is absolutely unnecessary and a waste of the public funds. It is placing upon the people a burden that will be continued for years to come; because, as we start in now, we are going to pursue that road from this time on. There will be no going back to the conditions that have existed heretofore. It is perfectly idle, in that view of the situation, to appeal to ancient history or the eloquence of Demosthenes to justify the passing of this kind of legislation.

'Of course, if it were necessary to establish and maintain a large navy in order to protect the country from aggression on the part of any foreign nation or nations, then the people would be perfectly willing that this money should be expended in that way. So would I.

But I want to see some reason for it, and I want to see some indication of danger that justifies this sudden and enormous increase of the naval power of the country at such an expense to the Government.

'Now, sir, I did not expect to discuss this question further, and I should not have done so except for the position taken by the Senator from Idaho, particularly, and by other Senators. The Senator certainly has not understood my opposition to the bill. I think, perhaps, he has not understood the opposition of other Senators to legislation of this kind. It is not, with me, a question of money alone. It is not a question of relations with foreign countries. It is a simple question of the effect of such legislation upon our own country, and the probable effect it will have upon our own free institutions.'

A month later the bill to establish a United States Shipping Board for the purpose of encouraging, developing, and creating a naval auxiliary, naval reserve, and a merchant marine was under discussion, which he voted against for the reasons given in the following statement which he made in the running debate on the subject:

'We are opening the door to the admission of foreign-built ships into our coastwise trade. We are taking a step which has never been taken by any nation in the world up to this time. It is a natural thing for a people to control their own coastwise business. I think it is the most ill-advised step that can be taken in connection with all our shipping interests.

'I am in favor of the establishment of a shipping board, not with the powers given this board, which are restricted and coercive and which will not, in my judgment, enlarge the merchant marine, but a shipping board with suitable powers. I am in favor of building auxiliaries for the Navy, at the proper time and under the proper conditions; and if we build a sufficient number for the Navy we are sure to have more than we can use in ordinary peace times; under those conditions surplus ships could be leased or chartered to private individuals, to be used in commercial pursuits. That was the general purport of the bill to which the Senator from Alabama referred, which I introduced.

'If the pending bill were limited to those two provisions, I should be glad to vote for it. But the other provisions of the bill are so restrictive that they will prevent what the sponsors for the bill hope may result from it; that is, something in the way of development of an American merchant marine.

'Taking everything into consideration, I do not think we could do anything which would be more certain than the passage of this bill to reduce the volume of our merchant marine and almost certain to put our shipyards partially, if not entirely, out of commission. That this is not a Democratic policy, as the fathers knew it, I want to demonstrate by reading from Thomas Jefferson what he said about building our own ships. Mr. Jefferson said, in 1794, "To force shipbuilding is to establish shipyards; is to form magazines; to multiply useful hands; to produce artists and workmen of every kind who may be found at once for the peaceful speculations of commerce and for the terrible wants of war. . . . For a navigating people to purchase its marine afloat would be a strange speculation, as the marine would always be dependent on the merchants furnishing them. Placing, as a reserve, with a foreign nation or in a foreign shipyard the carpenters, blacksmiths, calkers, sailmakers,

and the vessels of a nation, would be a singular commercial combination. We must, therefore, build them ourselves." And yet, under the provisions of this bill and
almost certainly after the war is over, any ships that
are purchased or built are going to be built in foreign
shipyards or are going to be foreign ships, purchased.

'It is for all these reasons, which seem to me to be
sufficient, that I oppose this legislation, and particularly
oppose the amendment which has been offered by the
committee, which will admit to the coastwise trade
foreign-built ships.'

On September 2, 1916, the Senate considered 'An
Act to establish an eight-hour day for employees and
carriers, engaged in interstate and foreign commerce.'
Mr. Weeks participated in the discussion and said,
among other things:

'Mr. President, this is the most important legislative
crisis I have faced during my twelve years in Congress,
and while I am well aware that what I say is not going to
influence the action which the Senate will take to-day, I
cannot let the occasion pass without a brief presentation
of my views. The legislation we are considering is of a
most unusual character and results from a most difficult
but not unusual situation. Information in the press
during the past year has given the general public an ink-
ling of the differences which were said to exist between
the managers of railroads and the train men: but there
was no definite information on the subject, either known
to the public or in the hands of Congress, until a few
days ago when the President summoned the train men
to Washington to consult with them in regard to their
contentions. The result of this consultation was a defi-

nite proposition, made by the President, approving the eight-hour day, compulsory arbitration, and the power to compel the operation of railroads, which, with the exception of the eight-hour feature, are not included in the bill which the Senate is now considering.

'In his address to Congress this week the President stated that the controversy had been existing for more than a year. The natural inquiry one is led to make is, If the situation had been brought to the attention of the President and he had information that there were likely to be serious results, why has he neglected to bring it to the attention of Congress, which has been in session nine months, and, in that way give Congress an opportunity to calmly and deliberately consider every phase of the question and to determine a course of action which might satisfy not only the parties in interest but, more particularly, the interests of the general public, which are involved in any legislation of this character? It must be apparent to the President, as it is to every one else, that no fair and sane consideration can be given to such questions as these in the midst of a political campaign, not to mention the fact that no time has been given to Congress to give the subject any real study. It is true that hearings were held day before yesterday and that they are now in print, but they covered a period of nine hours, and there is not a Member of this body, not connected with the committee, who has had an opportunity to read and digest them.

. . . .

'The whole question has finally reached the stage where it puts the railway train men in the position of demanding that Congress shall stand and deliver. I do not mean to imply that they have willingly put themselves in this position. I have no doubt they would prefer to settle their own differences with their own employers and in their own way, but the President, by inviting the managers and train men to Washington, has not only involved himself and the Administration in this controversy, but, by his recommendations to Congress has involved it as well. The employees, standing on their own rights, insist that unless their contentions are granted before Monday, the 4th, they will carry out their purpose of striking. We need not analyze the probability of this threat being carried out, because we are going to pass the legislation; but I for one do not believe that a majority of the train men wish to strike. I am confident and have proof that many of them are satisfied with present conditions.

.   .   .   .

'I should be glad to provide the means to make a careful investigation of this whole question, and, when a report has been made, to vote for legislation which is justified or is based on the facts; but I will not take any part in putting Congress in the position of standing and delivering. If it has the result which I believe it is going to have, it is a step which every one who is instrumental in bringing it about is going to live to regret, and therefore, without attempting to pass on the merits of this controversy, and even if I approved of every phase of this bill, I would be forced to oppose it for the reasons stated.'

The bill passed the Senate by a strict party vote on the same day. A prominent newspaper said at the time of the event: 'Congress, yielding to a hold-up, pure and simple, the blackmailing of the whole nation under the threat of a strike, the extortion from a Nation's legislature of a special act granting the demands of the brotherhoods without time to inquire into its justice or its practicability, puts upon the country an intolerable humiliation.'

In commenting upon the attitude of the Republican members of the Senate, Mr. Weeks wrote at the time: 'Republican Senators did not shrink from the responsibility of bringing about a strike, but, knowing that they could not defeat the bill without a protracted filibuster, they did not propose to discuss it a sufficient time to enable the President in the midst of a political campaign to charge that they were responsible for it. If we had continued the discussion until midnight, Saturday night, and the strike had been ordered, then the President and the Democratic press would say that the Republican Senators were responsible for the strike, that if they had carried out his recommendations there would have been none; and in the limited time before election, with all the harm which might have come from the strike, there was a general agreement among Republican Senators that it would have been a bad move, from the standpoint of our cause. I want you to know, however, that I did not and do not agree personally with this proposition. I would have killed the bill if I could have had my way, by talk or any other method, because I doubted then and I do not believe now there would have been a strike if the bill had not been passed.'

CHAPTER IX

In the second session of the Sixty-Fourth Congress, beginning December 4, 1916, and ending on March 4, 1917, when, on February 22, 1917, the Senate had under consideration a bill to provide revenue, to defray the expenses of the increased appropriations for the Army and Navy and the extension of fortifications and for other purposes, Mr. Weeks proposed a substitute bill and in the course of his remarks said:

'We need not only to develop our efficiency and provide reasonable protection to enable us to meet the competition of our foreign commercial rivals, at the end of the war, but we must prepare ourselves to face new conditions when this great European struggle is over. For example, we have several millions of men in the United States engaged in the manufacture of munitions. The minute the war is over their employment will cease and they will come into competition with the other workmen in the United States. It is probable that more than 30,000,000 — possibly 40,000,000 — of men are in the armies of the European countries, at war or engaged in the manufacture of munitions of war. They have been taken from their normal pursuits. As soon as the war is over they will return to their employments; they will find their places occupied to some degree by a new element in industrial life, and this element will materially increase the competition for employment which will exist in those countries. As a result of this competition during the readjustment period, it is almost certain that the average wage paid, in European countries, will be even lower than before the war.

'Exactly the opposite condition obtains in the United States. Wages are abnormally high. A reduction in wages and adjustment to new conditions always means that some interest is pinched and that many difficulties must be met during the readjustment period. Moreover, European countries are going to be poor. Poverty does not promote the purchase of products. You can only sell to those who have money to buy; and we should not, for a moment, be deceived by the specious story that European nations are going to need many of our products to rehabilitate themselves, because of the destruction which has taken place. As I have suggested, this destruction has been confined to a very limited area. It will take a long time to replace it, but the replacement is going to be carried on by the people at home. In any event, they will not have the ready money to rehabilitate themselves immediately, and I predict that the purchasing power of Europe will be found to be materially lower than it was before the war.

. . . .

'I am going to give a few illustrations of the effect of the application of this proposed law, and I think they will fairly demonstrate the contention I make, that the bill is unfair; that it is sectional; that it does not apply with the same force to the wealth of the country as it does to the efficiency of the country; and that from every standpoint it will be vicious in its results.

'(1) The bill is objectionable because it is class legislation. The incomes derived from agriculture and from personal service are to be exempt. Thus, a wealthy farmer or a professional man who may be a lawyer, receiving large fees, escapes altogether.

'(2) Although there is a flat exemption of $5000, there would still be many partnerships or close corporations upon which this tax would be a burden, for in many cases the capital invested may be small, the business having been built up entirely by personal effort.

'(3) Capital investment is defined as actual money paid in and actual property owned, together with undivided surplus. To ascertain this would involve great difficulty in some cases and would probably necessitate governmental inspection. The latter would be another step toward centralization. In short, the doctrine of "the less government the better," under Democratic rule, is being thrown to the winds.

'(4) The legislation is punitive in effect. It is leveled at the profits of business, at the effective results of capital and surplus. It is a tax upon the efficiency of the Nation.

'(5) In theory, an income tax is an ideal one, because the fundamental idea upon which it is founded is, that taxation should be imposed according to ability to pay. But there should be as nearly as practicable equality of sacrifice among the taxpayers, and a tax levied at a uniform rate cannot produce equality of sacrifice.

'The proposed law is in effect an income tax possessing some of the vices and few of the merits which that form of direct tax contains. The only sound income tax is one which reaches every one in a proportionate degree.'

.　.　.　.　.　.　.　.　.　.

The excess profits feature of this bill is unfair for the following reasons:

'1. It is discriminatory.

'2. It is unfair.

'3. It will discourage initiative; it will prevent development of resources and industries.

'4. It will favor certain classes or groups.

'5. It will cause great confusion in its interpretation.

'6. It fixes an arbitrary cash basis of value which, under the capital-stock tax rulings, is unsound and unreasonable.'

On February 15, 1917, Mr. Weeks expressed himself as follows in a letter:

'I have had a great many protests against the excess profits tax. . . . Of course, I am going to make as strong a statement as possible against this tax and if it had not become a party programme there would be no trouble about getting rid of it. The Democrats themselves prefer a bond issue, at least, most of them do, and it is only the action of the Treasury Department, backed up by the President, which is imposing this particular tax on us. It is, however, consistent with all of the legislation which has been passed by this Administration in that it imposes the burden of taxation on a few and, as a result, the many clamor for appropriations.

'I do not see anything in the situation which warrants optimism in the slightest degree. I think we are drifting into war, which has evidently gotten into the blood of all the inhabitants of the earth. It looks now as if we were going to have trouble in Cuba as well as Mexico, Germany, and Austria, so that we may expect expenditures of great amounts of money and some human beings before there is a readjustment of the world's affairs.'

An illustration of Mr. Weeks's sound business sense, which marked everything he said may be found in a further discussion of this bill on February 28, 1917, when he said:

'Now, Mr. President, what should be done with this $64,000,000 of bonds and all other maturing bonds, is to pay them in some way. I suggested the other day in my argument relating to the issuing of bonds that the only safe and proper way to issue them, in order to insure their payment when they mature, is to issue serial bonds. I am not going to take time to go into a long discussion of the relative merits of a bond issue maturing at its termination without any sinking fund, a bond issue with a sinking fund to retire them at the time the bonds mature, or bonds issued as serial bonds, so that if the longest bond in the series terminates in twenty years, one twentieth of the issue will be paid each year. All I have to say, Mr. President, is that all the statistics, bearing on this subject, indicate that the serial bond is very much cheaper from the standpoint of the issuing party than any other form. I submitted the other day some tables indicating the saving that could be made by issuing serial bonds. Those tables had been prepared with great care, and they can be depended upon by Senators as being as accurate as it is possible for such statistics to be.

'One of my amendments relates to that particular subject. As I have said, provision is made in this bill for refunding these bonds in fifty years. Instead of refunding them in fifty years, I would handle the question in this way: On page 11, line 21, after the word "authorized," strike out down to and including the words "per annum," on page 12, line 1, and insert the following proviso:

'"*Provided further*, That in lieu of any of the bonds provided for in this act the Secretary of the Treasury is hereby authorized and directed to issue serial bonds of the United States, maturing in equal amounts from date of issue to 20 years from date of issue, bearing interest, payable semi-annually, at a rate not exceeding 3 per cent per annum: *Provided further*, That the mandatory provision in this paragraph may be waived if the market conditions are such that the obtainable rate on serial bonds is more than one-fourth per cent per annum higher than on bonds of other forms of issue."

'The reason I suggest that last proviso, Mr. President, is that it has been charged that serial bonds would not sell on as advantageous a basis as would bonds of other forms of issue. I do not think that that claim is justified. I believe that serial bonds, running from one to twenty years, as is provided in this amendment, will sell as well as an issue of bonds running for twenty years and all maturing at that time. So I do not think it possible that there could be any other result than getting the best possible price for the bonds; and yet, in order to protect the Treasury Department, I have provided that, if it is found necessary to pay more than one fourth of one per cent more, or to sell on a quarter per cent higher basis than would be the case with any other form of issue, the Secretary of the Treasury is not bound to sell the serial bonds.

.   .   .   .

'I am sorry there are so few Senators listening to what I am saying about this matter of issuing serial bonds, for I wish the Senate might understand what it really means, and the very material savings that can be made. Just for example, I took from one of the best-known bond men a statement which I did not include in my remarks the other day, which is a fair indication of what can be done. This is Mr. Chamberlain, who says, in his Principles of Bond Investments, that it costs $418,305 more to issue $1,000,000 of fifty-year, four per cent bonds, to be retired at the end of that time, at a three per cent basis for the sinking fund — which is the usual average return — than if the issue were made serially, and one fiftieth of the bonds retired annually. Just think of it! An issue of $1,000,000 of bonds would cost $418,000 more than if issued in serial form, and one fiftieth of them paid each year.'

When the Naval Appropriation Bill was under discussion in March, 1917, Mr. Weeks spoke as follows, as to the superiority of private over public yards for the construction of major ships:

'The reason why I am asking particularly about this matter is because I have been informed that some steps have been taken relating to the Boston Navy Yard. Personally I am not in favor of equipping navy yards for the construction of major ships except in one or two instances, so that the Government may, in ordinary times, have a means of competing with outside bidders, if the outside bids seem to be unreasonable. I am perfectly satisfied that the privately controlled yards can build ships in ordinary times much cheaper than they can be built at navy yards, and I regret ordinarily to see any construction of that kind carried on at the navy yards. I am perfectly content to have some preparation made for the construction of major ships, because I do not wish a price imposed upon the Government which is going to be extortionate. I think it should have facilities to protect itself in that way, but I think there should be a fair consideration by the best experts the Navy has, about where these preparations should be made.

'We build capital ships at the New York yard, and if one other yard were fitted for that purpose, in my judgment it would be sufficient; but I think there should be some definite plan, and it should be in the hands of Congress as to where this money is to be expended, how much is to be expended, and how much is to be expended at each yard, so that we may have accurate information upon that subject.'

On March 2, 1917, Mr. Weeks expressed privately the following views on the legislative situation: 'We have discussed in a legitimate way appropriation bills and other matters during the last few days, so that it is going to be impossible to pass very much of the legislation, which must be adopted, before the first of July. This will necessitate an extra session of Congress, and I approve of it. What the President should do is to call a session at once, with an agreement that only certain specified legislation should be considered during the extra session. That, I think, could be arranged without any trouble. I spent a good part of last night in trying to make such arrangements, but the President is perfectly pig-headed and I think his party associates are all afraid to put up to him the situation as it really is, so that we do not get anywhere in any matter in which he is involved.' And again on March 6, 'when he last appeared before the Senate and House of Representatives he stated that he could do, what he was asking Congress to furnish him the means of doing without any other authority, but now he has discovered a law which prevents his doing so. It seems incredible that he could not have known all about the law, to which he refers, when he delivered his address. It was mentioned two or three times in the debate in the Senate, and almost every one who is familiar with international affairs knew that such a law existed. I suspect it is another case of faking.'

The first session of the Sixty-Fifth Congress continued through October 6, 1917.

On April 9, Mr. Weeks introduced a joint resolution providing for the appointment of a Committee to be known as the 'Joint Committee on the Conduct of the War,' which had been declared on April 2. This proposed Committee was to consist of six members of the Senate, four Democrats and two Republicans, and six members of the House, three Republicans and three Democrats. This followed a precedent established in the conduct of the Civil War.

In presenting the resolution, Mr. Weeks said:

'Mr. President, it is my purpose to ask that the joint resolution be referred to the Committee on Rules. Before doing so I wish, however, to say that this is following the general course which was followed by Congress during the Civil War. It furnishes a direct connecting link between the executive and the legislative branches of the Government.

'It seems to me that we should correlate all the forces of the Government and all the forces in civil life, for the purpose of supporting the Government at this time. It is reported in the press that we are to be asked to appropriate vast sums of money, five or six billion dollars, without any direct indication where and how that money shall be expended. I believe that it is a part of the duty of Congress to have some knowledge of the methods of expenditure and to determine whether the expenditure is being made in accordance with the purposes of Congress.

'This is no reflection on the President or on the Secretaries whose departments will have the expenditure of the money, but we are extremely careful, in ordinary times, to make specific every appropriation and require by law that the money shall not be spent for any other purpose. We are going into a great war, and it appears to me that we should take every precaution to prevent any improper expenditure of money and to keep before the people, at all times, the methods which are being taken to expend these large amounts of money, as well as the conduct of the war in every particular.'

The resolution was subsequently reported upon adversely by the Committee.

Speaking on April 23, 1917, upon a Senate Bill, to authorize the President to increase temporarily the Military Establishment of the United States, Mr. Weeks said at the conclusion of his speech, in which he dwelt upon the need of universal military training: 'Now we have not had universal military training and we want it — or most of us do — and we want universal service at this time. There ought not to be a single slacker in the United States. Either every man should be engaged in the military service or he should be engaged in some other way in supporting the government at this time.'

Speaking of the conditions in Washington Mr. Weeks wrote on May 5, 1917:

'Of course, legislatively, I know something about it, but we have no information about what the Administration is doing or is likely to do. My impression, however, is that the first troops we send to France will be regulars and that they will be followed by the best-trained men outside the regular organization. Naturally, under present conditions, these would be members of the National Guard. The General Staff was inclined to wish the National Guard sent first, after a period of intensive training here and then on the other side. Marshal Joffre, with whom I talked the other night, advocated the former plan; that is, assuming that we would send regulars first, that they would be gotten together here, transported as soon as possible, and then trained in modern fighting tactics, after they reached France. He was very insistent that we should send one division without delay, believing that its presence in France would stimulate the whole French nation much more than the value of its fighting capacity, and that it would have exactly the reverse effect on the Germans.

'I have not any idea that the President will commission T. R. even if the Senate and House conferees agree to the volunteer proposition, which was inserted in the Army Bill by the Senate. He made application for a commission and to enlist a volunteer force some time ago, which was refused.

'As we really get into the war and begin the development of the different requirements, the magnitude of the whole undertaking becomes apparent, and the question of supplies, transportation, food products, etc., is going to be quite as important as the fighting. There is pretty nearly nothing in sight which gives me any great satisfaction, and I am as antagonistic to this Administration and its methods as ever. While Republicans are doing their duty as they see it, the war is being fought as a Democratic proposition. The President has nothing to

do with Republicans, even when they are the element
that enables him to carry out his policies.'

When the Agricultural Products Bill was under consideration on May 31, 1917, Mr. Weeks made the following characteristically blunt comment upon it:

'Mr. President, in my judgment there is very little of
this bill that is not worthless. There is very much in the
bill that may be extremely harmful. I do not think it is
based on sound governmental principles. The amendment offered by the Senator from Washington is, to my
mind, about the only good thing in the bill. I would be
glad to vote for any proposition which will punish a man
for speculating in food products under such conditions
as obtain to-day, but I do not want the Government to
enter into this course for any other reasons.

'The amendment which has just been offered by the
Senator from Florida seems to me to be as virtuous as
most of the propositions in the bill. I am particularly
interested in it because I have been devoting a considerable part of my time to-day to prevent the Navy Department from taking over two steam trawlers which have
just been built and are ready to be put into operation
by a codfishing firm. It would produce a very large
volume of fish if they are allowed to go into service. The
Navy Department proposes to take them over, for some
purpose connected with naval affairs. If they do that it
will very materially reduce the fish supply in the United
States, because these two modern trawlers would probably secure ten times as many fish as the ordinary
vessels used in that service.

'Now, what kind of logic can it be which will suggest
to one department of the Government to take away

from the fishing service the vessels which are constructed for that purpose and empower another department of the Government to undertake the catching and curing of fish? It would disjoint it, at best, and be unwise, it seems to me, in every particular. I hope the amendment will not prevail.'

On June 4, 1917, Senator Weeks issued the following patriotic appeal regarding registration, under the Draft Law:

'To-morrow is registration day, and the youth of the nation will be called upon to perform the first of many patriotic duties growing out of the present war. The registration is compulsory, but the spirit back of the registration will decide whether the individual man is a conscript or a volunteer. Let every man and boy, who signs his name to a registration slip, have back of him the patriotic pride and encouragement of those he loves, and our new army of 1,000,000 men will strike the blow that will help to bring peace and liberty to the entire world.

'There will be a few slackers, but they will suffer the shame they deserve. For the first time in many decades, the nation needs the services and support of its entire man-power, and June 5, 1917, should go down into American history as a day unparalleled for patriotic fervor and devotion to American ideals.

'This is not the time or occasion for the exercise of individual opinion on the merits of a proposed governmental action. In this emergency there are but two classes — those units who uphold their government, without question, and those who wilfully or for some mistaken reason do not. Don't make the irretrievable mistake of putting yourself in the second class.'

On July 16, when the Senate resumed consideration of the bill to provide further for the National security and defense by encouraging the production, conserving the supply and controlling the distribution of food products and fuel, Mr. Weeks said, referring to a charge that citizens who composed the different parts of the advisory commission were in Washington for the purpose of letting contracts to themselves, and as evidence of the need of the creation of a 'Joint Committee on the Conduct of the War,' which he had previously proposed:

'Mr. President, I think the Senator from Iowa just suggested that rumors of this kind which have come to him and come to others should be investigated for every public reason. This morning the Senator from Maine referred to the same matter, very pertinently, it seemed to me, and he suggested that unless I were going to offer as an amendment to this bill the proposition which I introduced in April, relating to a committee on the conduct of the war, he thought seriously of doing it. I want to say, Mr. President, that I think I have shown reasonable patience in waiting for a report of the Committee on Rules on that proposition.

'Any one who knows anything about the situation here, knows the reason it has not been reported back to the Senate; the fact remains that it has not been done, and it is my purpose to offer it as an amendment on this bill. Every day there are questions coming up here which demand public consideration, about which the public is entitled to information. There is one question which is bound to come up for investigation; it appears pretty nearly every day in the newspapers — I refer to the operations of the Shipping Board. They have literally become a public scandal. The most important development which we have before us is the creation of enough shipping to take the place of that which is destroyed every day; and yet contracts have been tied up for three months, owing to disagreements about which I do not propose to express an opinion here, now, but which have prevented action. Now, the public, which is perfectly willing to appropriate hundreds of millions of dollars for these purposes, is entitled to some action; and if the President does not take it, then there should be a committee in session which will investigate, without any further motion from any one, such matters of public importance.'

On July 20, 1917, the Senate, again, had under consideration the bill to provide further for the National security and defense by encouraging the production, conserving the supply, and controlling the distribution of food products and fuel. Mr. Weeks expressed himself, in part, as follows:

'So the question itself is most involved. It cannot be charged that the coal miner is alone responsible, or in many cases even largely responsible, for this situation. The needs of New England are not the needs of Ohio, which mines its own coal, or the needs of Illinois, which mines its own coal. The transportation questions are much more involved than in those States.

'When I listen to these amendments and the propositions of the committee I feel like saying, "A plague on all your houses!" I do not know how any one of them can answer the purposes which they claim to be able to do. It is utterly repugnant to me to think of the Government taking over the coal mines and operating them. In my judgment it would curtail rather than increase the coal supply of the country.

'On the other hand, I do not see how any man is going to be wise enough to fix a price for coal which will not do a material injustice to one section of the country, even if it does justice in another section. I do not believe there are men living who are wise enough to handle that kind of question without doing as much harm as they do good. If we were doing the wise thing, or if we had done it months ago, we would have undertaken to prepare this country for the transportation of its products. If we had devoted our money and our time to the transportation questions and forgotten all these other correlated ones, we would, to-day, and next winter be infinitely better off than we are going to be. It is too late now to build cars, it is too late to build vessels for this purpose, and it does not make any difference how many committees or commissions you have — the only possibility of relieving the New England situation is for the railroads to stop doing one kind of business and devote their equipment to the coal business.

'I presume, to some degree, that may be done and will be done under the direction of the committee connected with the advisory commission, as it has been in other cases, but this very advisory commission may not be all-wise.

'The New Haven Railroad has just been asked to send 1500 freight cars to Florida to transport the products of Florida, which are ready for market, to the Northern market. That delays every kind of business in New England, because the New Haven has not any more equipment than it needs, probably less than it needs. So while we are saving one industry or one product we may be doing irreparable damage in another case.

'I never was as much at sea on what seems to be the

best course to take, on any question, as I am on this one relating to fuel. I think in the final analysis if we would do what we can now to provide transportation facilities, if, for example, Congress would appropriate $100,000,-000 to build coal cars, we could not spend that money as wisely in any other way, because the car industry of the country is not overworked. If that industry could obtain material, without any question it could turn out a great many cars before the snow flies next winter, and if the motive power could be obtained, and those cars were available, we could care, very largely, at least, for the situation as it exists.'

Speaking upon the same bill on July 21, Mr. Weeks said:

'Mr. President, the psychology of this situation is such that I expect the bill will be passed, and I propose to vote for it, when it is perfected; but I do so without any anticipation that it will satisfy any considerable number of people, even if the wisest men are to be given control of the legislation. I do not believe that a bill which violates substantially every law of trade, with which it comes in contact, can possibly be administered to the satisfaction of the people who have been promoting the legislation.

'For more than sixteen hundred years there have been attempts made to regulate the prices of products by governmental action, and they have invariably proved failures, and I suspect will prove a failure in this case. This being the case, I have but little hope of action as a result of this legislation, which will be greatly beneficial, but I am willing to give it a trial. It seems to me there should be something in the bill which will be really beneficial to the people of the United States. For that reason I have introduced, as an amendment, a proposition for a committee on the conduct of the expenditures of the war. I am addressing the Senate briefly on that subject now, because I suspect, looking at the clock, that I will not have an opportunity to do so if I do not do so now.

'When I introduced my resolution providing for a committee on the conduct of the war, nearly three months ago, I did so because I believed, that, as the war progressed, a great many controversial matters would develop and that there should be some vent through which differences arising might be investigated, giving to Congress, the public, and the executive departments accurate information relating to the controversy. I believed then that many disinterested, loyal, and useful men would be attacked for reasons which would not bear investigation and that there would be many cases of inefficiency in the Government service, resulting in waste, extravagance, delay, and even graft, which could be better and more effectively investigated by a legislative committee than by the appointing power or department heads, heavily burdened, as they must necessarily be, with a multitude of important problems. Moreover, it seemed to me there should be some method of bringing about a more complete coöperation between the legislative and executive branches of the Government in promoting the conduct of the war. All of these presumed reasons for such a committee have already developed, although the war from our standpoint is in its infancy and not a single American soldier is yet on the firing line.'

On August 1, 1917, the Senate resumed the consideration of a resolution proposing an amendment to the Constitution of the United States on nation-wide prohibition. On that day Mr. Weeks stated that it was his purpose to vote against submitting the proposition to the States and he closed his speech as follows:

'I am now, and always have been, a believer in local option, and firmly believe that this is a question which should be decided by the people of the several States in accordance with their own wishes. The police powers are inherent in the States, and the question of controlling the sale of spirits largely comes within that constitutional provision.

'Formerly there was some logic in the position taken by many that, if liquor were sold in any States it could be shipped into other States against the wishes of the people of the States that had adopted prohibition. That condition has been cured by the Webb-Kenyon Bill, for which I voted, which prohibits the shipment of liquor into dry territory; and the act making this prohibitive has been declared constitutional by the Supreme Court, so there is no possibility of such complaint, if the officers of the States are attending to their duties.

'Moreover, in order to prevent or discourage the purchase of liquor in dry territory, a bill passed Congress last winter prohibiting the carrying by mail of newspapers into dry territory, if they contained liquor advertisements. I voted for that bill, and I shall vote for any other legislation to protect the desires of those living in territory which has become dry.

'One of the serious weaknesses of this proposed measure is that it may be brought before the legislatures of the several States as many times as its proponents desire, or until the legislatures of three fourths of the States are found favorable to the proposition. If it were submitted at one time, it might be found that the legislatures of twenty-five or thirty States would be favorable to it and the legislatures of the other States unfavorable; but it can be brought up again and again in the States which have not adopted the provision, until a legislature may be found, years hence, favorable to it. By that time, there might be legislatures in some of the States which had adopted the amendment unfavorable to it, but they could not retrace their steps. That makes the whole question a constant irritant, in connection with our elections, distracting attention from the issues which divide political parties, and very largely breaking down the party spirit and action which I believe essential to the best interests of the Republic. I need not cite any other instance of that condition than that found in the State of Maine, where prohibition has prevailed for substantially fifty years — a prohibition which most people admit has not prohibited, largely because the law officers have not performed their full duty, but really because the sentiment of the State, or of localities within the State, has been against prosecutions for violations of the law.

'No law can be enforced unless it accords with public sentiment; in fact, when a law does not conform to public sentiment, ordinarily there is no attempt to enforce it. We have a good illustration of that in the law passed a few years ago by Congress regulating the speed of automobiles in the District of Columbia, limiting their speed to twelve miles an hour, and this law was passed largely at the instance and urging of those unfamiliar with automobile traffic. It is unnecessary to say to the Senate that this law is violated by every automobilist in the District of Columbia every day he uses his automobile, and unless an automobilist indulges in excessive or unreasonable speed no attention whatever is paid to it. Therefore, while the law is neglected, it becomes positively harmful, because it begets a disregard for all law and creates a tendency to evade reasonable statutes.'

relation of the prohibition and suffrage questions to the I & R vote.

'I cannot see anything but harm coming from woman suffrage. I have not found a man among those representing States which have adopted woman suffrage who does not admit that it has made no material change in legislation or other conditions in their State. It adds greatly to the burden of conducting elections, and there are so many substantial reasons, in my judgment, against it that I shall never support it, whatever may be the judgment or the votes of others. There are too many ill-informed people voting in this country rather than too few. What we want is a more intelligent suffrage rather than a less intelligent one. I do not believe that you will claim that women have more judicial minds or are better fitted for anything relating to passing upon the questions in an unprejudiced way than men. If this is true, then giving them suffrage is going to weaken rather than strengthen government in this country.

'I am perfectly willing to subscribe to prohibition when the people of Massachusetts decide they want it, but I am opposed to having the people of Nevada pass on that kind of a question for us. Personally I would be very glad if I thought the world had reached a point where it would use any kind of spirits in moderation. I think it is approaching that condition, but I do not believe that it has reached it yet, and passing any kind of law without public support behind it is always ill-advised. However, I am perfectly agreeable to submitting the prohibition question to the voters of the State, and if they vote in favor of it, I shall say Amen and be quite willing to observe it, as I am any other law adopted as a result of the sober judgment of the people.'

Mr. Weeks could not be moved from his opposition to woman suffrage. He more than once said, and in most emphatic language, that he would rather be defeated at the then approaching senatorial election than abandon his convictions. Serious argument and playful comment were alike powerless to move him. One of his friends, disposed to a humorous view of the situation, sent him the following lines:

> 'While the lamp holds out to burn
> The vilest sinner may return' —

which is another way of saying,

> Unless you choose to be stone blind
> 'Tis not too late to change your mind —

or, if you prefer,

> Unless you wish to be a goat,
> Oh, why not let the women vote?

The second session of the Sixty-Fifth Congress covered the period from December 3, 1917, through November 21, 1918, during the latter part of which occurred Mr. Weeks's campaign for reëlection, in which he was defeated by David I. Walsh, an account of which will be given later.

On December 18, the Senate took up a bill providing for an amendment to the 'Farm Loan Act.' In commenting upon it, Mr. Weeks said:

'Mr. President, I am a member of the Committee on Banking and Currency, which considered this legislation, and I am one of the members of the committee who voted against reporting it favorably. I assume that as long as the bill comes here, with the approval of the administration and the large majority of the Committee on Banking and Currency, no other than affirmative action will be taken, but I think it due Senators, when such an unusual step is being taken, one which has never been undertaken before, that they understand just exactly what is being done. It is for that reason I hope to have an opportunity to express to as many Senators as possible my view of this legislation.

.　.　.　.　.　.　.　.　.　.　.

'How is the purchaser of a Liberty bond going to feel when he is importuned to buy a bond, either by the sacrifice of some security which he has or by failing to invest his money in something that will pay him better, if he is told that the money is not to be used to prosecute the war, but it is to be loaned to another one of his fellow citizens simply because that fellow citizen can borrow it at a lower rate of interest than he is now paying on his indebtedness? That is the gist and the essence of this proposition. That is exactly what is going to happen. Senators, if you subscribe to the next Liberty Loan, you must feel that some part of your subscription, instead of being used to prosecute the war, is going to be loaned to some of your fellow citizens at a lower rate of interest than they are now paying and for that reason only. Fundamentally, of course, that is bad morally. It is bad from the standpoint of the Government at such a time as this, and it is bad finance as well.

'Personally I have very little faith in any of these schemes which put the Government into business with the assurance that we are going to get better results than heretofore. It is true that there are farm-loan banks all over Europe, but they are all under private auspices, and in no case is the Government involved in any way. I want the Government in this case involved as little as possible. Therefore I am going to offer an amendment to this bill, which I will read: "That until all bonds so purchased by the Secretary of the Treasury have been redeemed or repurchased, no loan in addition to those now approved shall be made by Federal land banks except under special rules prepared by the Federal Farm Loan Board, limiting further loans from funds derived from the Treasury to those made for the sole purpose of increasing farm products."

'In other words, while this situation is bad, it seems to me it will be simply disgraceful if there should be continued the loaning of money for the sole purpose of enabling a man to get his loan at a lower rate of interest than he is now paying. There may be an excuse if it is going to result in an increase of farm products.'

On February 15, 1918, Mr. Weeks spoke at length upon 'A War Cabinet and Director of Munitions.' I quote here the opening and closing paragraphs of his speech.

'Mr. President, I have delayed making any comments in the Senate relating to the examination of the operations of the War Department, until the investigation, which was undertaken in December, had been substantially completed. I now wish to submit some remarks in advocacy of the constructive legislation proposed by the Committee on Military Affairs as the result of its investigations — the War-Cabinet Bill and the bill providing a centralized head of purchasing. In order to make these comments intelligently, it seems to me I cannot do otherwise than point out to the Senate some of the reasons for proposing this legislation and why members of the committee believe these bills should pass.

'Before the convening of Congress in December, and since the beginning of the war, members of the committee have received a great number of complaints and criticisms against the manner in which the War Department was conducting the preparations for our participation in this great conflict. Naturally complaints have come to all Senators, but a much greater number have come to members of the Committee on Military Affairs. These complaints can be divided into three classes: First, those coming from disappointed contractors or seekers for Government work. Second, those coming from young men who have enlisted or been drafted into the military service and who found themselves living under conditions to which they were unused, unfamiliar, and to which they did not readily adjust themselves. Third, those criticisms which seemed on their face to furnish evidence of a failure on the part of some one to do something which should have been done.

'No member of the committee expected to find perfection in the operations of the War Department, under the trying conditions existing during the past ten months. It was not humanly possible to take the military organization we had at the beginning of the war, expand it to many times its original size, and bring it to what it is to-day without making mistakes. The same thing would be true of any enterprise of a business character, for any one familiar with business operations must realize that the failure of individuals to comprehend a situation or measure up to it, necessarily means

mistakes in carrying out even the best-digested plans.
I do not place any great reliance on individual failures
or cases indicating errors due to the human equation,
but when such failures are of sufficient number, in any
particular activity, to demonstrate a lack of proper
planning, coördination, systematic effort, or careful
supervision, then they become an indictment of that
particular activity.

.   .   .   .

'It has been charged that Congress is meddling in the
war and trying to curtail the authority of the President.
The President will name these men; Congress will not do
so, and there is no possibility that it will furnish a means
for Congress to interfere with any activity over which
it has no jurisdiction. Can it be possible that the President will be embarrassed by such a cabinet, as he has
suggested he would be? It would seem as if he would be
embarrassed to a greater extent by a perpetuation of the
disjointed system which now exists, a system which has
failed to produce ships, notwithstanding the shipping
plans; which has failed to deliver sufficient fuel, notwithstanding the unbounded coal supply we have;
which has been responsible for a failure to protect our
soldiers against sickness and furnish them with suitable
clothing. We are the inventors and leaders in aeroplanes,
and yet we have no aeroplanes. We have the greatest
steel works in the world, and yet we have few guns.
We lead the whole world in automobile manufacture,
and yet we are just commencing to obtain motor trucks;
and the worst of all, the system we have had is responsible for camp hospitals not having heat, water, or
sewerage.

'Congress has resolved that every resource of the

country shall be devoted to the successful prosecution of the war, and, as far as possible, this pledge has been fulfilled. Can any one claim that it is not the duty of Congress to see that the resources it has provided are so expended that a consummation of the purposes for which they are given is insured? How are we to know that this is being done in a manner satisfactory to the Congress and the people of the country, unless investigations are held and the details of the work of the administration scrutinized? Moreover, we owe everything to our men on the other side and to those on this side training to take their place at the front. They are to be plunged into the vortex of the most deadly military operations men have ever had to encounter. Every conceivable device to kill, maim, and torture is in operation on that great battle front. What excuse can we make to our soldiers if we are neglectful of their security, their comfort, and, in the final analysis, their lives? The loyal man in the United States is not he who complacently assumes that everything is as it should be, who is willing to accept general statements for detailed information, but on the contrary is the one who is ever alert to do and to see that there is done, not our bit, but our very best. We owe this to our fighting forces, our country, and to ourselves, and should not be diverted from that course by unreasoning or uninformed criticism from any one, whatever his position may be.'

When the Post Office appropriation bill came up in the Senate on June 29, 1918, Mr. Weeks expressed his opinion in no uncertain terms in regard to the action upon pneumatic tubes, in which Boston was interested. He said:

'Mr. President, I should like to say one word which I did not have an opportunity to say on account of what seemed to me to be the haste of the proceedings relative to the passage of the Post Office bill.

'I do not propose to take any definite time to discuss what has transpired, in connection with this bill, but I should not be doing justice to myself if I did not enter my protest against the action which has destroyed several millions of dollars of property and has destroyed the mail facilities in five of the largest cities of this country, and those cities produce a net revenue of sixty-odd millions of dollars a year. There is not, and never has been, a word of testimony against that service from any man who has been getting the benefit of it, but, on the contrary, universal testimony in favor of its continuance.

'In the name of those people, who have been paying such a large revenue to the Government for all these years, and who wish the service of the pneumatic tubes continued, I enter my protest against the high-handed method which has been adopted in this connection, destroying the property of the companies and destroying the mail facilities of the people who have been enjoying them.'

And on September 17, he again advocated the issue of serial bonds for the Fourth Liberty Loan, in a speech of which the following are the open paragraphs:

'Mr. President, our Government is about to issue a Fourth Liberty Loan, larger than any of the previous issues, and therefore a greater strain on the financial resources of the country than we have had heretofore to meet. I assume that the country will respond as patriotically in this instance as it has in the past, and that there will be no question about a full subscription to the $6,000,000,000 of bonds which are to be offered to the public. I am interested in the manner of issuing these bonds, and it is that question which I wish to bring to the attention of the Senate. It is an inopportune time, I am sure, if an audience is expected on the floor of the Senate, but it will be a matter of record, which, I think, may justify the effort.

'In February last year, when the finance bill of that month was under consideration, I submitted to the Senate some observations, included in which was a statement relating to the manner of issuing bonds in serial form. I thought at the time, in fact I was confident at the time, that many Senators who had not had the opportunity to study this question were impressed with the value of the suggestion; but for some reason of which I am not informed the Treasury Department decided not to take advantage of the forms and figures which had been prepared and which were included in the "Record." It is to see, once more, if I cannot obtain enough interest in this important subject, which in my judgment will save more money than all the savings that can be made between now and the end of the war, without in any way impairing the possibility of placing loans, that I now address the Senate.

'One of the striking actions taken in connection with that bill was the refunding of the bonded indebtedness incurred in prosecuting the Spanish-American War. Some sixty-eight millions of bonds were issued at the time of the Spanish War, to supplement the additional taxation which was laid to provide for the expenditures incident to that conflict. Those bonds were to mature in twenty years, and the provision was made for their renewal for fifty years. In other words, and there could be no better example of the folly of such a system, the grandchildren or the great grandchildren of those who were active in affairs in 1898 are going to be obliged to either pay for the expenses of a small war, fought at that time or renew again the indebtedness then incurred, and all the generations living between 1898 and 1968 will have to bear the burden of paying the interest on that indebtedness.

. . . .

'. . . We should not lose sight of the fact that every effort should be made to strengthen the Nation's credit, for by so doing we add an additional surety to our position as a military, as well as a commercial power, and a large indebtedness for which no provision has been made for payment cannot but produce a bad impression and will result in lessening the Nation's credit. Moreover, bonds issued under the serial method, properly and justly distribute the cost of the war over the time it is determined as being necessary to pay the entire indebtedness. No part of this or succeeding generations, until the entire indebtedness is paid, will be able to escape its measure of the responsibility and that, in itself, will have a good effect on the Nation and a stabilizing effect on the price of bonds. We are necessarily spending enormous sums of money and there should be no hesitation to make every expenditure which is legitimate, but there should be no opportunity lost to make a saving wherever it can be done without in any degree lessening the effectiveness of the prosecution of the war, and I maintain that all of the methods combined which might be discovered to produce economies in our expenditures would not equal the saving that can be made to the Government if the serial-bond method is adopted. It may be said that the printing of the bonds for the Fourth Liberty Loan has already been undertaken; even if it has, the plates and every preparatory step which may have been taken could very well be discarded to bring about the enormous savings evidenced by the figures which I have submitted, the correctness of which I believe cannot be successfully disputed.

On September 27, 1918, Mr. Weeks introduced a resolution creating a committee of six Senators and six Representatives to be known as the 'Joint Committee on Reconstruction.' He spoke, in part, as follows in introducing the resolution:

'Mr. President, the Hun is evidently on the run; and while we may not be able to see the end of this war, the end is coming. It may come sooner than we anticipate; and when it does come, we should be prepared for the conditions which we shall have to face.

'I wish to submit to the Senate, briefly, and in a form which does not cover anything like all the subjects to which I have referred, some of the reasons why I think action should be taken on this resolution.

'When the United States declared war against the Imperial German Government, in April, 1917, although the more observing had for many months believed this step inevitable, practically no preparation had been made, and, as a result, it was necessary to prepare for war at a time when war actually prevailed. This failure has had many decided disadvantages. It not only delayed our active participation in the war, but it has and will cost us tens of thousands of additional lives and hundreds of millions, indeed, billions of dollars. The actual material, with which we have had to supply ourselves since the spring of 1917 will have cost many billions more than it would, if it had been provided in prewar times. I am not saying this in the way of criticism. Quite likely a majority of the American people did not visualize the situation which was developing, and as a result there may not have been sufficient public pressure demanding that more active steps be taken in making preparations. We know, however, that the successes of the German armies, in the first years of the war, were largely due to the very thorough preparation made by the German Government and that the weakness of the Allied armies was their unpreparedness when war was declared. Although the Allies were better prepared than the United States, when it entered the war, it took them, especially Great Britain, a long time to become effective fighting forces.

'While the end of this great conflict may not be in sight, we hope it is, and we know now what the end will be. When it does come, it will not give us any time for preparation; indeed, in one day the whole world scene will change. Unless we take advantage of the present to provide for the future, we shall be caught in exactly the same condition, as regards peace, as we were when we declared war — unprepared. It will be infinitely more reprehensible if we fail to make preparations for peace, because we shall have lost our opportunity to take advantage of the great lessons we have learned from this war. There might have been some excuse from the viewpoint of many people for not making ample preparations to fight, but with that failure before our eyes, the example of the failures of other nations, and, more important, the provisions these nations are making for peace, there is no excuse for our country not preparing itself to meet the great after-war problems. Every nation now engaged in war has been and is now getting ready for peace conditions. Nearly three years ago conferences were held by the Allies at which certain general principles were adopted, in regard to trade conditions after the war, the relationship of one power to another, the relationship of the Allied nations to friendly countries, neutral nations, and the enemy governments. Similar conferences were held by the Central Powers. Quite likely the conclusions reached at that time may have to be modified, but these conferences indicate the far-sightedness of European governments and the tendency on the part of the other nations, engaged in the war, to do those things which every one must recognize as absolutely essential.

'Since early in 1916, in addition to these international conferences, the various belligerent nations have been investigating and studying every conceivable question relating to after-war conditions, their relation to the social and industrial life of the country, and have, at least tentatively, adopted plans for carrying out the policies required by the new era we must face. This is especially true — and the evidence is at hand — in the case of Great Britain and, to some degree, Germany. In these countries the investigations have advanced to such an extent that separate ministries have been established to assume charge of the necessary reconstruction. In Germany, if the evidence I have is correct, three such ministries have been organized and one has been created in England. I do not believe an identical course can be followed to the best advantage in this country — at least we should reach it through gradual stages — but we must, without delay, take such steps as may be necessary to provide for the innumerable new problems we must face the day peace is made. Because we do not need coal in the summer, is no excuse for not filling our bins for the coming winter.

'The resolution I have introduced provides the authorization and means to make the necessary investigations. It may not completely cover all the questions to be considered, and it may be necessary, later on, to introduce additional resolutions covering particular subjects; but as I do conceive it to be the business of Congress to give its active attention to this subject, and to do so at once, I hope there will be no delay in the consideration or adoption of this resolution.'

On September 30, 1918, President Wilson addressed the Senate and strongly urged concurrence in the Amendment, already approved by the House, proposing the extension of suffrage to women, as vitally essential to the successful prosecution of the Great War.

Every argument in favor of the Amendment, based on reason or sentiment, was made in the debate. When the vote was taken on October 1, 1918, with his reelection to the Senate to be decided in a little over a month, Mr. Weeks was one of the thirty-one to vote in the negative, fifty-three having voted in the affirmative, less than two thirds, and therefore the resolution did not pass. A change of three votes from the negative to the affirmative would have been sufficient for the passage of the resolution. It was quite to be expected that women urging the Suffrage Amendment, the country over, should have been infuriated at the result and determined to oppose the reëlection of Senators voting in the negative.

During Mr. Weeks's campaign for reëlection to the Senate, which occurred during the closing months of the second session of the Sixty-Fifth Congress, former President Theodore Roosevelt said publicly: 'As for Senator Weeks, not merely the regard of Massachusetts for her own reputation, but her high interest in the honor and welfare of the nation, will insure her returning him to the Senate. His abilities are such as are peculiarly necessary at this particular crisis. He has stood for the unflinching and efficient prosecution of the war, until it can be ended by the unconditional surrender of Germany. His own son is a gallant fighting man in our gallant fighting army over seas. He will stand as bravely and wisely for the right kind of peace as he has stood for the right kind of war.'

Mr. Weeks was defeated by David I. Walsh in the election of November 5, 1918, Mr. Walsh receiving 207,478 votes; Mr. Weeks, 188,287; and Thomas W. Lawson, 21,985.

The reasons for Mr. Weeks's defeat were many, some of which I will refer to. In the first place, Mr. Walsh was much better known personally throughout the State than Mr. Weeks. He had been Lieutenant-Governor for one year and Governor for two, and in those years had campaigned widely. He was a most vigorous and attractive stump speaker, and then, too, economic conditions were most favorable for him. The railroad and street-car men, who were receiving fabulous war-time wages, were quite satisfied with Mr. Wilson's Administration and were ready to express their satisfaction in votes. Mr. Weeks had been out of the

State for many years, busy with his legislative duties, and was little known, in person, outside of the Metropolitan District.

Mr. Weeks, in the Senate, had voted against two constitutional Amendments, that adopting prohibition, as a national policy and that extending the suffrage to women. The former affected his vote somewhat, the latter very seriously.

The State was flooded with anti-Weeks literature by the suffragist women, every one of whom was expected to provide a male vote against him. Then, too, there was, in certain quarters, and among those who usually voted the Republican ticket, a wish to support President Wilson, because of his advocacy of a League of Nations.

Mr. Weeks was not unmindful of the fact that some of his votes in the Senate would injure him politically, but when a colleague attempted to persuade him to favor the prohibition and suffrage Amendments to the Constitution, on the ground that his opposition would not prevent their ultimate adoption and would do him great harm politically, Weeks said, as I have been informed by one present at the interview, 'I don't believe in them and I won't vote for them. I will take defeat first.'

Senator Lodge said in a letter to a friend: 'It is beyond words and has fallen upon a fine man of whom I am so fond — alas, alas.'

Theodore Roosevelt wrote to Mr. Weeks: 'Of course you are a good loser! You are a good fighter, a straight American, a natural soldier, and the father of a natural soldier. I feel the deepest regret that I wasn't able to be of any real use to you. At least, my dear Senator, it wasn't from failure of desire on my part.'

CHAPTER XI

THE third and last session of the Sixty-Fifth Congress,
which brought to a close Mr. Weeks's service in the
legislative branch of the National Government, began
on December 2, 1918, and ended March 4, 1919.

On December 19, 1918, he condemned the foreign
mail service in the following severe language:

'I did not suppose there was a Senator on this floor
who would have the temerity to even apologize for the
foreign mail service. The Senate Military Committee,
as the Senator from Tennessee knows, has frequently
made inquiry about the matter. There has been a de-
luge of complaints from every source, complaints that
have been verified, and it has been acknowledged, on the
part of the War Department officials appearing before
the committee, that the service was bad and they did
not know, practically speaking, how to correct it. What
the Senator from Nebraska has said about it is absolutely true. It is not only a breakdown, it is a hopeless
breakdown, and it shows an incompetency which I have
not seen anywhere in the Government service since I
have been in Congress.'

On January 2, 1919, he spoke at length upon the delay in publishing the casualty lists. In closing, he said:

'It may be claimed that the real duty of the War Department and of our Army was to win the war, and no one can successfully gainsay that statement. Moreover, our troops have conducted themselves in this first requirement in a manner quite equal to our fondest expectations; but, in addition to this requirement, it was the duty of the War Department to keep stimulated not only the morale of the Army but the morale of the people at home, especially of the families of those serving on the other side, and to prevent, as far as possible, unnecessary distress and apprehension. You cannot read the papers, or the numerous letters, or the testimony given at the hearing of the Senate Committee on Military Affairs on this subject without coming to the conclusion that there has been a failure on the part of the War Department to meet this requirement. Every Senator will undoubtedly corroborate the correctness of this conclusion. I do not say this from a desire to be critical, but I do believe that, having made an examination of the conditions surrounding this activity, it is the duty of some one to put on record the result of that investigation and to call attention to the reasons for the failure of this branch of our military service, a failure which has caused unnecessary mental suffering and anxiety on the part of many of our people.'

When, on January 20, 1919, the Senate had under discussion a bill providing for the relief of such populations in Europe and countries contiguous thereto, outside of Germany, as may be determined by the President as necessary, Mr. Weeks said:

'When we take the whole question, by and large, when we consider that the President is on the other side representing the United States, when he is on the ground and knows the situation, when he is presumably going to make every effort to bring about a just peace, I think we are rather in duty bound to take one more of these steps which have always been accompanied by the "trust me" statement since the beginning of the war. I do not wonder that Senators are irritated by the situation. I do not wonder that they hesitate about doing it, when they think of all the arguments which may be made against it; but I do think that there is ample reason in this case, considering our situation in Europe — the fact that the war is not over, the fact that we want to get our soldiers home as speedily as possible — for our supporting this appropriation, and, as far as I am concerned, I have concluded to follow that course.'

On February 5, 1919, Mr. Weeks introduced a resolution relating to the prohibition of the importation of certain articles by Great Britain:

'Mr. President, I do not introduce this resolution in any spirit of antagonism to Great Britain, but I do it for the purpose of calling to the attention of the Senate how very greatly our foreign trade may be affected by this additional prohibition, which includes the great variety of articles mentioned in the list just read. I think the time has come when we must give some attention to our own domestic affairs, when we must determine whether we are going to protect our foreign commerce. Possibly something is being done in connection with this subject by the State Department, but I think it is proper that the Senate should be informed what action, if any, has been taken or is being taken relative to this action of the British Government. I do not charge that this action is aimed at the United States. It is general, if I am correctly informed; but it is a process of attempting to build up British industries, and, of course, at the expense of those who have sent similar goods into that territory.

    ·   ·   ·   ·   ·   ·   ·   ·   ·

'I do not know that finally I will be in a position to criticize Great Britain for the action which has been taken, but the Senator from North Dakota very truly says they are trying to protect their industries and keep their people employed. I said two or three times, that very action prevents us from employing our people in this country. When I see men walking the streets in the Massachusetts shoe cities, because the trade with Europe has been cut off — the million dollars of business we were doing in that line with Great Britain was stopped suddenly two years ago, and the embargo has not been removed — I say that I prefer, if one is necessary, to see the workmen of Great Britain walking the streets rather than the workmen in this country.'

When, on February 15, 1919, the Rivers and Harbors appropriation bill was under consideration, Mr. Weeks made the following statement of what Massachusetts had done to improve her rivers and harbors:

'Mr. President, I heard the Senator from Utah, a day or two ago, ask some Senator if his State had made any contribution to the improvement of rivers and harbors, in which they were directly interested, and thinking he might ask me the question, I brought with me this morning a statement showing what Massachusetts has done.

'My judgment is that Massachusetts has done and is doing about as much and more than it should, and that many of the expenditures the State has made are properly national expenditures; but, as I have the opportunity to do so, I wish to put in the "Record" the result of the operations along these lines. . . . I have not all the expenditures that have been made by the State of Massachusetts, for rivers and harbors, of course. It would take a long time to compile them; but I have a letter in my possession relating to the proposition, now pending in Congress, to make a forty-foot channel in Boston Harbor, in which it is stated: "The United States has expended on Boston Harbor and its tributary rivers, etc., from 1825 to 1915, a period of 90 years, the sum of $12,668,474.99, an average of $140,760.83 per year. The State of Massachusetts has expended and actually entered into contract to expend on Boston Harbor and its tributary rivers, etc., from 1870 to 1915, a period of 45 years, the sum of $15,477,360.62, of which amount all but $2,784,152.94 has actually been expended, making an average of $343,719.03, per year, by the State."

'During forty-five years the State of Massachusetts has expended upon Boston Harbor and rivers tributary thereto over $3,000,000 more than the National Government has expended since the beginning of the river and harbor appropriation.

'I do not contend, Mr. President, that all States should do as much, but I do contend that there should be, in doubtful cases, coöperation between the local community and the General Government. I do not think it should be the case in Boston Harbor, for example, which is distinctly National; nor in a great improvement like the Mississippi River or New York Harbor, but I do think in improvements, essentially local, there should be a plan of coöperation between the General Government and the local government which would modify, to some degree, this system of rivers and harbors improvements.'

On February 15, 1919, Mr. Weeks again urged that a reconstruction policy should be adopted and spoke, in part, as follows:

'Last September there was introduced a resolution which, in considerable detail, brought to the attention of the Senate this whole subject. That resolution has been referred to by the Senator from Iowa. Indeed, a revised resolution, prepared by the committee of which he is a member, has been submitted to the Senate. It is not a question of form or in what shape or, indeed, to what extent this resolution should carry the movement, but it is of vital importance to this country that something be done. The day I introduced the resolution — the 27th of last September, I think it was — there was a hasty gathering of the clans across the aisle.

'The suggestion was made that something ought to be done about this; and a bill was prepared, which was introduced by the Senator from North Carolina. At that time both resolutions were referred to the Committee on the Judiciary. I have no doubt that at that time there was some purpose, on the part of the majority in this Chamber to take action, but for some unknown reason — which may be guessed, but which I do not care to repeat — it was decided to take no action. Therefore those resolutions have been lying, in the Senate Committee on the Judiciary, from that time to this, without any action whatever, while we have known that every day, important committees of the British Parliament and of British citizens, important committees in France, important committees in Italy, and in every other European country, were working out schemes they considered necessary, not to bring the industrial world back to the conditions existing before the war, because any one with any judgment must have known that that would be impossible, but to prepare the world for the new industrial conditions, prevailing after the war. After-war normal conditions will never be the same as pre-war normal conditions.'

I have quoted very liberally from many of Mr. Weeks's speeches in the House and Senate to indicate not only the large number of subjects he spoke upon, during his fifteen years of service, but the quality of the contributions he made to every discussion in which he took part. No stronger impression can be gained from them than of his conservatism and sound judgment and yet his progressive inclination is manifest in many of the positions he took, notably in the creation of the White Mountain-Appalachian Forest Reservation. That he had a deep coloring of sentiment in his nature and was willing to take an extremely advanced position upon the right and duty of the National Government to exercise, in a good cause, its control over matters of interstate concern, is manifested in the influential part he took in securing legislation to protect migratory birds. His independence of thought and action is frequently displayed as when, for example, he stood in a minority of four in the House, in 1906, against the passage of the rate bill — strongly urged by President Roosevelt —

until it was amended, and in his position in the Senate on the legislation establishing the Federal Reserve System when, in opposition to most of his Republican colleagues, he voted for the bill, prepared in a Democratic Congress, after he had contributed more than any other member of the Senate in perfecting it. His position was, in a word, that, while he preferred the bill prepared by the Monetary Commission, the legislation proposed was far better than no legislation.

Another occasion on which he exhibited his independence was in his vote on repealing that provision of the Panama Canal Act of August 24, 1912, which exempted vessels engaged in the coastwise trade of the United States from payment of tolls. President Wilson was strongly for repeal. Mr. Root and Mr. Lodge took the same view; furthermore, it seemed a very magnanimous act, and that consideration would appeal very strongly to a man of Mr. Weeks's generous nature, but he believed that we were entitled to the exemption, under the terms of the treaty, and that, as a trustee for the American people, he could not acquiesce in a surrender of the right.

Perhaps the most striking illustration of Mr. Weeks's courage was in his opposition to the Amendment to the Federal Constitution extending the suffrage to women, a month before he came up for election to the Senate for a second term — nothing he could do, and he knew it, would prevent the ultimate adoption of the Amendment, indeed it was approved by the Senate at the following session, but he would not vote for a measure that he did not believe in.

A careful review of his legislative career demonstrates that he was a statesman rather than a politician. No better statement can be made of the principles which governed him in his legislative relations than that made in a letter to his son, who was about to become an Alderman in the city of Newton, dated January 3, 1923, and which is, in part, as follows:

'There are two or three things I want to impress upon you as it is your first experience in a legislative body. Success in such a place, more than in almost any other, depends on knowledge. A man is a leader, legislatively, when he knows more than those who are serving with him. He does not have to be an orator, have wealth or any other qualification, than to have the facts, and therefore you ought to take some part of the work, perhaps all of it if you have time, and know all about what is going on. Study the rules which are used, so that you will be entirely familiar with them. Attend committee meetings, so that you will be entirely familiar with the work of the committee, and above all things do not attempt to speak unless you know exactly what you are talking about. There is no place in the world where you get sized up quicker than you do in a legislative body. If you are on your feet every few minutes talking about something which all the others know as much about as you do, you do not acquire but lose influence. If you get the reputation of knowing what you are talking about, then every one will listen and will be likely to accept your views. I have seen hundreds of cases which confirm this statement. The greatest orator who has been in Congress since I have been in Washington is ——. Members and others listen to his speeches, because he is a great orator, but he has no more influence, and never has had, than the most inconspicuous Member, because he has the reputation of not having carefully and fundamentally studied his subjects, but depends on verbiage rather than information.

'Do not get into the habit of quarreling with men who do not agree with you. They are entitled to their opinions as much as you are to yours. The thing to do is to convince them that they are wrong, and that will apply in general politics as well as in the Newton Board of Aldermen. The way to cure a communist is not to suppress his speech, but to argue him out of his position. If you cannot argue him out of it, he may be right and you wrong.

Mr. Weeks left the Senate on March 4, 1919, with the affection and respect of all the members, Republicans and Democrats alike.

Elihu Root said of him:

'I had a very warm regard for John W. Weeks, based upon my observation and experience, as one of his colleagues in the Senate. He was a very valuable member of that body. His judgment was sound and naturally unbiased. He was always kindly and considerate and his serene and friendly disposition enabled him to express his opinion clearly and positively, without causing any irritation. Of course petty jealousies and quarrels among the members of a legislative body, and especially among the members of the dominant party in that body, are fatal to legislative progress and wise legislative action.

'Weeks always took the broad and never the petty view, and he had an extraordinary faculty of lifting other people up onto the platform on which he stood and leading them to forget their small irritations and suspicions.

'One of the weaknesses of our legislative bodies, in this country, is that so great a part of the members have no sense of obligation to help make the Government work. They proceed upon the probably unconscious assumption that all the responsibility for making things go in the Government rests with the Executive, leaving their own interests to be expended upon local matters relating to their districts or upon subjects which will attract the voters. That is one great reason why our legislative bodies fail to lead the public and spend a large part of their time in trying to avoid being led themselves. Weeks always acted under a strong desire to get his utmost possible best in making the Government of the country effective and successful, and without any preaching on his part, his presence and action, when in the Senate, constantly tended to create the same standard of conduct on the part of his associates.

'He was a great loss to the Senate and his death was a great loss to the country, but the reflection that we are still capable of producing such men for public service is cheerful and encouraging.'

Secretary of the Treasury Andrew W. Mellon, speaking of him, at a later period, both as a legislator and a Cabinet Officer said:

'John W. Weeks was one of the most useful men of his generation in public life. He was a man of great ability, sound judgment and absolute integrity. He had a first-hand knowledge of a great variety of subjects. As a result of his early training at the Naval Academy and his subsequent experience as a banker, he was especially qualified to deal with naval and financial questions. Throughout his long and distinguished public career as Congressman, Senator and Cabinet Officer, he made a study of the problems connected with national defense, banking reform and taxation. Often, in Cabinet, I was impressed with his clear insight into these problems and with the sound and practical plans which he offered for their solution.'

Theodore E. Burton, now a Representative, formerly Senator from the State of Ohio and closely associated with Mr. Weeks, in legislation upon monetary matters, speaks as follows:

'I knew him intimately both in the House and Senate, and there was no one with whom I was more friendly. He had lovable qualities, was loyal to his friends but without blindness as to their faults, always ready to do a favor or coöperate when he was sure it was right. As a legislator he was constantly alert and had a ready judgment which enabled him to reach decisions upon a great variety of problems presented to Congress. Thus his conclusions were always respected by his colleagues.

'If I may mention any one trait in his personal character more prominent than another, it was his poise. He did not lose his head at any time. He was not readily swept on, by any sudden impulse. It would be a mistake, however, to say that he did not keep in touch with all the movements of the time.' Lee S. Overman, Senator from the State of North Carolina for twenty-five years and a representative Democrat, wrote of Mr. Weeks: 'He and I were friends. I liked him for his amiable and kindly qualities and I admired him for his fine abilities. He was a very, very good Senator: able, industrious, and active in all public matters that engaged his attention. On our side of the aisle he was very popular and his views and opinions highly respected. He helped us handsomely in the passage of the Federal Reserve Bill.'

I have earlier called attention to the fact that during

the last twenty years great changes have been made in
our Constitution and in the character of our legislation,
which has tended greatly to increase the responsibilities
of the National Government and the area of its activities.

Four Amendments have been added to the Constitution: the Sixteenth in 1913, giving Congress the power
to lay and collect taxes on incomes from whatever
source derived, without apportionment among the several States; the Seventeenth in 1913, providing for the
election of Senators by the people; the Eighteenth in
1919, the so-called Prohibition Amendment; the Nineteenth in 1920, giving women the right to vote.

During or nearly within this period, 1906–27, perhaps the greatest extension of federal authority has
been in enlarging the police power of the National Government, under the authority conferred upon Congress
by Section 8 of Article 1 of the Constitution, which declared that 'the Congress shall have power — to regulate commerce with foreign nations, and among the
several States, and with the Indian tribes.'

'Until the year 1903, Congress had confined the exercise of its powers under the Commerce Clause, almost
entirely, to the subject of intoxicating liquor, common
carriers, and trusts. In that year, however, the decision
of the Court in the great case of Champion v. Ames,
188 U.S. 321, upholding the Act of 1895 by which Congress forbade all transportation of lottery tickets in
interstate commerce, disclosed the existence of a
hitherto unsuspected field of National power. While the
Court expressly stated that, in sustaining the right
absolutely to prohibit interstate commerce in lottery
tickets, it must not be understood to uphold a general

right to exclude any and all articles from such commerce, nevertheless, the reasoning on which the opinion was based left a very wide discretion to Congress. Hitherto, it had been largely left to the States, under the exercise of the police power, to decide, each for itself, what articles of commerce should or should not be brought within the State or produced within the State for transportation elsewhere. Now the Court announced the doctrine that Congress might decide to what extent and under what regulations such articles might be transported.

.   .   .   .

'The practical result of the case was the creation of a Federal police power — the right to regulate the manner of production, manufacture, sale and transportation of articles and the transportation of persons, through the medium of legislation professing to regulate commerce between the States. Congress took very swift advantage of the new field thus opened to it. In 1903 and 1905, it passed the Animal Contagion Disease and the enlarged Animal Quarantine Acts; in 1906, the Pure Food Act; in 1905 and 1906, the Metals Hallmark Acts; in 1905, 1912, 1915, and 1917, the Plant Quarantine Acts; in 1907, the Meat Inspection Act; in 1909 and 1914, the Narcotics Acts; in 1910, the White Slave Traffic Act; in 1910, the Insecticide Act; in 1912, the Apple-Grading Act and the Adulterated-Seed Act; in 1913, the Serums and Toxins Act; in 1916, the Warehouse Act and the Grain Standards Act; in 1916, the Child Labor Act.'[1]

In litigation involving this Child Labor Act, in the

[1] *The Supreme Court in United States History*, Charles Warren, 1926, vol. 2, pp. 735-37.

case of Hammer v. Dagenhart, 274 U.S. 251, 1918, the Court said and finally settled that there was a limit to Congressional power under the Commerce Clause, speaking in part as follows:

'In our view the necessary effect of this act is, by means of a prohibition against the movement in interstate commerce, of ordinary commercial commodities, to regulate the hours of labor of children in factories and mines within the states, a purely state authority. Thus the act in a two-fold sense is repugnant to the Constitution. It not only transcends the authority delegated to Congress over commerce but also exerts a power, as to a purely local matter to which the federal authority does not extend. The far-reaching result of upholding the act cannot be more plainly indicated than by pointing out that if Congress can thus regulate matters entrusted to local authority, by prohibition of the movement of commodities in interstate commerce, all freedom of commerce will be at an end, and the power of the states over local matters may be eliminated, and thus our system of government be practically destroyed.'

When the fight for the ratification of the treaty of Versailles was on, in the summer of 1919, Mr. Weeks was no longer a member of the Senate, but he made his views known in the following address:

'The one great foreign question absorbing the public interest at the expense of all others, although I think I see that the public is desirous of hearing the last of it at as early a day as possible, is the pending peace treaty with Germany and especially the League of Nations covenant.

'I have a very strong feeling that our entering into any permanent alliance with European or other nations is a serious mistake. What the United States Senate is now discussing is the most important question which has been before that body since the civil war. It practically changes our entire relationship with the rest of the world.

'Instead of restricting our activities to our national affairs, we are to become involved, by the proposed League of Nations, in a great number of matters in which we have no direct interest, with which we have heretofore had nothing to do and against which we have been warned by the Father of Our Country.

'I suppose most people have read Washington's "Farewell Address," but few understand that that address was more than the individual and spasmodic expression of opinion of a great leader. It was the concerted effort of all the great leaders of that time, without regard to their individual ideas of government. It was reviewed over and over again by such men as Jefferson, Madison, Monroe, and the other great statesmen of that period. Having first been written by Washington himself, after all of these men had carefully examined it and suggested their views of changes which might be desirable, it was rewritten by Hamilton. It was then taken by Washington and carefully reviewed. Every word in it was weighed and carefully considered, so that it was the combined judgment of the founders of this Government. I have heard it suggested that it is out of date, that conditions have changed. To my mind it is no more out of date, because it is one hundred and thirty years old, than the Ten Commandments because they are thousands of years old. Age has nothing to do with it. It is a fundamental American doctrine which is entitled to the respect of all generations of Americans, and I wish to express the opinion that future generations of Americans will regret, whether or not the provisions of the League of Nations are modified, that we ever became a party to it.

'If our enormous strength — and we are the great, rich and powerful country of the world to-day — needs to be exerted for the benefit of mankind elsewhere, it should be exerted as the individual case may develop, like our entrance into the European war, or the Spanish-American War. Such conditions will develop, and we should be prepared to do our duty toward mankind, when our assistance is needed, but we do not increase our power or our usefulness, in deciding such questions by being a party to them.   Indeed, we decrease our relative importance and influence.

'An individual does not increase his powers of usefulness, in preserving peace, by engaging in every brawl which may be taking place on the street. He is in an infinitely better position to remain on the outside as an adviser or arbiter and decide what his course shall be, as circumstances may warrant, rather than become an active participant in what is being done, and I think that idea will apply with equal force to the nation.

'Personally, I hope the reservations proposed by Mr. Root may be adopted as quickly as possible.

'There is some force in the contention made by the President in his various interviews with Senators that it is undesirable to open up the question again, but the President should not have gotten the country into this position, without the advice of the Senate before he had taken the final step. He has acted in this matter, as in many others, purely as an autocrat, and he now wishes to force the country to accept the result of what he has deliberately done. While we were engaged in war it was our duty to support him, even if the action taken did not meet our individual views. When our country is at war the President is the Commander-in-Chief, and, in the final analysis, he must be obeyed; but that time has passed, and there are tens of millions of other Americans who should be consulted, either directly or through their representatives, in matters affecting the nation in time of peace. That was not done, and if it is embarrassing to open the Paris conference again, it is the fault of the President and not the fault of the Senate.'

Mr. Weeks went to Lancaster, New Hampshire, for the summer of 1919, returning to Boston, in the early fall, to undertake work for the Republican National Committee. He spent the autumn of 1919 in Boston and took an active part in the gubernatorial campaign of that year. After the State election in 1919, he returned to Washington, and subsequently spent a large part of the winter in Florida. During the early part of the summer of 1920 he was in Lancaster and, later, was present at the Republican National Convention in Chicago, when the Massachusetts delegation elected him a member of the National Committee, an office from which he resigned on May 3, 1923. He was succeeded by William M. Butler. In the early part of September, Mr. Weeks took charge of the New York Headquarters of the Republican National Committee. In the Convention of 1920, he was not active in the support of any candidate. He was highly thought of by all and would certainly have been selected for the Cabinet by General Wood or Mr. Lowden if either had been elected, as he was by Mr. Harding.

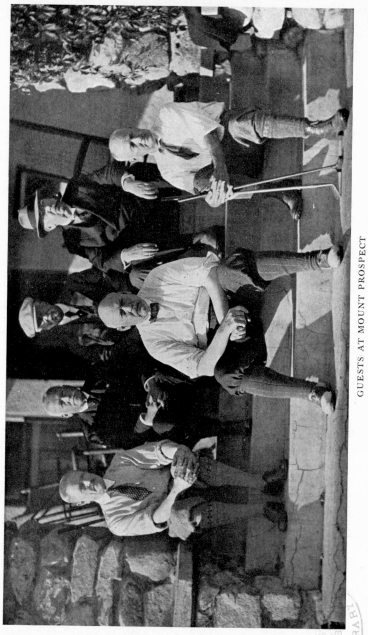

GUESTS AT MOUNT PROSPECT

Left to right: Gen. John G. Pershing, Charles G. Washburn, William B. H. Dowse,
John W. Weeks, John W. Dwight, Gen. J. G. Harbord

Mr. Weeks took his seat in the Cabinet as Secretary of War on March 4, 1921. He had the confidence, respect, and affection of his associates. The then Secretary of State, Charles Evans Hughes, speaks as follows of their relations:

'I had not known John W. Weeks intimately before we became colleagues in President Harding's Cabinet, but I was deeply gratified by his selection as Secretary of War, as I knew the importance and difficulty of the task that had to be performed. His reputation for acumen, fairness and knowledge of affairs, was of the highest. He was distinctly a civilian, although he had studied at Annapolis and had served in the Spanish War. He had won distinction in the House of Representatives and in the Senate because of his straightforwardness and mastery of problems of finance and administration. He had political sagacity, but he was not a trimmer. His ability was constructive, and he went straight to the merits of the questions before him. He was an ideal Secretary of War to make the adjustments necessary, in the liquidation of war activities and in the reorganization of the Army under the National Defense Act of 1920. He was a man who won your respect at once and held it always. He inspired complete confidence.

'I associate John W. Weeks with the qualities of probity, hardheadedness, thoroughness and courage. These qualities, with extraordinary keenness of perception in financial affairs, gave him success in business, in politics and in administration. He mastered his work and was hailed as a master. He had none of the ingratiating qualities of a politician. He did not strive to please, or bend the knee to power, whatever its source.

He won his way because he held the general esteem of all those who knew him, and this knowledge and respect of one's intimates, gradually spreading through the community, gives to one in public life, despite all the perversities of criticism, the most solid and unassailable reputation.

'He was a quiet man, not given to much public speech, but when he did speak in public or in private, he spoke his mind. He was not a model of discretion in speech, but he said what he believed; he had thought out his subject and had convictions. Whether you agreed with him or not, you had to listen, for he knew his facts, and with respect to principles he spoke with entire sincerity and had his definite reasons for his way of thinking. Such a man, in whatever situation, in or out of office, is a true leader in democracy.

'We were born on the same day of the year, although not in the same year, and, with former Representative Samuel E. Winslow, of Worcester, Massachusetts, also born on the same day of the year, we had for several years our birthday dinners. The last of these was in 1925, held somewhat earlier than the anniversary date, as I was about to leave Washington. Secretary Weeks had not been well and the future was not promising. When I saw him, a few months later, in Boston, after his severe illness, I was profoundly impressed by his calm courage. It was not an attitude of mere resignation, nor was it one of unjustified optimism. His spirit was indomitable. He had suffered intensely; he was too wise to be deceived. But he was conqueror, the man of undiminished strength of will, who looked at both life and death with even eye, unfearing. It was a rare privilege to know him and to be his friend.'

On Armistice Day, Friday, November 11, 1921, Secretary of War Weeks took a prominent part, in a most impressive ceremony in the National Cemetery, at the burial of the 'Unknown Soldier.' Nothing was lacking to lend great impressiveness to the occasion. Secretary Weeks spoke as follows, in introducing President Harding to the great and distinguished company:

'We are gathered, not to mourn the passing of a great general, but an unknown soldier of the republic, who fought to sustain a great cause, for which he gave his life. Whether he came from the North, the South, the East, or the West, we do not know. Neither do we know his name, his lineage or any fact related to his life or death, but we do know that he was a typical American, who responded to his Country's call and that he now sleeps with the heroes.

'We, who are gathered here in such numbers, are simply representatives of the United States, who are here in spirit and whose sentiments have been more deeply stirred by this event than by any in the life of our Country. These sentiments can be adequately expressed by only one citizen — The President of the United States.'

On this occasion Secretary Weeks walked in the procession from the Rotunda in the Capitol to the Cemetery at Arlington. It is believed that his strength was unduly taxed by this experience, which was followed, almost immediately, by a severe attack of angina pectoris.

Mr. Weeks, when Secretary of War, sent in June, 1924, the following letter to the United Spanish War Veterans, assembled in State Convention at Middletown, Ohio:

MY DEAR COMRADES:

I send greetings not only as Secretary of the Department, under which you served, but as one who served with you during the Spanish-American War.

That was the most altruistic war in the history of the world. We took Cuba and Porto Rico from Spain and turned over to the Cubans and Porto Ricans every dollar of taxes received from the people.

We took the Philippines from Spain, and sent them an army of teachers and turned our soldiers into teachers, to give them the foundation of a free, self-governing community.

We sent doctors to all three to free them from pestilence and plague; lawyers to assist them in framing and administering their laws; economists and financial experts to draft sound revenue systems and direct commercial expansion.

We asked no war indemnity from Spain. Instead we paid back to the conquered country the money she had expended on public improvements in Cuba, Porto Rico, and the Philippines.

Search history and you will find no similar action, excepting that which our country again took after the World War, asking neither territory nor indemnities, but sending relief expeditions to feed the hungry of the vanquished countries.

You were crusaders who brought in a new order and gave new hope to all peoples, for the World War proved that your sons were loyal to the new faith.

Surely it is not necessary to point out that such victories do more to establish peace and justice on earth, than all the resolutions that were ever adopted or all the plans that were ever conceived. Actions speak louder than words — always.

You, through whose services our country first became a world power, with righteousness for its offensive strength, want the United States of America to continue this leadership among the nations.

This only can be, as you know, if we, as a nation, are defensively strong. Our position cannot be maintained by a weak or decadent nation.

For these reasons I hope you will get behind the new Army of the United States, join on September 12 during the 'Defense Test,' with its citizen soldiers who are your successors, and explain to your neighbors our peaceful and patriotic plans. From the fullness of your experience you have learned what a preventative of war, what a factor of safety in war and what a stabilizer after war, is adequate preparedness during peace.

While Mr. Weeks's conduct of the War Department will be dealt with hereafter by others, his own recital of what was accomplished in the year 1924 is most interesting:

'The year 1924, in the history of the American Army, has been a year of record-making. Nor are the records made and the achievements attained merely by the trans-continental dawn-to-dusk trip of an Army flier or the round-the-world flight of Army aviators. During 1923, it had been felt that the progress of readjustment and reorganization and peace-time growth, following the armistice, had come to sufficient fruition to enable us to make tangible plans and approach a fairly stabilized training basis for our forces. So for the first time in our history, we created, in 1923, a general mobilization plan providing for the automatic action of all the citizen forces of the nation in the event of an emergency. Dur-

ing the year 1924, all components of the Army of the
United States — regulars, guardsmen, and reservists —
devoted the major part of their attention to the preparation of unit mobilization plans as part of a general
attempt to familiarize each member of each component,
with what would be his duties and his responsibilities,
in case of a major emergency. Training activities went
on with constantly accelerated enthusiasm. Interest in
the National Guard grew to such an extent, that enlist-
ments exceeded the appropriation authorization and
the brakes had to be put on. Military training began
to appeal so strongly to the American youths that
recruiting activities had to be checked, to keep the
Regular Army within its budget strength. Forty-nine
thousand young men applied for admission to summer
camps, with facilities and funds for only about thirty-
three thousand. The reserve officers of the country
constantly asked for more training and more active
duty. The colleges have taken so strongly to the Reserve Officers' Training Corps idea, that they have been
asking for new units and for additional officer instructors. The defense system of the country, as outlined in
the Act of 1920 and put into effect by slow progressive
stages, has during 1924 finally begun to reach a defini-
tive stage. In September of the year just closed, the
War Department held a Defense Test in order to check
up on the facilities, equipment, personnel, and plans of
operation of all units of all three components of the
Army. This Test, participated in by 333,675 military
personnel, actually represent more than 1,215,528 one-
day volunteers, and more than 6534 separate communities, and, practically, universally endorsed by editorial
opinion the country over, proved conclusively — not

PRESIDENT COOLIDGE AND SECRETARY WEEKS GREETING THE WORLD FLIERS ON THE COMPLETION
OF THEIR FLIGHT, SEPTEMBER 9, 1924

only that the people of the United States are desirous of adequate national defense — but also that the democratic citizen army idea, with its volunteer enrollments, and part-time training in citizen components, is a sound method of insuring the defense of the country and is in conformity with American social idealism and with the current condition of American social and economic life. During the last month of the year, in presenting my report to the President, I indicated certain points at which additional effort must be directed, to keep our defense system in proper shape and explained at length a number of coördinated projects, for future development, that have been the subject of General Staff study for the past three or more years. The general idea of maintaining, in excellent condition, the physical equipment and installations of the Army has met with popular approval, and it is hoped that the major projects, prepared by the Staff and mentioned in my report will be fitted into a progressive and economical programme for the military establishment. This is the tangible history of the year 1924 in the War Department, successive progression from plans to practice, from actual application to investigation and report on the state of our defense forces, and finally, from the investigation and report, to a concrete programme for the years to come.

'This work of reorganization, the entire project for the Defense Test, and the preparation of the program for the future, have been initiated and executed, principally because of the insight and energy of General Pershing, whose retirement for age, last September, imposed an almost irreparable loss on the Army and the War Department.'

CHAPTER XII

Appreciations of Mr. Weeks's services as Secretary of War by Vice-President Charles G. Dawes, Secretary of War Dwight F. Davis, General of the Armies John J. Pershing, Major-General James G. Harbord, retired, and the late Governor-General Leonard Wood.

As General Harbord deals more particularly with the military duties of the office of Secretary of War, his statement, substantially as it was written, will appear first.

General Harbord says:

'The real preparation of Secretary Weeks for his important cabinet work began in the character of those ancestors who, for nearly a century before his birth had endured harsh climate and frontier poverty on the upper reaches of the Connecticut River, among the foothills of the Presidential Range of the White Mountains. Among the inspiring surroundings of that noble region, he was born. He loved it all his days, and his life ended within sight of his birthplace at Lancaster, New Hampshire, as doubtless he wished it. His character and physique took on likeness of that rugged environment and he was big in body, soul and brain.

'Trained for the sea at the Naval Academy, the periodical poverty of our military establishments, always in cycles of action and reaction, sent his class into civil life by discharge, at graduation. First in Florida and then in his native New England he achieved a successful business career. With a competence, by the time he reached middle life, he took up public service and went to Congress as a Representative from a Massachusetts district, and then as Senator from the same state.

'In over fifty years he was the first Secretary of War, trained in one of the National Academies, with a sense of discipline instilled in him during the impressionable days of his youth — a tremendous qualification for handling an establishment, of which discipline should be the very soul. Many distinguished lawyers had headed the War Department during that half-century and some who had achieved success in commercial life but none other had brought to it that invaluable asset of experience and acquaintance in both houses of Congress. In a great executive department with activities touching almost every phase of our national life, with many thousands of soldiers, officers, and civilian employees on its military side and, perhaps, a larger number in its purely civil activities, congressional experience is almost above appraisement. Dependent upon Congress for the outline of its policies, in many instances, and looking to that source for the appropriations that support it, the Secretary must know the best methods of presentation of matters that require legislative action. Skilled in the art of polite refusal and patient listening, he must know who is who in Congress and, in a thousand instances, weigh the relative importance of those with whom he deals, for his Department. In such experience and the use of it Secretary Weeks was unexcelled. His popularity among his former legislative colleagues, of all parties, made an informality possible in dealing with them that greatly facilitated business. Practically every communication that left the War Department for a Senator or Representative, during his time, was signed by the Secretary himself. Thus responsibility for political action was borne by the head of the Department, as it should be. The morning hours of every working day were devoted by the Secretary to receiving congressional callers, practically to the exclusion of other business.

'The reconstruction period following the Great War has witnessed probably the greatest administrative activity the world has ever seen. Excluding the economic and financial problems, which have occupied our late allies and enemies, it is doubtful if any administrative official was ever confronted with a greater task than faced Secretary Weeks, when he took office on March 4th, 1921. The liquidation of our effort in the War had been slowed down, in all the Executive Departments, by the long illness of President Wilson, and in the War Department the major military problems still remained to be solved. In the number and complexity of its activities, even in ordinary peace times, the task of the American Secretary of War is one of the most difficult and arduous in the world. The office of The Adjutant General, which is the principal channel of communication between the War Department and the remainder of the military establishment, for example, in 1925, handled over four million communications. To his appropriate duties as War Minister, responsible alone for the fiscal policy of his Department, and practically commanding the military forces of the Nation, in representation of the President, Congress has in a century and a half added a multitude of detailed responsibilities that he cannot delegate to others, and which entail a slavish burden on the Secretary, sometimes to the disadvantage of the United States Army. Probably three fourths of the flood of affairs that come before him for decision are purely civil in character and many others are merely incidental to the military establishment.

'The supervision of the tremendous appropriations for rivers and harbors; buildings and grounds in the District of Columbia; the Federal Power Commission; the inland waterways; the National Soldiers' Home; real estate transactions, resulting from the abandonment of military posts not transferred to the Interior Department; military cemeteries in Europe and National Cemeteries in the United States; amnesties for political and military prisoners, encarcerated during the war; the administration of Muscle Shoals and similar plants, pending action by Congress; the lowering level of the Great Lakes; the administration of the Panama Canal Zone, of Porto Rico, of the Philippines; the thousand angles from which Senators and Representatives approach the War Department for themselves and their constituents; the daily contact with the political phases of the administration, which is shared by all cabinet officers — these are all duties on the civil side of our War Office. They are time-consuming, often nerve-racking, and generally, mentally exhausting. The mental machinery of the Secretary is now in high, now in low, now at the intermediate, then in reverse, continually changing gears, watching traffic signals, changing loads, and familiarizing itself with new speed laws.

'These civil duties of Secretary Weeks were generally those which confront every Secretary of War in time of peace. There existed, everywhere, the necessity of prompt retrenchment and economy, to which policy the new administration was committed, and which inevitably follows every war. Otherwise, except in the insular dependencies of Porto Rico and the Philippines, they were the usual class of civil administrative duties.

In Porto Rico, President Harding had made an unhappy choice for governor, but one to which he long adhered, with that fine but sometimes misguided loyalty which characterized his attitude towards his friends. While this situation was being worked out, that little island government consumed a disproportionate amount of the Secretary's time and thought. In the Philippines the situation was more serious. During the eight years of the Wilson Administration the Philippines were largely crowded from the attention of the home government by the events preceding and during our participation in the World War. The Governor-General, for several terms a member of the House of Representatives, and whose place of seniority, on an important committee in the House was popularly supposed to have been desired for a Southern Democrat in 1913, went to the Islands without executive experience. His administration witnessed the inauguration of the Jones Act, the speedy disintegration of an excellent civil service, built up during fourteen years of colonial administration and a premature but almost complete Filipinization of the Government service; the embarkation of the Philippine Government upon disastrous financial ventures, including its entry into various forms of commercial business; the weaving of executive orders into legislation; and a general lowering of that tone and efficiency which had, from the time of our occupation distinguished it under five Governors-General of both political faiths. These facts, now generally admitted, did not result from the Jones Law, though its wisdom is not beyond dispute, nor from lack of proper direction from Secretary of War Newton D. Baker, whose instructions in the premises were adequate and definite, but they brought about a situation in the Philippines, which, though ameliorated, still exists, intolerable either from the American or the Filipino standpoint. Very early in his administration Secretary Weeks sent former Governor-General Forbes, one of the outstanding constructive administrators we have had, out there, and Major-General Leonard Wood, who had twenty years before distinguished himself in the government of Cuba, to study and report upon conditions in the Philippine Government. Upon the submission of their report, which revealed the unhappy situation in the Islands, General Wood retired from active military service and was named as Governor-General of the Philippines. Through the Insular Bureau of the War Department, Secretary Weeks extended consistent support to the Governor-General, while sustaining harmonious relations with the Philippine delegation in Congress, and the several Independence Missions that visited the United States during his time. He believed that America should govern or get out of the Islands. The presence of the insular government in business was, of course, repugnant to him. He realized the necessity of preventing encroachment upon the prerogatives of the executive. As a believer in our own institutions the effort of Filipino statesmen to turn their government into one responsible only to the legislature did not meet with his approval. He was, nevertheless, a friend of the Filipino and every proper aspiration of that people, undoubtedly, had his sympathy. But he saw their problems with the advantage of his own broad governmental experience and wide reading of political history.

'In time of peace the United States Army is a going concern, with its problems more or less interwoven or tangential to each other. When Secretary Weeks entered the War Department, there was the customary routine of business to be carried on but in addition there were four military major matters that commanded his attention and upon his successful handling of which rests his fame as a great Secretary of War. Like the ordinary routine, these more or less overlapped and the boundaries between them marked indistinct frontiers. Those major military policies were:

'1. The creation of a General Staff, modelled on that built by General Pershing in the American Expeditionary Forces and which had so largely contributed to carry the American effort to a victorious conclusion.

'2. Retrenchment and economy, following the tremendous expenditures of the War and disposition of the surplus supplies left from the war footing of the Army.

'3. The successful initiation of the National Defense Act approved June 4th, 1920.

'4. Reorganization and reduction of the regular military establishment.

'When General Pershing sailed for France on May 28, 1917, his General Staff, which was later to number hundreds, consisted of but three officers. In addition to the tremendous duties always devolving upon a commander of great armies in war, he was obliged to create the General Staff acknowledged, by all capable military students, as an essential to the conduct of modern war. Future historians will recognize this creative effort of General Pershing as a distinct accomplishment, over and above his successful command of the American Expeditionary Forces. The General Staff, thus brought together, so left its impress upon the events of the time that the return of our troops to America was followed by a general feeling among thoughtful citizens that its organization should be crystallized in the military establishment, in order that the lessons of the World War be not lost, and future emergencies not find our Army so lamentably unprepared, with the necessary General Staff. Secretary Weeks was of this conviction and on taking office announced his intention of creating such a General Staff. Previous to the World War, the War Department General Staff organization had been unscientific and tended to group itself around the personalities of individual members. So little was its true function appreciated that, in the summer of 1917, the ambitious staff officers were allowed to break up the organization by seeking line assignments, and the War Department General Staff for some months, practically, ceased to exist. The following winter the new Chief of Staff, General Peyton C. March, built a War Department General Staff to meet the demands of the moment, and, under his tremendous executive drive and dominating personality, it successfully accomplished the great task of getting the necessary men and munitions across the Atlantic. Under the circumstances of its creation it was inevitable that it drifted into the assumption of administrative and operative duties that should have been performed by the permanent staff and supply agencies, that have long existed.

'In the pre-war General Staff, no provision was made for one portion to take the field with the commander of the armies, in event of war, while another remained to carry out the equally essential duties connected with the mobilization of men and material. It had been so absorbed in the routine of peace-time administration, that its Chief and the Staff itself had given little time to

preparation for war. It was perhaps inevitable, therefore, that the system saw a pathetically insignificant
number of General Staff officers, accompanying the
Commander-in-Chief to France, and in the War Department a mobilization machinery depleted and dis-
organized at the moment of its greatest opportunity.

'Within a few weeks after taking office Secretary
Weeks announced his intention of making General
Pershing Chief of Staff of the Army, having particularly in mind his unrivalled experience as fitting him to
mould the new General Staff. A Board of officers, of
wide experience, was named within a week after General
Pershing became Chief of Staff, which studied the War
Department General Staff and recommended an organization which received the approval of Secretary Weeks
in August, 1921.

'It took as a fundamental principle that, if efficient
execution of plans is to be expected, under the stress of
war, those who have formulated and prepared them,
must be, in general, charged with their execution. Under the law, defining the duties of the General Staff,
they fall into two spheres; that of mobilizing the men
and material of our country, including their preparation, concentration and delivery to the field forces; and
their use in war against an enemy.

'Secretary Weeks had been emphatic in his instructions to the Board, which recommended the new organization that there must be in the staff a section which,
charged with the formulation of plans for the actual
employment of our armed forces against an enemy,
should, at the outbreak of war, take the field as the actual nucleus of the General Headquarters of the Field
Forces. With this addition, the new organization fol-

lowed very closely that of the General Staff of the American Expeditionary Forces. Including the section just described, it created five divisions of the War Department General Staff, the other four dealing, respectively, with personnel, intelligence, operations and training, and supply. These four affect the mobilization of men and material for war, and deal with duties of a routine nature, necessary in both peace and war.

'The Chief of Staff was charged with the larger problems connected with the training and organization of the Army of the United States, including the National Guard and Organized Reserve under the new National Defense Act, while the routine business of the army was to be supervised and transacted by a Deputy Chief of Staff. In event of war the Chief of Staff would take the field with the portion of the General Staff which had prepared the plans of campaign, while the Deputy would become Chief of the War Department General Staff, retaining that portion of the staff, charged with the plans for mobilization of men and material.

'It was characteristic of Secretary Weeks that this new organization was not approved and put into effect until after full discussion of all its details with the chiefs of permanent staff and supply bureaus of the War Department and full agreement as to its workability. Five years have changed it in no important particular. General Pershing went to his well-earned retirement in 1924, the Chiefs of Staff have in turn succeeded him. There are but few Chiefs of permanent bureaus left in the War Department, of those with whom Secretary Weeks discussed the General Staff nearly six years ago. There is perhaps no General Staff officer on duty in the War Department of 1927 who was there in the same capacity in 1921. Hundreds have come and gone, including the great Secretary himself, but the organization in which he took such keen interest promises to survive.

'The reduction of a great war establishment is one of the most difficult of administrative tasks. Even with every American soldier anxious to turn his face homeward after the war, it was difficult to get the last man on the last truck, leaving a French village, and start the convoy for the port of embarkation. After every war a similar difficulty has confronted the War Department, in its effort to reduce the numbers of civilian employees, camps, posts, hospitals, leased holdings, schools, piers, docks, and even ships. Each chief of bureau views the diminution of his establishment with a sense of personal loss. Each officer and clerk believes his own work to be essential. No one sees, without regret, the discontinuance of activities, to which he has given his best of body and brain. Retrenchment is a duty as melancholy as it is necessary. Pending the action of Congress on the National Defense which was not taken until June, 1920, the War Department was not aware of the probable size of the army and could not, therefore, proceed with freedom on a policy of reduction of its accessory establishment. In March, 1921, Secretary Weeks found the principal work of retrenchment still to be done. He had known the necessity of economy in his youth and brought to the task frugal instincts, inherited from New England ancestry.

'Taking the pre-war number of 45,911 civilian employees in and out of Washington, as a standard to be reached, he, by July, 1921, reduced the field service of the War Department by 22½ per cent. By January 31,

1924, these employees had been reduced to a total of 42,458, or 3453 below the clerical force employed, in and out of Washington, on April 6, 1917.

'By October, 1922, fifty-eight army stations had been eliminated, by movements, into permanent posts, releasing the real estate to be rented under, revocable license, or sold. After the salvage of buildings and material six of the great war cantonments were turned over to states for national guard use. Seven of such cantonments were retained for training areas, but only under caretaking detachments. Nine great Quartermaster depots and nine temporary Ordnance Reserve depots were abandoned. Six Air Service plants were sold and seven others reduced to caretaking status. Sixty-seven parcels of real estate in the several Corps Areas were ordered sold during the same period.

'Continuing retrenchment, begun by his predecessor, a Special Panama Canal Commission, convened by Secretary Weeks, in October, 1921, went carefully into costs of operation, rates of pay, labor policies, sanitation and other activities on the Canal Zone, making recommendations which were approved by him for increase of efficiency and decrease of expenses. As a consequence employees were reduced from 17,000 to 11,000, a yearly saving of $1,750,000.

'As an example of economies effected in the operation of Quartermaster Depots, at New York General Intermediate Depot, the cost of operation was reduced, during 1921, by $575,279 per month, effecting a yearly saving of $6,903,348.

'One of the features of the retrenchment policy of Secretary Weeks was the sale and transfer of surplus stocks left over from the War. Immediately after

Peace, Congress authorized the War Department to dispose of surplus stocks to foreign countries, except foodstuffs. Considerable judgment had to be exercised in disposing of these stocks, having in mind the preservation of markets for American manufacturers. This was no doubt a determining factor in the sale to the French Government of our stocks in France. The provision against the sale of foodstuffs abroad, except those just mentioned, was doubtless expected to bring down the high cost of living in the United States. This narrowed the potential market, but the stocks were finally sold, a single food item being 119,000,000 pounds of canned meat, sold for over five and a quarter millions of dollars. Between March 4 and June 30, 1921, a total of $117,-400, 179.41 was sold to the public or transferred to other departments of the government. Between the armistice and March, 1922, all surplus stocks of wool were sold, amounting to a total of $249,740,727.28.

'With an efficient Director of the Budget and a watchful Congress, itself bent upon economy, retrenchment and the sale of surplus stocks in the War Department could not be continued indefinitely at high speed. During his first year in office Secretary Weeks effected economies to the amount of over forty millions of dollars. The great work of retrenchment was largely accomplished during that year, but the policy of rigid economy continued to the end of his administration, and the impetus he gave it still carries it on. His was a business administration by a business man.

'The National Defense Act, as we have it to-day, was approved by the President on June 4, 1920. In the words of Secretary Weeks the military policy provided by the National Defense Act is: "One harmonious army for the United States, consisting of the Regular Army, the National Guard and the Organized Reserves." Again: " It is the first comprehensive military legislation in our history. It provides for the organization in frame work, of an adequate citizen army, in time of peace, and for a regular establishment, only large enough to make the training and development of the citizen army effective and to perform certain special duties that can be performed only by professional soldiers."

'While the administration of Secretary Weeks was to see an immense amount of thought devoted to the working-out of the details of the National Defense under his direction — and it was well done — his great individual task was in explaining the purpose and advantage of the law to our people. Such a system must be sustained by public opinion, if it is to be efficient and permanent. Such public opinion can only be formed through the education of the people. Secretary Weeks, with his magnetic personality, his great prestige, and wide popular following, spoke with authority on the need for National Defense and the way the present law meets that need. The opinion of no other public man carried so much weight. It was as the voice of one, crying in the wilderness of pacifism and reaction, following the Great War.

'Besides the division of the country into corps areas, on the basis of population, for the purposes of administration, training and mobilization, which had been accomplished before Secretary Weeks took office, the law provided for an adequate and trained General Staff, with well-defined functions and duties, which have been described in the preceding paragraph. Under the law both National Guard and Organized Reserves are represented on the General Staff, in the preparation of plans and policies affecting them. Provision is made by the Act for the mobilization of the national and industrial activities, required in event of war, for the organization and coördination of supply, for the development of an officers' reserve corps and an enlisted reserve corps. The personnel of these reserve corps is to be organized into military units, for service in a major emergency, which with the National Guard, will preserve a portion of the military strength developed during the World War. The Act provides for the annual establishment of training camps for the instruction of civilians. It placed the coördination of supply and the mobilization of industry, under the Assistant Secretary of War. The Reserve is not subject to duty, except in time of major emergency, and for training periods of not more than fifteen days per year. Training camps are also held in conjunction with academic training given in a great many schools and colleges through the country.

'Secretary Weeks approached the development under the National Defense Act with abhorrence of war, but with a full realization that conditions may arise which make it, with all its horrors, the only alternative to a dishonorable peace. Said he: "National defense, however, does not mean necessarily always remaining on the defensive. A proper defensive can be sometimes best attained, and with less cost of men and money, if the initiative in attack is taken by the defender.

'"The welfare and protection of the nation — not the protection and advancement of the interests of any special class or group of citizens — is the first and paramount duty of the Government. Time has not lessened the wisdom of Washington's advice, 'In time of peace, prepare for war.' It is as essential in the preservation of the Republic, in 1921, as it was in 1780.

'"To prepare for war in time of peace would imply the necessity of the adoption of a military policy taking into consideration and making provision for every contingency, which might arise in time of war, and not only must such a policy be formulated, but the success of its operation depends upon its clear understanding by those, in whose interest it has been created, and who, in the final analysis, must furnish the driving force for its execution. If a definite business policy is necessary to the successful conduct of a great industrial concern, certainly a definite military policy is essential to the proper protection of the nation. A business of any size that only plans its operations from day to day seldom survives. Every successful business operation is carried on according to definite policies, determined and consistently followed by those responsible for its conduct. In the years of plenty the wise business man makes provision for possible lean years in the future. The wise nation makes preparation, in time of peace, for possible wars in the future, and, while the nation that fails to make preparation for war may survive a conflict, into which it has been unwillingly forced, it can only do so at an enormous cost of life and wealth, which, in effect, makes it the murderer of its own people.

'"The past is history — the future, mystery. It would be folly to let our hopes for the future blind our eyes to the facts of the past. History demonstrates that this world, since its very creation, has revolved in a cycle, in which peace ends in war just as war, in turn, ends in peace. While I want to see our country lead in every proper means to bring about an understanding between the nations of the world, which will ensure the world against another war, I hope to see it prepared to defend its rights, its sovereignty, and its citizens, until the day comes, if it ever does, when all nations by mutual consent dismantle their fortifications and scrap their navies.

'"I am well aware that a great many good people in this country, indeed in the world, believe the time has come, when the world should undertake a general disarmament. I am personally entirely in sympathy with every wise and sane endeavor to bring about the adoption of a world-wide movement, with that result in view; but we must remember that the passions of war and the disturbances to society, as well as to individuals, cannot be overcome or forgotten in a day. Only time, and a great deal of time, will bring people and nations back to a normal condition. Every one knows that we are far from a condition of normalcy, even in this country where our citizens did not come in direct contact with the actual horrors of war, until our shattered and maimed boys returned to their homes. If that is true of America, how much greater it must be, over, practically, the entire area of continental Europe. A great conflict, which came so near to destroying civilization, as we have known it, could not but leave the nerves of the world in a shattered condition.

'"At the end of the war, every one had a panacea to suggest for every contingency or probable contingency that might arise. Sometimes a real movement, proposing an unwise or hasty change, was developed so that it has been necessary to urge caution, to plead for it, and to endeavor to bring into active participation, in attempting a solution of the many and difficult problems confronting humanity, the best men available.

'"I believe there is a great improvement in conditions, both at home and abroad, and that the world is gradually returning to a state of mind, where, with a vivid recollection of the horrors of the past war, it can take definite action in bringing about a reduction in armament and possibly complete disarmament. Under present conditions, however, it would be the height of folly for the United States to be the first to disarm. Worldwide disarmament must come, as the result of an international agreement and must be done simultaneously. Prudence would not permit disarming, while others hold weapons in their hands."

'Aside from the requirements for national defense, which justify popular military training as contemplated by the National Defense Act, Secretary Weeks believed that the physical, moral and educational value of military training more than justified the cost of the training. Said he: "I have always believed that suitable military training is of material advantage to the citizen, that it gives him a physical and mental poise, which he does not obtain elsewhere, that it makes him a better employer and a better employee, and that we cannot, as a government, do more for the young men of the country in preparing them for citizenship than in furnishing them with the comparatively simple training which will come from their connection with the National Reserves. As a business man, about to take an employee, I would not hesitate, other conditions being equal, in giving preference to the man who had received military instruction and training. I think that is the conclusion reached by every employer who has given attention to that phase of the employee's qualifications."

'The National Defense Act contemplated a regular

army of 18,000 officers and 280,000 enlisted men. In his work of carrying out the Act, Secretary Weeks saw this force reduced by Congress, in three bites, to 12,000 officers and 125,000 men, nominally, but actually to 115,000 men, due to appropriations inadequate to maintain the nominal strength. This shrivelled and dwarfed the fruit that the Act might have borne, but its effect was accepted by Secretary Weeks in that calm philosophy of citizenship with which he inevitably bowed to proper authority. His personal interest never slackened, and his efforts to carry out the Act, to the best of his ability, never diminished.

'The Reserve Corps of officers with careful standards for qualifications was built up by him to over seventy thousand officers. This Corps was largely initiated with veteran officers who had served in the War, with expectation that as this body of experienced officers disappeared, with time, their places would be filled from the men receiving military training in schools and colleges and in the Citizens Military Training Camps. By September, 1921, initial steps had been taken, for the formation of the Organized Reserves, into three field armies, comprising nine army corps and twenty-seven divisions. The sixteen National Army divisions of the World War were retained in the Organized Reserve — their World War histories remaining to inspire their traditions. The responsibility for the Organized Reserve was largely decentralized to the nine Corps Area Commanders, all of them officers, who had exercised high command during the recent war. Provision, always subject to proper appropriations from Congress, was made for fifteen days' training for approximately a third of the reserve officer personnel each year. A limited number of them were given more than fifteen days' training, in connection with the General Staff and the Service Schools of the Regular Army, and as instructors at training camps. Both the Reserve Officers and the Civilian Military Training Camps, under Secretary Weeks, developed a popularity, with numbers seeking admittance far beyond the limiting strength of the appropriations.

'Regulations for the Organized Reserve were published and enforced. Officers were assigned to the units, with which, it is expected, they will mobilize in event of war. Examinations to determine fitness for appointment and for subsequent promotions were inaugurated. Assignments were determined by fitness as shown by previous experience and in some cases by knowledge of professions or occupations, in civil life, along the lines of certain duties in the army. Training was not limited, alone, to the fifteen days permitted by the appropriations, but correspondence schools were established, and individual interest and effort stimulated. Reserve Officers were permitted to attend the Service Schools of the Regular Army and, in some cases, did so at considerable personal financial hardship.

'The central idea of the whole Reserve plan is that, when a national emergency arises, the units of the Reserve Division will immediately begin intensive training and be ready for action in weeks instead of months, without the waste of time and money which was necessary in the system of mobilization, which was in force at the beginning of the World War. The Organized Reserve is the organization under the National Defense of the "unorganized militia" of our Constitution. Secretary Weeks brought the Organized Reserve to a place where it now has a voice in our military counsels and a post of honor in our National Defense with the National Guard. It is the expression of the American idea, that we intend to fight our own battles, and with the insignificant size of our Regular Army, in proportion to our area and population, goes far toward the state contemplated by Thomas Jefferson when he said: "None but an armed nation can dispense with a standing army."

'In the mobilization plans, prepared in 1921, six Field Armies were contemplated, the first three comprising one, to be formed from units of the Regular Army and two from the National Guard, and the second three, as already stated, to be formed of the Organized Reserves. In a major emergency it is expected that the first line of our defense will be formed of the Regular Army and the National Guard, which will cover the mobilization and training of the Organized Reserves, which must be expanded by volunteers, or preferably by the draft.

'In the National Guard reorganization programme, as shaped by Secretary Weeks, lessons of the World War were taken into account and the present National Guard differs very materially from that of pre-war days. It is no longer forty-nine allied armies, but is now *the* National Guard. It is a well-developed component of the army of the United States, with a proper ratio of troops of all branches of the service, including all calibers of heavy artillery, anti-aircraft artillery, tanks, airplanes, balloons and motor truck units, each with its defined mission, so that in the event of war all may take their places in the field with a minimum of confusion. Eighteen National Guard divisions are allotted to the Nine Corps Areas, besides a number of Corps, Army and General Headquarters troops. Cavalry strength, to the amount of four divisions, is in course of organization.

Under the law the National Guard is computed on a basis of 800 for each Senator and Representative in Congress, or about 450,000 men. Actually about half that total has been reached. Six states have complete divisions, in addition to some Corps, Army and G.H.Q. troops. Almost without exception the state authorities have shown interest, and the National Guard reached a higher point in numbers and efficiency under the Weeks administration than it has ever known before.

'Secretary Weeks was an ardent believer in the summer training camps, and they received his fostering attention throughout his administration. In the summer of 1922, for the first time, all elements of the three-part Army of the United States participated in field training. Throughout our country the outstanding feature of the training camps was the enthusiasm with which all concerned threw themselves into the work, and the consequent high level of accomplishment. Regulars, National Guardsmen, Reserves, Reserve Officers' Training Corps units from the schools and colleges, and civilians of the Military Training Camps worked, side by side, with appreciation of their respective rôles in the team-work of the National Defense. So successfully was this feature of our insurance against possible national disaster initiated that its future depends almost entirely on the provision by Congress of the absolutely necessary funds each year. It was a feature of our National Defense very close to the heart of Secretary Weeks.

'Beginning with a strength of 18,000 officers and 280,000 men, the first two years of the Weeks administration saw the Regular Army reduced to 12,000 officers and 125,000 men. This resulted in almost constant reorganization of the army and, of course, interfered with its efficient operation. The constant and final opinion of Secretary Weeks was that the Regular Army could not properly perform its mission with less than 13,000 officers and 150,000 men. While its strength diminished its mission remained unchanged. Secretary Weeks defined that mission to be:

'1. To train and develop the National Guard and the Organized Reserve, the two great branches of the citizen soldiery.

'2. To maintain the necessary schools for the training of officers and enlisted men of all three components of the Army of the United States.

'3. To maintain the administrative overhead for the three-part Army.

'4. To provide peace-time garrisons for our continental coast defenses.

'5. To provide peace and war-time garrisons for our overseas possessions.

'6. To maintain a well-trained force for emergency purposes and to serve as a model for the two bodies of citizen soldiers.

'The strength to which he was required to reduce the Regular Army is 155,000 less than that authorized by the National Defense Act, which resulted from the lessons of the World War and assigned the above mission for the Regular establishment, and 102,000 less than the authorized pre-war strength before the three-part army was created.

'A few less than thirty thousand men are required for the overseas possessions; the Regular Army being responsible not only for the maintenance of law and order and the protection of life and property, but also for the holding of those strategic positions, without reënforcements, in case of an emergency.

'In the distribution of troops for the continental United States, the greatest reduction had to be made in the coast defenses and in the mobile force, the latter being that portion which is used for emergency purposes, for protection of the southern border, as a model and demonstrating force for the citizen soldiers, and as a basis of expansion, in the event of attack from outside sources. It was not possible to much reduce the allotment for the overhead of the three-part Army, to the school system, and to special duty with the National Guard, Organized Reserves, and the Reserve Officers' Training Corps.

'Actually but approximately 43,000 were finally available for the mobile force, which necessitated the abandonment of the Secretary's cherished plan of an organization of nine mobile divisions, which were to be allocated, one to each Corps Area, concentrated to form a force in each Area available for immediate use. These divisions were to have been the great practical schools in which officers and men should learn, from experience, the art of command and the functioning and coördination of all arms, with maneuvers in the appropriate season for their own instruction, and that of the remainder of the Army of the United States as contemplated by the National Defense Act.

'In the reduction but one division could be retained as a concentrated unit, two others being nominally retained but with widely scattered units, and the remainder as divisions disappear — to be again revived possibly in a time of national danger and at emergency cost. Thus the vicious circle again begins. Unpreparedness piling up a big war debt, necessitating economy, with resulting unpreparedness, promising a similar waste of blood and treasure in a future war. As Secretary Weeks remarked: "We should not overlook the fact that the National Defense Act itself is a great economic measure deliberately designed to provide adequate defense at a minimum of cost."

'In his reduction of the Regular Army, it is of interest to know that the administration for which the Secretary had to provide includes the War Department General Staff, the offices of the Chiefs of Branches and the other executive and administrative offices of the War Department, the Headquarters of nine Corps Areas, Supply and Remount Depots, Arsenals, General Hospitals, Disciplinary Barracks, Recruiting Service, Finance Officers, Construction and Transport Services, Military Attachés, River, Harbor and Fortification Works, District of Columbia Commissions, Federal Power Commission, Alaskan Commissions, Canal Zone Government, Porto Rico Government, Coast and Inland Waterways, American Red Cross, Relief Administration, Veterans' Bureau, Bureau of the Budget, Bureau of Standards, Washington–Alaska Cable and Telegraph, Soldiers' Home Hospitals and similar activities. These include offices and agencies maintained in time of peace, prepared for immediate and effective functioning in event of mobilization. Thus only can we avoid the historic delay and confusion which, in the past, has always resulted from a peace-time organization not adaptable to the quick expansion necessitated by the emergency.

'The World War resulted in the creation of many services previously unknown to armies. In his allocation of his officer strength, Secretary Weeks had to provide over two thousand officers to carry on the military

study, research, instruction and dissemination of knowledge for the Army of the United States, essential to a
standardization of training. This includes officers for
duty at the United States Military Academy, War
College, General Service, Infantry, Tank, Field Artil-
lery, Cavalry, Coast Artillery, Engineers, Signal, Air-
ship, Communication, Mechanic, Observation, Pilot,
Photo, Balloon, Motor Transport, Animal Transport,
Administration, Subsistence, Shoe, Bakers and Cooks,
Medical Field Service, Flight Surgeons, Veterinary,
Chemical Warfare, Finance, Ordnance, Chaplains, and
Army Music Schools.

'Over three thousand officers were assigned to develop,
organize, instruct, and plan the mobilization of those
elements upon which the main reliance for National Defense is placed, being the National Guard, Organized
Reserves, Reserve Officers' Training Corps units, in
schools and colleges, and the Citizens Military Training
Camps.

'Over five thousand officers were assigned to the portion of the Regular Army used in the continental United
States, and over six hundred more to the coast defenses.
Nearly three thousand were sent to the overseas garrisons which, in event of emergency, cannot be aug-
mented by the citizen soldiery.

'In the reduction of the Army the Secretary strove to
alleviate the feeling of unrest and instability which is
inevitable among the commissioned personnel, when reductions are in process or contemplation. The entire
army had confidence in his justice and fair dealing.
The permanency of the officers' commission, during good
behavior, and the certain maintenance of the army retired list were recognized by him as deferred compensa-

tion, which fact alone enables the Government to retain in service a very high class of men at much lower salary cost than is paid for similar men in civil life. Notwithstanding the increased cost of living and the reduced purchasing power of the dollar, Officers of the Army, Navy and Marine Corps received no increase in salary from 1908 to 1922, when a bill, earnestly supported by Secretary Weeks, was passed. The wretched housing conditions in the Army, following the World War, and the rising cost of living at military stations, were a constant concern to him and he neglected no effort to remedy them.

'The story of the work of Secretary Weeks in the War Department is not complete without some reference to his contributions to the political doctrines of his time. He stood very high in the confidence of the two Commanders-in-Chief under whom he served. He was not a believer in the direct primary. He believed in universal military training. The retirement of disabled emergency officers he opposed only if they were to be placed on the Regular Army retired list, otherwise he favored it. The purchase of the Cape Cod Canal he urged as a measure of naval preparedness. He denounced the bloc system as dangerous to American institutions, permitting rule by minorities, and dividing the country into hostile groups and factions; and he favored universal conscription of man-power, labor and wealth in time of war. He believed in a modification of the Volstead Act to permit the sale of light wines and beer. He was opposed to the use of the Army in the enforcement of prohibition. The initiative and referendum were disapproved by him. The plans for industrial mobilization, in event of war, had his consistent, steady support. He believed in the control of radio by a single governmental agency, with a monopoly of some sort, under government control and regulation. The plan for a single department of National Defense did not appeal to him. He demonstrated that but two and one half cents of every dollar paid by the American citizen for governmental purposes goes to the support of the Army.

'Secretary Weeks brought the ideal temperament for the solution of the problems of the War Department, in the critical reconstruction period following the World War. Straight and honest by inheritance; schooled in self-discipline from his youth; courageous and unafraid; dignified and deliberative, though frank and prompt in decision; a politician, in the high sense of the term, accurate in his judgment of the character of men and women; a veteran of much legislative experience, not to be stampeded into hasty decisions; firm but kindly, with a certain gentle tolerance; he had the rare ability to make adverse decisions and retain the confidence and friendship of the loser. Loyal alike to friend and country, his noble face with its fine eyes, firm chin, and kindly smile, more often grave than mirthful, marked him as a leader of leaders.

'His work in the War Department, thus told in imperfect and inadequate measure, was the crowning glory of his long career as a statesman and patriot. One who worked under him and loved him can in these final words scarcely command the restraint in expression which dignity to his memory demands. Others will write of his successful business career; of his youthful training as a sailor and of his love for the Navy which endured to the end of his days; of his greatness as a representative and senator; of his standing in his home community; of the purity and beauty of his family life, and he was kingly in all these relations. But for us, who knew him as the Secretary of War, during the last four years of his life, there lingers the charm of his rare personality, and endures the memory of his greatest work, so greatly done.'

Secretary of War Dwight F. Davis says:

'Adequately to appreciate the accomplishments of John Wingate Weeks, while Secretary of War, during that disturbed period of governmental reorganization, immediately following the World War, one must first have knowledge of the great scope and wide geographic extent of the activities and functions of the Department. Military posts — over 250 in number — are located in the United States, Alaska, Porto Rico, Panama Canal Zone, Hawaii, the Philippine Islands, and China. Upon the War Department rests the responsibility for the clothing, feeding, equipping, training, and welfare of the Regular Army troops of these widely scattered garrisons, which extend from Fort McKinley, Maine, to Tientsin, China, and from Chilkoot Barracks in Alaska to Fort Amador in the Canal Zone. Nearly 4000 National Guard units, located in approximately 1400 cities and towns in the United States, Porto Rico, and Hawaii, and units of the Organized Reserves, allotted to 2700 municipalities, within the continental limits of the United States, also come under War Department supervision. Units of the Reserve Officers' Training Corps are located at over 220 institutions of learning, while Citizens' Military Training Camps are held in each of the nine corps areas every summer. Linking the activities of the War Department with the capital cities of the world, are the offices of over twenty military attachés.

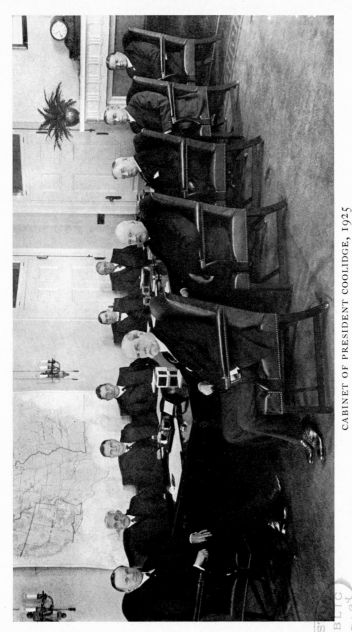

CABINET OF PRESIDENT COOLIDGE, 1925

Left to right: The President; Andrew W. Mellon, Treasury; Harlan F. Stone, Attorney General; Curtis D. Wilbur, Navy; Charles E. Hughes, State; Howard M. Gore, Agriculture; James J. Davis, Labor; John W. Weeks, War; Harry S. New, Postmaster General; Hubert Work, Interior; Herbert C. Hoover, Commerce

'Army installations are so varied as to include in-dustrial and service schools; Quartermaster, Engineer and Ordnance depots; arsenals and proving grounds; hospitals and medical centers; flying fields; motor transport repair centers; sea-going mine planters; ferry systems and a transport service; and remount stations. Other War Department activities relate to the building and maintenance of roads, trails, and bridges in Alaska; cable, radio, and telegraph systems; flood control pro-jects; the improvement of rivers and harbors; national military parks; national cemeteries; the erection of national monuments and buildings; homes for disabled soldiers; an inland waterways corporation; and colonial governments. Such a recital portrays very incompletely the manifold and exacting responsibilities which Mr. Weeks shouldered at a time when the War Department was undergoing transformation from a war to a peace basis. In addition to these duties, which were distinctly related to War Department activities, the Secretary was called upon to assume many other non-military offices. He is the representative of the President of the United States, directly charged with the general super-vision of the administration of the Panama Canal and the operation of the Panama Railroad Company and its subsidiary, and the Panama Railroad Steamship Line. He is Chairman of the Federal Power Commission; President of the National Forest Reservation Com-mission; President of the President's Committee on Outdoor Recreation; and Chairman of the Committee appointed by the President to determine the policy of the Federal Government with respect to our Merchant Marine, governmental control, and American shipping in general. He also sits as a member of the Federal Oil

Conservation Board and is chairman or member of numerous committees or commissions to which are delegated the supervision and maintenance of monuments, national parks, and other similar projects.

'To the administration of the War Department, Secretary Weeks brought a wide and varied experience. He was possessed of unusual qualities of perception and accuracy of judgment. He could listen to an involved and intricate argument with patience and, with a few rapier-like questions, strip the subject of any subtlety and present the substance with startling vividness. His decision once made, he accepted full responsibility for his action. Fully aware that no one man — no matter how endowed with intellect and energy — could possibly control all the activities of his great department, he placed large responsibility upon his subordinates, clothed them with corresponding powers, and then held them to strict accountability. He inspired not only great personal loyalty, but keen personal admiration. John Wingate Weeks was a leader of men, in every sense of the word. It was the possession of this intangible quality of leadership that, more than any one factor, enabled him to carry the War Department and the Army through those discouraging years of curtailment of activities, reductions, demotions, and disinterestedness on the part of the public, which are an inevitable reaction to all great wars.

'Among the duties of the Secretary of War are the general direction of the prosecution of work for the improvement of rivers and harbors and navigation, the supervision of works for flood control, and the enforcement of laws for the protection of navigable waters.

'During the period that Mr. Weeks headed the War

Department, the necessity for increasing the transportation facilities of the United States and at the same time reducing the cost of transportation, was becoming more and more apparent. His active and intelligent interest, and participation in the development of river and harbor improvements and of water transportation facilities, was evidence that he fully appreciated the seneeds. He realized that the War Department, through its river and harbor work, and through the activity of the Federal Barge Line, was in a position to furnish, in large measure, the needed facilities and also to demonstrate their value.

'During his administration there was expended on the various river and harbor improvements, prosecuted by the War Department, nearly $200,000,000. His supervision of this work was active. His decisions indicated an intelligent and impartial judgment of the needs of all sections of the United States, and an understanding of the manner in which available funds could best be applied to meet these needs.

'One of the principal works of construction undertaken by the Federal Government in recent years is the Wilson Dam at Muscle Shoals, Alabama. Mr. Weeks was largely responsible for the completion of this work. Undertaken as a war measure, as part of the programme for the production of nitrates, this project was later discontinued. One method of demonstrating whether it would be advisable to resume the work was to determine its value, and, in compliance with the direction of the Secretary of War, letters were written asking for offers for the property. Among those received was one from Mr. Henry Ford. The receipt of a bid from so successful an industrialist convinced the Secretary that the completion of the Muscle Shoals project would be wise.

Under the direction of Mr. Weeks, work was resumed, and the structure has since been, for all practical purposes, completed.

'While he was keenly appreciative of the commercial importance of river and harbor work, he understood fully the very intimate relation that such development bore to the question of national defense. Commercial interests involved in this work are usually in accord with those of the national defense. In the few cases, however, where conflict of interests arose that could not be reconciled, Mr. Weeks held that the question of National Defense should be the deciding factor, and for that reason, among others, was convinced that the development of our rivers and harbors should come within the jurisdiction of the Secretary of War.

'On assuming office, Mr. Weeks, in common with the majority of successful men of large affairs, was opposed to the extension of governmental operations in business and industry. He was one of the first advocates of the after-war slogan of "less government in business; more business in government." Nevertheless, when he found himself charged by law with the responsibility of promoting, encouraging and developing waterways and of fostering and maintaining, in full vigor, both rail and water transportation, when he found himself the governing head of the Inland and Coastwise Waterways Service, the instrument created for the observance of the declared policy of Congress in transportation matters, he immediately undertook a serious study of the question. As is true of all who have made an intensive study of the problem of revising traffic on waterways, upon the development of which the Federal Government has expended well over a billion dollars, Mr. Weeks became actively interested in the project and the means for its accomplishment. The longer he studied his problem, the more clearly he perceived the intricate mass of hindering and useless restrictions placed upon operations, as then conducted. When the proposal of the formation of a corporation to eliminate these obstacles was presented by him, he devised means to eliminate all superfluous ideas, until there was evolved a workable plan to present to Congress.

'Through letters and conversations, and by his appearance before committees of Congress, he materially aided in having embodied into concrete law the Act which created the Inland Waterways Corporation. The corporation is now functioning successfully, under the Secretary of War, demonstrating to the public and to private capital that our national policy of creating navigable waterways, in the belief that cheaper transportation would result therefrom, was one based upon a firm foundation, and that the public at large and carriers as well can be benefited by cheaper transportation, through all water routes, joint rail-water routes, and rail-water-highway routes.

'His judgment in the revocation of certain contracts of lease, involving many boats, and his action in the seizure of such boats, has been upheld by the United States Supreme Court and is regarded by the legal profession as a landmark establishing certain government rights and responsibilities which had theretofore remained in the "twilight zone" of legal speculation.

'Secretary Weeks maintained his interest in this corporation up to his last days in the War Department; he took great pride in the enlargement of its operations and in its growing success. Every member of the Advisory Board of the Inland Waterways Corporation succumbed to his charm of manner and yielded to his judgment. At their very first meeting with Mr. Weeks, they were convinced that the Secretary was infinitely well-equipped to solve the problems involved in the operation of this new governmental public activity. Every member of the Advisory Board was his loyal admirer and friend.

'From the beginning of the construction of the Panama Canal to the present, the Secretary of War has been charged by the President with personal supervision over canal affairs, including those of the Panama Railroad Company. Secretary Weeks always took deep personal interest in matters affecting the canal and railroad. He visited the Isthmus in the spring of 1923.

'Many important questions of policy were settled by him during the time he was Secretary of War. These included matters pertaining to the relations between the canal and railroad organizations and their employees; the commercial operations of the canal and the Panama Railroad; and questions involving relations between the government of the United States and the Republic of Panama. He recommended the abrogation of the so-called "Taft Agreement," which was done by Executive Order, and approved, broadly, most of the provisions in the new treaty with the Republic of Panama which, when ratified, will partly supersede the "Taft Agreement."

'Secretary Weeks also appointed a Special Commission which visited the Isthmus in the summer of 1921 for the purpose of making a thorough investigation into all of the phases of the activities of the Canal and Railroad, including the steamship line. He did not approve all of the recommendations of this Commission, but as a result of its report, and with the approval of the Government of the Panama Canal, which had previously recommended some of the changes suggested, he authorized many improvements in the canal's administration. Among those effected were those reorganizing the accounting system; making moderate charges for rental of quarters occupied by employees; reaffirming the policy that the rates of pay authorized by law, of not to exceed twenty-five per cent over the rates paid for similar service by the Government in the United States, should be continued on the Isthmus; and encouraging agriculture by authorizing the opening of small tracts of land, in the Canal Zone, to the local population.

'The reorganization of the accounting system on the Isthmus was based on the following instructions issued by Mr. Weeks on October 18, 1921: "A careful study shall be made of the cost of the canal, in order to establish, if possible, a capitalization, to determine a fair commercial value that should be fixed for the canal and its various allied activities. When this has been arrived at, the actual cost of the canal and its activities should be written down to this figure, and thereafter be used in the operation and official report as capital account, upon which returns and expenditures should be justified. Having arrived at this figure, it will be subdivided and an allocation be made to each auxiliary activity, under the canal administration, and thereafter the sum allotted to each of these activities shall be the one that must be used in justifying the continued existence of the activity concerned. But in case the operations show a loss, the Governor may present to the Secretary of War a statement of the reasons why the activities might be longer continued. There are certain activities, such as sanitation, hospitalization, fire and police protection, and other similar governmental functions, which obviously are not activities from which commercial returns can be expected. These should be attached to Canal Operations proper and the cost thereof be borne by Canal Operations. By capitalizing the canal and its various subdivisions as herein noted, it is believed that many desirable results will obtain, and thereafter not only the canal as a whole, but each of its auxiliary activities will be given a measure by which the efficiency of its operations should be determined.

'". . . In the system of accounting there shall be provisions made for a complete and independent showing by each separate business activity throughout the Zone, and invested capital (subject to the revised set-up value as elsewhere directed) shall be set up as a direct charge thereto, the accounts showing the actual result of each unit."

'As a result of this reorganization, the Panama Canal accounting system was placed on a businesslike basis, which met both the commercial and governmental requirements. Wisdom, moderation, and justice, marked all Mr. Weeks's decisions in connection with matters relating to the administration and operation of the Panama Canal, and his interest in this monumental work never waned.

'As soon as he entered upon his duties, Mr. Weeks showed a pronounced appreciation of the problems which faced the War Department, in connection with the demobilization of the Army. He was among the first to appreciate that the discharge of the war army would not end the War Department's problems. Vast accumulations of supplies would constitute fully as difficult and embarrassing a question. To his subordinates he soon outlined comprehensive plans for the return of the Army to a normal peace-time status. He knew that appropriations must soon be reduced to a basis more closely approximating that of the pre-war period. Consequently, he at once gave directions to eliminate the "overhead." At that time the Government had immense quantities of supplies on hand, which not only necessitated caretakers but required a large amount of rented storage. On the other hand, it would be unfair to industry to unload the surplus at such a rate as to materially affect market values. Therefore, with a fine discrimination, Mr. Weeks directed disposition of the surplus — some by transfer to Government departments, some by wholesale disposition at a low price that did not affect the market. He realized that it was better to make some sacrifices in price rather than continue to eat up values in warehouse charges. The remaining property was transferred to government warehouses, care being exercised to make transfers at minimum transportation charges.

'As a result of Mr. Weeks's recommendations, under dates of December 19, 1922, and May 7, 1924, Congress authorized the disposal of sixty-two military reservations or parts thereof, with an estimated sales value in excess of $3,500,000.

'These reservations were recommended for disposal, for the reason that the War Department felt that it should not be encumbered with property which no longer possessed any military value. Moreover, the War Department Appropriation Act for the fiscal year 1925, provided that the Secretary of War should submit to Congress, at its next session, a comprehensive plan for necessary permanent construction at military posts, based on the use of funds received from the sale of surplus War Department real estate, and for the sale of such property, then owned by the War Department, as in the opinion of the Secretary of War was no longer required for military purposes.

'There were also a number of war military camp sites and plants, disposed of by Mr. Weeks for which legislative authority already existed, the more important of which were: Camp Gordon, Georgia; Chicago Ordnance Depot, Illinois; Baltimore Quartermaster Depot, Maryland; Midland Brine Plant, Michigan; Amatol Arsenal, New Jersey; Morgan Ordnance Depot, New Jersey; Curtiss-Elmwood Plant, New York; Rochester Gun Plant, New York; Erie Howitzer Plant, New York; Neville Island Gun Plant, Pennsylvania; Portsmouth Water Development, Virginia; and Camp Zachary Taylor, Kentucky; with an aggregate of 12,511.38 acres and a sales price of $5,193,846.78.

'This authorization and the availability of this sum enabled the War Department to formulate a comprehensive construction policy, whereby the temporary greatly dilapidated and sometimes dangerous war-time buildings, in which troops were housed, could be replaced by comfortable and modern barracks and quarters. The knowledge, throughout the army, that this replacement would be begun and completed with all possible dispatch had an immediate, beneficial effect on morale.

'During his term of office Secretary Weeks took an active interest in the burial places of our military dead. He approved the permanent retention of the American Military Cemetery at Waereghem, Belgium, to be named the Flanders Field Cemetery, and the burial ground at Séringes-et-Nesles, France, to be named the Oise-Aisne. His action brought the total number of American military cemeteries in Europe to eight.

'He also gave personal consideration to the plans for arrangement and ornamentation of the European cemeteries, the buildings to be erected, and their architecture. The latter is in harmony with that of the region of location.

'Negotiations for the sites for these cemeteries were completed, and the construction of buildings and utilities, and landscaping begun and practically completed during his administration, in accordance with the plans he approved. The total expenditure for these purposes was $856,680.

'The slab design of headstone of white marble which is now being furnished for all dead of the Army, Navy, and Marine Corps in the United States, with the exception of deceased veterans of the Civil and Spanish-American Wars, was approved by Secretary Weeks during his term of office. This design was originally intended for the graves in the overseas cemeteries, but after much discussion it was changed, so far as the European cemeteries were concerned, to the cruciform design for Christians and Star of David design for Jews, thus reproducing in enduring marble the temporary white wooden markers first placed at the American graves. This form of marker was strongly advocated by patriotic societies, especially by the Gold Star Mothers Associations, whose views appealed to Secretary Weeks. He, therefore, readily agreed to the change, although final details of the markers were not completed by the American Battle Monuments Commission until after the expiration of his term as Secretary of War.

'The entombment of the World War Unknown, in Arlington National Cemetery on Armistice Day, November 11, 1921, took place during Secretary Weeks's administration and he was the official Master of Ceremonies. The wonderful impressiveness and solemnity of this ceremony has passed into history as the greatest event of its kind in all time.

'Two new national cemeteries were established while Mr. Weeks was Secretary of War. One was the burial place of President Zachary Taylor near Louisville, Kentucky, containing about seventeen acres, donated by the State of Kentucky. Here a beautiful mausoleum was erected by the Government to which, on May 6, 1926, the bodies of President Taylor and his wife were transferred, with appropriate ceremonies, from an old vault. The second was an old burial place at Sitka, Alaska, in which had been interred the bodies of sixty-two soldier, sailor, Marine Corps, and Coast Service dead. It was on Government land, had been long neglected, and was in an exceedingly chaotic condition. When the matter was brought to his attention, Secretary Weeks at once requested the Secretary of the Interior to withdraw the tract from entry and transfer it to the War Department. This being accomplished, he declared it a national cemetery so that funds from the War Department appropriations could be expended upon it. The War Department was aided in this work by the Navy Department, the Alaska Road Commission, and the Sitka American Legion Post.

'Secretary Weeks favored and encouraged the movement to preserve Fort McHenry, Maryland, where

JOHN W. WEEKS AND LLOYD GEORGE
At Arlington Cemetery, 1923

Francis Scott Key was inspired to write "The Star-Spangled Banner." As a result, Congress passed the Act approved March 23, 1925, authorizing the restoration of this historic fort and its permanent preservation as a national park and memorial shrine.

'The following structures were, on his recommendation, proclaimed National Monuments by the President, under the Antiquities Act of June 8, 1906, because of their historical interest and significance: Fort Wood (Statue of Liberty), New York Harbor; Castle Pinckney, Charleston Harbor, South Carolina; Fort Pulaski, near Savannah, Georgia; Fort Marion, St. Augustine, Florida; and Fort Matanzas, near St. Augustine, Florida.

'Secretary Weeks encouraged and approved the movement to fittingly dignify the burial place of Captain Meriwether Lewis of the epoch-making Lewis and Clark Expedition, near the town of Hohenwald, Lewis County, Tennessee. As a result of this movement, a tract of fifty acres of land in Lewis County, on which are the grave of Captain Meriwether Lewis, a monument erected under the provisions of an Act of the Tennessee Legislature in 1848, and other objects of historic interest, was tendered to the Government by the Meriwether Lewis Memorial Association of Tennessee on October 30, 1924. Upon recommendation of the War Department, the tract was accepted by the Secretary of the Interior under the provisions of the Antiquities Act of June 8, 1906. It was declared a national monument by proclamation of the President on February 6, 1925, and placed in charge of the War Department.

'While Mr. Weeks was Secretary of War, he initiated

an investigation with a view to returning to the states, in which located, government owned or controlled roads leading to national cemeteries and national military parks, which were used more by the general public as highways than as approach roads to the national cemeteries or national military parks, to which they appertained. Mr. Weeks was strongly in favor of the return of these roads to the States concerned and procured the passage of legislation to accomplish this purpose. As a result, Congress passed the Act, approved March 3, 1925, which authorizes the Secretary of War to convey to the States, in which located, government-owned or controlled approach roads to national cemeteries and national military parks.

'None of his predecessors came to the War Department so well equipped as he to meet the problems resulting from the supervision of the civil affairs of the Philippines and of Porto Rico. In the Senate he had been a member of the Committee on the Philippines and, in that position, was a diligent attendant at the various hearings and discussions which led up to the enactment of the present organic law of the Islands.

'He found the problems of these Islands to be largely financial. His experience as a banker and business man enabled him to meet these problems in a manner highly beneficial to the Islands. The adoption by the Philippine Government of a suggestion of Secretary Weeks as to the handling of the funds of the government resulted in a saving estimated conservatively at $8,000,-000, during his incumbency of the office of the Secretary of War, and since then of $800,000 per annum.

'One of the first duties which devolved upon Secretary Weeks was the preparation of the instructions to

General Wood and Governor Forbes, who were made a commission by President Harding to report on conditions in the Philippine Islands. These instructions manifested an intelligent understanding of the situation which one, coming new to the problems presented, would have been years in acquiring.

'In 1922 a mission of prominent Filipinos came to Washington representing the Independence Commission of the Islands. Mr. Weeks's experience in dealing with men was such that it was easy for him to deny practically every request — certainly every unreasonable request — of these representatives, not only without giving cause for offense but, instead, acquiring the deep respect of the members of the mission.

'In 1922 Mr. Weeks visited the Island of Porto Rico and saw, at first hand, the people with whom he was to deal and for whom he was to labor. He desired to visit the Philippine Islands, but the pressure of public business in Washington prevented.

'Mr. Weeks left the War Department with the affection and respect of the people of Porto Rico and the Philippines. He had never been too busy to give to their official representatives and private persons from the Islands, having to do with the Federal Government, his attention and time and, when necessary, his help.

'When his health forced his relinquishment of his Cabinet portfolio, sympathy and regret were nation-wide. Few departmental chiefs in so short a space of years had so impressed themselves upon their associates and received such sincere affection. Mr. Weeks loved the Army; the Army loved Mr. Weeks. The abiding and loyal affection of such a great number of citizens for their departed chief is the most fitting monument to his memory.'

General Pershing has said of Mr. Weeks:

'My official relations with him, as Chief of Staff under his administration of the office of Secretary of War, could not have been less formal. They were, to me, really personal, with hardly the thought that there was any official distinction between us. Our consideration of the various matters that come up was as though we were interested in some great enterprise in which we were associated as friends and for the success of which we were both equally responsible.

'He was quick to see the force of an argument or to point out its weakness. His broad experience as a man of affairs and as a public official had been such that scarcely a problem could be presented for which he did not have a parallel. Questions of administration, apparently knotty, were approached and handled with little hesitation by his practical mind. While he was Secretary the department was managed in a most business-like manner. There was no waste of government money, but, while the Army was run on an economical basis it was not at the sacrifice of efficiency. It can be said that full consideration was always given to the best interests of the Government.

'In his decisions, he never overlooked the effect his action would have upon the morale of the Army as a whole. A more considerate or kinder-hearted man I have never known. Even under the most aggravating conditions he never lost his poise. He was even-tempered under all circumstances. He often resorted to a story to illustrate his attitude, but never evinced disapproval in any but the most matter-of-fact manner. Being wholly loyal himself, he inspired and received loyalty from his subordinates.

'It was perhaps in his private life as a plain citizen and man that he made the greatest appeal to his associates and acquaintances. I had the good fortune to visit him twice at his summer home near Lancaster, New Hampshire, and, while there freed from official cares he was the most companionable of men. He mingled with the people of the village, and none were too humble to share his consideration and even his solicitude.

'John W. Weeks was one of those men, of whom there have been many, who came up from humble surroundings through their own efforts. There is no mystery in greatness; it does not overawe; it has friendliness, kindliness, appreciation and understanding. These qualities he had, and these added to a character strong and pure, such as his, constitute true greatness. He will always hold a place among the great men of his time.'

Vice-President Charles G. Dawes wrote of him:

'His work in the War Department was unique. He stood that test of a strong man which inheres in the ability to surround one's self with strong men. In calling those two great leaders, Generals Pershing and Harbord, just back from the management in France of America's greatest war effort, he welcomed what a weak man would have avoided — that contact, as a superior, with acknowledged leaders which would invite immediate comparison. As a consequence, without knowing what they have written, I venture to say that in your book no higher tributes are paid to the leadership of Secretary Weeks than by these two men. Not only was his leadership respected by the many officers of the American Expeditionary Forces, whom he assembled under him in his work, but he inspired their affectionate loyalty.

'What he accomplished in his administration of the War Department for our regular army organization and its adjuncts is historical, and will be found in the future to have profoundly influenced our national life.'

Governor-General Leonard Wood wrote me a few months before his death: 'My associations with Mr. Weeks were closest while he was Secretary of War and I on duty as Governor-General of the Philippine Islands, and I saw a good deal of him in the old days when he was Senator and I Chief of Staff. Mr. Weeks's Philippine policy was a sound one and he gave me strong support in my efforts to get the Government out of business and to maintain a sound policy here and carry out a rigid observance of the Organic Act which is, in fact, the constitution of the Philippines. I had hoped very much that he would be able to visit the Philippines during my stay here, but his unfortunate illness prevented it. His record as Secretary of War is an excellent one and he gained the respect and esteem of those with whom he came in contact. In a word, one can say that his Philippine policy was a sound one and had for its object the best interests of the Filipino people, indeed all residents of the Philippine Islands — Americans, Filipinos and others. He was strong for the maintenance of American sovereignty and its recognition by the people of the Islands. Our relations were always most cordial and his death brought with it a sense of real personal loss.'

CHAPTER XIII

Mr. Weeks's address 'I Didn't Know That' — Honorary degrees —
Society of the Cincinnati — His physical condition — Resignation as
Secretary of War — Journey to South America — Railroad accident —
Journey to the Hawaiian Islands — Death on Monday, July 12, 1926 —
Funeral at West Newton — Address of Reverend George A. Gordon, D.D.
— Dedication of John W. Weeks Memorial Bridge — Interment in the
National Cemetery at Arlington.

WHILE Mr. Weeks was Secretary of War, he made an
address, 'I Didn't Know That,' at the annual dinner of
the Boston Chamber of Commerce, on November 14,
1922, upon certain of the activities of the War Department. It was printed in the 'Congressional Record' of
December 11, 1922. It is so full of valuable information,
and illustrates so well Mr. Weeks's capacity for making
a clear and convincing statement that it is reprinted in
the Appendix.

During his term of service as Secretary of War, Mr.
Weeks received the honorary degree of LL.D. from five
institutions of learning: New York University, June 8,
1921; Rutgers College, June 14, 1921; Tufts College,
June 20, 1921; Pennsylvania Military College, June 16,
1922; Brown University, June 20, 1923.

Mr. Weeks was a member of the New Hampshire
Society of the Cincinnati by reason of the membership
of Captain John Weeks, his ancestor. This is an heredi-
tary patriotic society, organized in 1783, membership
in which was accorded to all Continental officers who
had served with honor and resigned after three years'
service or who had been honorably discharged for
disability. As the officers of the Revolution were returning to their farms, which they had left to fight for

their country, they named their Society after their Roman prototype, Lucius Quintus Cincinnatus. Colonel Sinclair Weeks succeeded to membership in the New Hampshire Society in July, 1927.

Mr. Weeks had been under regular medical supervision since February 4, 1915, when he told his physician that he had never had a day's illness, that he had been examined the year before and been pronounced to be in perfect health, but that he was conscious of an uncomfortable feeling about his heart, which, upon examination, was found to be slightly enlarged. Nothing was found wrong with him during the next few years until, in November, 1921, he had a severe attack of angina pectoris followed by minor attacks in December, January, and February; but, under regulated conditions, he remained perfectly well through 1923 and 1924. In March, 1925, there were indications of a slight hardening of the arteries, and in April, 1925, partial paralysis on one side, recovery from which was slow and not entirely complete. Other complications followed which led to an operation, but by October, 1925, Mr. Weeks was in very good condition; his heart was satisfactory, the paralysis had practically disappeared, and his general strength was excellent.

He felt impelled, however, by reason of his physical condition, to resign his office, which he did in October, 1925, in the following letter to the President:

'I regret that it seems unwise for me to serve any longer as Secretary of War. Due to your kindness, I have continued in office during the past six months, hoping that, about this time, I would be able to resume active duty. While my health has greatly improved and I hope to recover it ultimately, I am not now in con-

MR. WEEKS AND HIS GRANDCHILDREN, 1925

Left to right: Martha S. Davidge, John W. Davidge, Sinclair Weeks, John W. Weeks, Martha S. Weeks, John W. Weeks 2nd, Frances Lee Weeks

dition to undertake the responsibilities of any intensive occupation, and my doctors inform me that I shall not be able to do so for some months.

'It seems to me that in justice to you, the best interests of the military service and the proper consideration of the important non-military problems, entrusted to the War Department, I should no longer hold an office I cannot adequately fill. I therefore respectfully tender my resignation. In doing so I want to express my entire confidence in the success of your Administration and my sincere regret that I cannot continue, officially, the extremely pleasant relationships I have enjoyed with you and your advisers. Thank you for the kind consideration you have shown me during my service as a member of your Cabinet.'

In his reply, dated October 13, 1925, President Coolidge said:

'Your favor notifying me of your final determination to resign as Secretary of War, on account of your health, has been received with a great deal of regret. I am pleased to know, however, that your physical condition is growing more hopeful each day and that with relief from official duties there is prospect of a good recovery. I recall that you were entering public life twenty-one years ago, when you came to Northampton to speak during your first campaign for election to Congress. You have had the distinction of serving your home city, being a member of the National House and Senate, and sitting in the Cabinet under two administrations. Perhaps no more valuable suggestion was made to the Congress during the war than the proposal you made for preparing for peace. It will remain, with the law for national forests, which bears your name, as a tribute to your statesmanship. I cannot dispute that this entitles you to feel that you have given all that could be required of you in looking after the welfare of your country. I value your ability so much, and appreciate so highly the familiarity that your long experience in Washington has given you, with the affairs of government, that I feel your retirement to be a distinct loss. My personal relations with you have been such that I feel that the country is losing a valuable public administrator and I am losing intimate contact with a friend. Your wise conduct of the office of Secretary of War has been a great satisfaction to me, and, in the well-earned leisure that private life will afford you, I trust you will fully regain your strength and find time to continue your interest in the well-being of our country. The administration of your office has been such that you will go down in history as a great Secretary of War.

'In accepting your resignation, I extend to you every good wish for your continuing welfare.'

Almost immediately Mr. and Mrs. Weeks, with a party of friends, went to South America. They journeyed down the east coast, stopping at Rio de Janeiro, Montevideo, and Buenos Aires, then crossed the Andes to Chile, spending a day or two in Santiago and Valparaiso, and up the west coast on one of the Grace Line boats, stopping a day to see General Pershing at Arica. They also spent a day at Lima and several days at Panama. From Panama they took one of the fruit boats to Havana, spending a day or two there and home by way of Florida — Mr. and Mrs. Weeks stopped on the way north for a week or two at St. Augustine.

As Mr. Weeks had never been in South America, he had a particularly good time. The ambassadors and consuls did everything possible to make enjoyable the stay of the party. The military attachés were particularly attentive and he seemed to be greatly interested in what they were doing and their problems.

Considerable time was spent in Buenos Aires and a very pleasant visit was had at Santiago with Mr. William Miller Collier, the American Ambassador.

At Lima, Peru, the American Ambassador, Mr. Miles Poindexter, spent the day with the party, the members of which saw that old city more thoroughly than would otherwise have been possible.

Mr. Weeks was very much interested in what he saw at Panama. The Commandant was an old friend of his and the party viewed, in a leisurely way, the canal and the various fortifications. He also enjoyed his visit at Havana, with General Crowder.

Of course, he had to be careful not to get overtired. This required much self-denial on his part, as he was invited to many dinners and other entertainments, all of which he would have enjoyed. He was, on the whole, pretty well all of the time and thoroughly enjoyed the whole trip.

On their return, going north from St. Augustine, in December, 1925, Mr. and Mrs. Weeks were in a railroad accident, in which both suffered from bruises and from the shock. Mr. Weeks was confined to his bed for ten days, but apparently was not in any way permanently injured.

In January, 1926, after their recovery from the railroad accident, Mr. and Mrs. Weeks, with a party of friends, went to Hawaii. They had a private car to Los Angeles, where they took the steamer for Honolulu. They remained there at the Moana Hotel for six weeks and were very generally entertained, all of which was much enjoyed by Mr. Weeks.

It was quite apparent, however, upon their return to California, in April, that, while he seemed to be in good condition, his strength had been overtaxed. He had a severe attack of angina pectoris, but recovered sufficiently to leave California on April 10 and reached Washington on April 17. While there, on April 21, he had an attack of paralysis, from which he made a very quick recovery, but did not regain his strength and seemed thereafter slowly to fail. On June 5 he went to Boston with a very strong wish to reach his home in Lancaster, New Hampshire, whither he went with members of his family and an attending physician on June 26. He died there early in the morning of Monday, July 12, 1926.

His earnest wish had been gratified. He died in the spot dearer to him than any other. The towering peaks of the majestic Presidential Range stood, almost like sentinels, at his bedside. He fell asleep in the land of his fathers.

He was brought to West Newton and lay in state during the morning of Thursday, July 15, with a guard of honor from the United States Army. The funeral services were at two o'clock in the First Unitarian Church and were conducted by the Minister, the Reverend Paul S. Phalen. It was a very representative body of men and women that filled the church to overflowing; all drawn thither by their affection and respect for their beloved friend. Members of the Cabinet and of both houses of Congress, the Governor of the Commonwealth and other State officials, representatives of the Government of the City of Newton, friends and neighbors in large numbers.

ON HIS WAY TO HIS LAST CABINET MEETING, OCTOBER, 1925

The service was simple, as he would have it. The great assemblage joined in singing 'Lead, Kindly Light,' and 'Nearer, My God, to Thee,' the familiar hymns he loved. It was a wonderful expression of the feelings of the hearts and souls of all those present. The atmosphere was surcharged with the note of triumph.

The noble address which follows was by the Reverend George A. Gordon, D.D., Minister of the Old South Church, Boston.

'Some one put the question to Frederic Denison Maurice, the great prophet of English faith in the nineteenth century, "Shall we know our friends in the other world?" The reply was another question, "Are we sure that we know them here?" We who are his friends and fellow citizens thought we knew John W. Weeks; we thought so while he lived; since he passed away from us we have discovered that we did not know him. The image of him, reflected in the national prints of the country, gives him back to us in a magnitude and a worth and an impressive power, that we did not appreciate.

'Now that he has been taken from us, we see through eyes purified by grief. Men of his caliber are like great forest trees; we do not know their size until they are down. To-day, therefore, we stand in the awe of a great surprise, and our first word is a confession of thankfulness for the vision that is now given us into the greatness and worth of the friend whom we thought we had known so long.

'In his time, Plato found it difficult to get the best men to take office, and his way of meeting the difficulty was to propose a fine, to be imposed upon the best men who refused to make the great sacrifice, and the fine was for the best men to be ruled by unfit men. There is the great political fine; when the best men refuse to make this great sacrifice, the fit men are ruled by the unfit. Here is the sacred pathway to the motive that lifted Mr. Weeks from the cheerful ways of his business associates, from the easy mastery of the life to which he had been bred for many years, the motive that lifted him into the service of his country.

'He desired to help fit men to govern this great country, by his labor, his courage, his faith and his devotion, with others who helped to make this republic mightier, more prosperous, happier and charged, as it fronted the future, with a great and reasonable hope.

'Like all men who perform the highest kind of service, the ultimate source of his power was his character. What should we think of any appreciation of Washington that should leave out of account the great fountain of his power, his monumental character? What should we think of any homage given to Abraham Lincoln that should fail to recognize the character which made possible his great career?

'When Mr. Gladstone died, distinguished men, all over the United Kingdom, vied with one another in the eulogy of his gifts, his power, and his influence; but when John Morley came to write the life of Gladstone, he selected the words of his great political antagonist, Lord Salisbury, as coming nearest, as he said, to the heart of the great solemnity. Lord Salisbury said: "Mr. Gladstone was the most brilliant intellect in the parliamentary history of his country, but his power lay deeper, it lay in the fact that he was a great Christian statesman." Those words came from an able and unrelenting political foe. The ultimate source of Mr.

Weeks's power was his character. He had an extraordinary physical endowment, he had an intellect, versatile, massive, and masterly, but his character was the great foundation of his power — high purpose, high feelings, courage, the capacity to consider himself last, his country first, devotion magnificent, to the welfare of the republic.

'We have been saying to ourselves during the last few days that he died too early; sixty-six years for such a man seems altogether too brief. But the great question about a timepiece is not how long it takes to run down; the great question is its fidelity to the sun and its trustworthy report of the progress of all the shining hours of the day. The great question about a human being is not how long he lives; it is, for what has he lived? Great ideals, great causes, the public good, the honor, the dignity, the might, of the American republic and its instrumentality in the hand of God for the liberation and service of mankind.

'As I think of the life of our friend, the poet's words come to me, of one

> "Whose life in low estate began
> And in a simple village green;
> Who breaks his birth's invidious bar,
> And grasps the skirts of happy chance,
> And breasts the blows of circumstance
> And grapples with his evil star;
> Who makes by force his merit known
> And lives to clutch the golden keys,
> To mould a mighty state's decrees,
> And shape the whisper of the throne."

'There is our friend's life. Conquest at every step, ascension to political power by the way of his character, the force of his purpose of spirit; and his life in all its

energy and worth has been received into the heart of
the nation, there to abide, part of the saving grace of
the nation, part of its redemptive power, part of the
great assurance through all time to come, of its integrity
and glory. Is this all? Are you satisfied with this and
no more? I am not. There must be something for the
servant who gave all that he had and who has been dis-
missed from life in this world. What has become of him?
What are his wages? The poet will tell us:

"Glory of warrior, glory of orator, glory of song,
    Paid with a voice flying by to be lost on an endless sea;
Glory of Virtue, to fight, to struggle, to right the wrong;
    Nay, but she aim'd not at glory, no lover of glory she;
    Give her the glory of going on, and still to be.

"The wages of sin is death, if the wages of Virtue be dust,
    Would she have heart to endure for the life of the worm and the
        fly?
She desires no isles of the blest, no quiet seats of the just,
    To rest in a golden grove, or to bask in a summer sky.
    Give her the wages of going on, and not to die."

'In this faith we lay to rest this great friend of the
American Republic.'

On the afternoon of Commencement Day, Thursday, June 24, 1926, President Lowell announced to the
Alumni, among the gifts to Harvard University, which
had been received during the year, one from former
business associates for the 'John W. Weeks Bridge.'
    The donors of the bridge were Henry Hornblower,
James J. Phelan, Edward L. Geary, John W. Prentiss,
Henry N. Sweet, Charles T. Lovering, Ralph Hornblower, James A. Fayne, James S. Dunstan, Herbert C.
Sierck, Paul B. Skinner, Percy W. Brown, Alfred R.

Meyer, James H. Wainwright, and Ovington E. Weller.

This footbridge was dedicated on Saturday, May 14, 1927. For an account of the exercises I have drawn liberally upon the veracious columns of the *Boston Evening Transcript* of that date:

'A tribute, in which the Federal and State Governments, Harvard College, the City of Newton, the City of Cambridge, and the business world of Boston joined, was paid, this afternoon, to the memory of Honorable John Wingate Weeks, former Congressman, Senator, and Secretary of War, when the footbridge across the Charles River, built by a group of his associates as a memorial, was formally dedicated and given into the care of the Commonwealth. It was presented by the donors to Harvard College, after which President Lowell, in turn, presented it to the Commonwealth of Massachusetts through the medium of Lieutenant-Governor Frank G. Allen, who took the place of Governor Alvan T. Fuller, who was unable to leave his home because of illness. Secretary of War Dwight F. Davis, successor of Mr. Weeks in the Cabinet, represented the Federal Government.

'Every branch of the national defense was represented — Infantry, Bluejackets, Marines, and Coast Guardsmen were in line, a battery fired a salute and Army and Navy planes circled overhead. The exercises were watched by thousands on both sides of the river. Amplifiers, erected over the speakers' platform, carried their voices to the outskirts of the throng. Mr. Weeks was a former Alderman and Mayor of Newton. The city was represented by the Mayor and the Board of Aldermen. The bridge spans the river from a point in front of the freshman dormitories to the new group of buildings occupied by the graduate school of business administration.

'At two o'clock, the Harvard Glee Club and the band of the Thirteenth Infantry, U.S.A., boarded a Navy barge at the Newell Boat Club and moved to a position in front of the large grand stand built on the north bank of the river.

'Ranged along that side of the stream, in close formation, were the band of the Fifth Infantry, with the field music of the Thirteenth Infantry to augment it; a battalion of the Thirteenth Infantry; a battalion of the Fifth Infantry; the Navy Yard band and battalion of Bluejackets, Marines and members of the Coast Guard. Opposite, on the south bank, were drawn up the Ninth Coast Artillery Corps band, a regiment of Infantry from the National Guard, a troop of National Guard Cavalry and a battery of Field Artillery from the same organization. Farther back, near the Graduate School of Business Administration, was the R.O.T.C. battery of Harvard College. A guard of honor composed of a platoon of the First Corps of Cadets was in line, directly before the grand stand, and the colors of the regular Army and Navy contingents were massed at the Cambridge end of the bridge. Enlisted men representing the Army, Navy, Marine Corps, Coast Guard and National Guard, were stationed at the ends of the bridge to unveil the tablets.

'The Fifth Infantry Band played from half-past two until three o'clock, and, at that hour, a bugler sounded attention. This was followed by a single bugle note as a signal, whereupon the colors of the Secretary of War were displayed at the center of the bridge, while the Fifth Infantry Band sounded four ruffles with flourishes.

President Lowell Accepting the Bridge

Troops Marching across the Bridge
DEDICATION OF THE JOHN W. WEEKS BRIDGE

The Grand Stand

Unveiling the Tablets

DEDICATION OF THE JOHN W. WEEKS BRIDGE

'At the first ruffle the enlisted men unveiled the tablets and the R.O.T.C. battery fired a salute of nineteen guns. Then the glee club, accompanied by the band, sang, after which the Reverend Paul S. Phalen, minister of the West Newton Unitarian Parish, of which Secretary Weeks was a member, offered prayer.

'Following this Henry Hornblower, speaking for the donors, presented the bridge to Harvard College in the following address:

'"It is my great privilege, in behalf of the former associates of Mr. Weeks, to present this bridge, connecting two important parts of the property of the University and creating one more link between the cities of Boston and Cambridge.

'"It is also a matter of profound satisfaction to these, his friends and long-time associates, that Mr. Weeks was informed of their wish and intention — so that a projected monument to a great public servant has become, upon his untimely death, a permanent memorial for all time."

'In accepting the gift in behalf of the President and Fellows of the University, President Lowell said:

'"A connection seems to exist between universities and the passage of streams. The very names of Oxford and Cambridge recall the reason that determined their situation; and it is hardly fanciful to assume that the site of Harvard was selected as the lowest point where the Charles could be easily traversed with the simple means the early settlers could command — the point where the handsome Anderson Bridge now stands.

'"Since that time many bridges have spanned the river; but being a tidal stream, the falling water showed the muddy banks until Charles Eliot, the landscape architect, had the imagination to perceive that by a dam, toward its mouth, the river could be made a thing of beauty. Now it has been adorned by this most graceful of bridges that we dedicate to-day.

'"A footbridge is much needed as a refuge from the automobile, the deadliest of man's inventions used in times of peace. Connecting the lands of the university on the two sides of the river, it is a great boon to its members and not less to the crowds who attend the games.

'"It is a privilege to accept this bridge and to express our gratitude to the generous partners and friends of the statesman in whose memory it is built. But every bridge over navigable water should be in public control and, therefore, it is an honor to be allowed to transfer it to the Commonwealth of Massachusetts, in behalf of the donors."

'Lieutenant-Governor Frank G. Allen said in his address of acceptance:

'"This beautiful bridge, made possible by the efforts and contributions of the associates and friends of a distinguished citizen of Massachusetts, by them presented to Harvard College and in turn by the president and fellows of that great institution presented to the Commonwealth of Massachusetts, as a memorial to John Wingate Weeks, is more than a material structure adding its facilities to those already spanning the Charles River. It suggests for the generations yet to come some thought of the dignity and power of public service, by a man who loved his country and labored for it in the vigorous years of his life.

'"This bridge, dedicated to the memory of a good citizen of this State and of this nation, is forever to bear his name. That name is written in American history through his public services. It is engraved in the hearts of friends, by his capacity for friendship. Now it is given here a monument, a memorial.

"'Future generations, pronouncing his name here, will not escape the thought that a man so served the public and so nourished friendship that, after he had passed from this world, there were those who were moved to erect this memorial to him.

"'Such memorials as this serve a high purpose. There will be men and women in the world to come who may know little of the details of his public service; for ours is a land wherein many men give service, and though their names go into the imperishable records of the Republic, human memory, in general, is unstable; so it will be with him as with others who have benefited their country and have passed from mortal life. The high purpose which this memorial bridge ever will serve, for long years to come, is this: It will attest the friendship of his contemporaries.

"'Men and women who cross here, and who may pause to consider the significance of its memorial lesson, will have the hope that their sons, or their daughters, may so win the esteem and the respect of their time that, after they have gone, some sweet memory of them will remain. Boys and girls playing here, or hurrying across this bridge, will feel some thrill reflected from the fact that this is a memorial, and some among them may be stirred by it to strive the better to serve their Commonwealth and their country.

"'I hope the memory will always remain, that this memorial bridge sprang from the efforts of personal associates and friends. I like to think of this bridge as a memorial of friendship. Of what constitutes greatness in this world there is much debate. Of the greatness of human friendship there has never been a question. To win the cold esteem of history may denote qualities of nobility; to win the friendship of associates is something that, perhaps, in final analysis is more noble than the first.

'"John Wingate Weeks, citizen, soldier, statesman, had many friends. This bridge is a memorial to him, to the quality of friendship. It links Cambridge and Boston. It links the old Harvard and the new. It links generation to generation. It binds cities and years closer, in eternal bonds of understanding and esteem. It offers an inspiring symbol to us and to posterity.

'"I am here to accept this bridge in the name of the Commonwealth of Massachusetts. To Mr. Hornblower, as representing the donors, I offer the Commonwealth's warm appreciation. To all the friends of John W. Weeks, who have made this gift possible, the Commonwealth gives thanks. To those who are to come in years ahead, I ask, in the Commonwealth's name, that they will keep his memory green, and learn increasingly to know the beauty of friendship and its potency for patriotism.

'"In the name of the Commonwealth of Massachusetts, I now accept the John W. Weeks Bridge, and counsel our successors ever to preserve and maintain it."

'Then followed the address of Secretary of War Dwight F. Davis:

'"It has always seemed to me that we honor ourselves whenever we honor a distinguished man. This homage we pay to a splendid figure who has passed, springs from something deep, fine and hopeful in all humanity. It is as if we would snatch from forgetfulness the noble life we have seen lived, and hold it up before us forever as a model and a guide. Certainly, as long as we do this, as long as this instinct lives, the future of humanity is safe enough. And, apparently, the instinct is as old, and will live as long, as man himself. In every age other men have delighted to honor and to imitate those who have lived, acted and thought in the interests of humanity. The pity is that we know such men so little while they are with us. So nearly always it has taken their death to reveal them.

'"No doubt many thought they knew well the man we honor here to-day. In his lifetime John W. Weeks had been highly honored. The people of his State and later the people of the Nation learned to know him as a statesman. But the true man behind the statesman was hidden from all but his intimate friends. It was only when he left us that we found him out in his true nobility — and found what a loss we had suffered.

'"Now that you would honor him with some adequate memorial, it seems to me you have chosen well, in giving his name to this bridge, across a stream long known to legend and song, and dear to all who live along its banks. No symbol more fitting could be found for the life that John Weeks lived. He bridged many younger men over their poverty, and many older men over their doubts and perplexities.

'"This was the spirit of John W. Weeks. It was little known during his lifetime, and it was only after his death that we learned how many were his acts of charity, how lavish he was with his means, and with his cheery encouragement and his kindly counsel.

'"Succeeding generations are not always satisfied with the memorials we raise to good and able men. Bronze statue and marble bust are often passed without a thought for the man whose effigy it is. But a bridge is a thing of daily utility to all. Nothing could better perpetuate the memory of John W. Weeks, for utility to others was the guiding principle of his life. The thousands, in the future, who cross this bridge and see his name will be constantly reminded of what he was and what he did. They will recall, with pride, the many qualities of this true son of Massachusetts.

'"It seems to me, standing here to-day, as if the bridge were the measure of all that belongs to the realm of human need. Between one individual and another, between all the individuals of the world, as a chasm that needs always to be bridged. Language is that bridge, yet how frail it is after all, and how poorly it serves us upon occasions like this. The written word — the book — is a bridge, yet not the greatest writer in the world can reach us with all the wealth of his thought. Poet, painter, preacher, philosopher — all try to bridge us across to new riches of understanding, for what is about us and within us. In a sense, we are all bridges, or builders of bridges.

'"So I say again, it seems to me eminently fitting that the name of John W. Weeks should be given to this bridge, for many are those whom he carried across a difficult place. As a younger man than he, with less experience in many matters, I was glad to make use of the helpful advice he was always ready to give in meetings of the Cabinet and elsewhere. I learned to have absolute faith in his judgment. He saw at once the point of any problem, and to this gift of insight he added a wide and thorough knowledge of human nature. Never, when I sought his counsel and followed it, was I led into a single false step.

'"At first John Weeks was not readily understood. To learn the real heights and depths of his mind, one had to become well acquainted with him. And because he was shy and inclined to hide his real gifts, this took considerable time. Yet at any time he chose he could have taken his place as a high and widely known authority on questions of economics and politics. What he knew he kept to himself, except as he was asked. Then he was only too ready to open to others, for their better understanding, the rich stores of his knowledge and thought.

'"Massachusetts has had many statesmen; few have had so many. From the beginning of the Republic, the Nation has looked to Massachusetts for minds trained to the problems of the hour or of the generations. The House of Representatives, the Senate, and the cabinets of many Presidents have been helped by the counsels of men from Massachusetts. Remove from American history the names of distinguished Americans born in Massachusetts and great gaps would be left that could never be filled. What would our history be like without memories of what we owe to Boston, Cambridge, Concord and Lexington? No other corner of our country has produced more honored names. But among all these, John W. Weeks will take a distinguished place.

'"He was as full of charity as he was of wisdom. Many another man he helped to greater success than his own. He helped them materially and helped them in spirit. Now that his modest wishes no longer have force, men will step forward from many quarters to tell what he did for them and for his country. He wrote no books, he made few speeches, but he poured out his wisdom like rain on thirsty soil, and let it reappear in other men's minds as if it were their own. In life he shrank from public notice, but wherever he went he was an influence, and many men speak wisely, because they listened to him. Massachusetts need have no fear for herself so long as she sends forth such sterling minds and characters to guide our national councils and enrich our national life. It is well that this State honors this man who loved her so well and did her such honor.

'"John W. Weeks was a man in every sense of the word. He was a good husband, a fine father, and a loyal friend. What more can be said of any man?"'

Further singing by the Glee Club, benediction by the Reverend Paul S. Phalen, and the playing of 'Auld Lang Syne' by the Thirteenth Infantry Band, and marching of troops across the bridge, brought the programme to a close.

But one event remains to be recorded here. On Thursday, October 6, 1927, the dust of our friend was reverently placed where it may be at rest until time shall be no more.

One gazing at the beautiful monument, in the National Cemetery at Arlington, which marks the spot, may well exclaim:

> O iron nerve to true occasion true;
> O fall'n at length that tower of strength
> Which stood four square to all the winds that blew,
> Such was he whom we deplore.

APPENDIX

APPENDIX

'I DIDN'T KNOW THAT'

ADDRESS[1] BY HON. JOHN W. WEEKS
SECRETARY OF WAR

MR. ROGERS. Mr. Speaker, under leave granted me to extend my remarks in the Record I am printing herewith a
speech delivered by the Secretary of War, Hon. John W.
Weeks, at the annual dinner of the Boston Chamber of Commerce, November 14, 1922. I have asked the leave of the
House to permit the publication of this address, because it
seems to me by far the clearest exposition I have ever seen of
the problems, accomplishments, and usefulness of the War
Department of the United States as a peace-time agency.
The speech is as follows:

In a recent issue of a well-known magazine I read with deep
interest an engaging article on the Netherlands, written by one of
her eminent sons, who is also our fellow citizen, Mr. Edward Bok.
With characteristic energy Mr. Bok pictured the ignorance of the
average American concerning that enterprising little country, which
he proved to be, however, not tiny at all, but indeed a great empire.
I confess that I was very much instructed by his picture. One must
admire the strategy employed to emphasize his very earnest and
praiseworthy purpose. I hope that I may, therefore, be forgiven for
attempting to employ Mr. Bok's method, while avoiding any pre-
tense of borrowing his inimitable style, to emphasize an equally earnest and, I trust, admirable purpose of my own.

Strange as it may seem, it is a fact that the average American
knows very little about his own Government. He is too busy with
his everyday affairs to give much attention to its activities. He
knows that it is divided into three branches, the executive, the
judicial, and the legislative. He knows the name of the President,

---

[1] Delivered at the Annual Dinner of the Boston Chamber of Commerce,
November 14, 1922. (Printed in the *Congressional Record*, December 11,
1922.)

the Vice President, probably two or more of the Cabinet, the names of the Senators from his State, and the Congressman representing his district. Every two years he goes to the polls — that is, if nothing more important interferes — and votes. Beyond this point he takes little interest in his Government until, perchance, he discovers through the medium of his daily newspaper something in the Government to criticize.

During my labors and studies, of the past year and a half, it has often impressed me that the average American knows scarcely more of the problems and accomplishments of his own War Department than he does of the geography and history of the Netherlands. He knows that there is a Regular Army; that its officers are trained at West Point, that there is a militia, that in event of an emergency he and his fellow citizens will become a part of the military force of the Nation, if their services are needed, and that, in time of war, an American Army will acquit itself with honor and credit. In times of peace, however, so little publicity is given to the activities of the Regular Army that it is very seldom, if ever, brought to the attention of Mr. Average Citizen, and if he gives any thought to it at all he is apt to think of the Army as an organization housed in very comfortable barracks, which drills a little, parades on national holidays, stands guard at forts along our coast, for which we may never have any use, has a number of vague and probably unimportant duties to perform, and costs a great deal of money which could well be devoted to other purposes. I have accordingly felt it to be one of my duties to bring to the attention of our citizens the varied and important activities of the Army. My efforts in that direction quite frequently draw the response, 'Well, I didn't know that.' This always encourages me in my efforts, since we appreciate that true self-government can come only through knowledge. It is my present purpose to endeavor to interest you, as I have been interested, in this instructional problem, with the hope that you might yourselves gain a deeper understanding of our difficulties and be better able to continue and possibly increase the loyal support which the members of the Boston Chamber of Commerce have always given to constructive programs of the Government.

You may not be aware that by the act of June, 1920, a definite military policy was adopted, based on the lessons of the World War, and that this program is the first permanent military policy the United States has ever had. The War Department is devoting itself very enthusiastically to the execution of the terms of this project, and the Secretary of War is charged with the responsibility for its proper administration. Under the requirements of law he has, however, an additional duty to urge upon our people a continued attention to their need for defensive preparation. In attempting to defend the activities of the department in this respect, I explain that what we advocate is really a most conservative policy of insurance against war and internal disturbance. When called upon, as I frequently am, to defend myself against the charge of militarism, I reply that I have no greater fondness for war than I have for fire, theft, murder, disease, and bankruptcy; yet I continue to urge the degree of insurance against the one that is recognized by most business men as sane policy of insurance against the others. It then is pointed out that the insurance offered is of the participating type. The investment in national defense has always brought full returns to the country in the physical and sanitary training of young citizens and in the constructive accomplishments of the War Department and its personnel. The question is sometimes asked, 'Why do Americans need this physical and sanitary training?' I reply, of course, that our experiences with the drafted men during the late war disclosed the alarming truth that approximately 50 per cent of our young men have physical defects, many of which would eventually prove disabling and most of which could easily be corrected by physical training and instruction, which is usually followed by the comment, 'Well, I didn't know that.'

This, I believe, is one of the most interesting aspects of military training. We are living in an age when most serious-minded men are studying the problems of race betterment. All about us are springing up organizations such as the 'better babies' movement, the 'Life Extension Institute,' and other activities whose purpose is the enrichment of our national life through physical improvement. What will be the influence upon our future of our physical evolution? Every American should ask this question, and there is no better source of pertinent information than in the writings of the Surgeon General of the Army on 'Military anthropology.' It is proven therein that the majority of our World War recruits were awkward, narrow-chested, under weight, and generally in poor physical condition. After a few months of training they were developed into broad-chested, two-fisted specimens of American manhood. These citizens received dividends from our defense investment in the form of definite and material gains in weight and in chest measurements. They were enrolled in the greatest 'Life Extension Institute' in the world. The War Department was given an opportunity of surveying the health of the nation. Many basic diseases and disabilities,

— such as weak arches, weak backs, malaria, social diseases, incipient tuberculosis, and countless other infections were discovered in time and eradicated. Camps were made models of neatness, and personal hygiene and sanitation were taught as primary studies. Inoculations against typhoid and similar plagues resulted in the establishment of new minimum records for prevalence. It cannot be questioned that the occurrence of these diseases, throughout our country, has been considerably lessened as a result of the training and medical administration of young men during the war. 'Is not this, Mr. Average American, a satisfactory dividend from military training?' 'Oh, certainly,' you reply, 'but I didn't realize that all this was true.'

Mothers and fathers frequently protest against exposing their boys to the 'dangerous' influences of military camps. They fear that the boys might become dissipated. We reply to these parents that the records of the Surgeon General show that there is a prevalence of social diseases among the young men of our country, straight from their own homes, that constitutes a shocking menace to our national existence. The influence of the military camp is a continual education against the dangers of intemperate life. While the soldier is in camp, he is protected in every possible way from these demoralizing diseases — by education, by disciplinary measures, and by prompt treatment of those who cannot resist nor escape. The American Army in France was, accordingly, able to establish such a low record of disease that our allies were astonished. We have continued to progress in handling this grave problem and I believe that one of the greatest benefits which can be conferred upon national life, through military training, will be the effectual control of this menacing evil. The first step is to instruct those who 'didn't know that.'

The statements that I have just made are sometimes questioned by individuals who remember the disease rates which prevailed in our armies in former wars. The reply is that we have been progressing. During the Civil War, smallpox claimed over 7,000 soldier victims; during the Spanish-American War and the Philippine insurrection there were 258 deaths from this disease; in the World War we lost 14 soldiers with smallpox, although there were 4,000,-000 of them in service. In the Civil War over 15,000 men died from malaria, while during the World War we lost but 25. In the Spanish-American War 20,000 soldiers, or 12 per cent of the total, suffered from typhoid fever; during the World War there were 2,000 cases, or about one-twentieth of 1 per cent. Had the death rates for typhoid in the World War been the same as in 1898, we would have lost 60,000 soldiers from this alone — more than we actually lost from all diseases.

It is difficult for the average American to appreciate that the Surgeon General of the Army is not merely the head of a small body of 'military' medical men. He truly represents the entire medical profession in the military field, just as the Chief of Engineers represents the engineering profession and as the Army itself represents the country. At the same time, the medical profession itself gives generous recognition to the wonderful pioneering work of Army surgeons. Our Medical Department has established certain basic principles that influence the prevention of disease throughout the world. Many of their achievements have resulted in the saving of innumerable lives and have actually made possible the free commercial intercourse between the countries on this continent. The countries to the south of us were once ravaged by yellow fever and malignant malaria. The French enterprise on the Isthmus of Panama was completely blocked by the fact that 75 per cent of the employees from France lost their lives from disease, within a few months after landing on the Isthmus. In 1901 a group of medical officers, headed by Maj. Walter Reed, determined definitely that yellow fever was transmitted by the mosquito. Within a very few months after this discovery Habana was cleared of the disease that had ravaged it for 150 years. Our greatest achievement in Panama was the conversion of this pestiferous district into a healthy region. Since 1906 one could live in Panama with equal assurance of protection against disease as if living, for example, in Boston. This was the work of the Army. When we took over the administration of Porto Rico the entire population was affected by 'tropical anemia.' The Army doctors demonstrated that this disease was a hookworm infection, and the measures taken accordingly have redeemed these people from a plague that would forever have hindered their development. There are many equally striking illustrations of the work of the American Army in improving the health of this country, our dependencies, and, indeed, of the entire world.

'That is all extremely interesting,' reply my questioners, 'but how about the other "constructive" accomplishments of the War Department? We thought that the purpose of the War Department was to wage war.' This is an almost ineradicable tendency — to believe that the War Department is hoping for war and uninterested in the pursuits of peace.

'Do you realize,' I respond, 'that until the middle of the past century the Army was the only public organization fully able to encourage and assist our citizens in their development of this great country?'

'Do you know that the great Lewis and Clark expedition that opened up the Northwest was conducted by the Army?'

The Army conducted nearly all preliminary explorations in the early days of the country. It constructed the early roads. It built bridges and canals. It alone was able to conduct the early surveys and make the maps which are so essential in the opening up of a new region. Army engineers initiated most of the accurate methods which are now employed in the geodetic, topographic, and hydrographic surveys of our possessions. The Army was virtually the pioneer of the pioneers. As our citizens moved west over the prairies and through the forests they traveled routes which were surveyed by Army engineers, constructed by the Army, and protected by military posts. They settled on locations which had been surveyed by the Army, and their titles were established and valid, only because of the surveys. In developing the land the settlers were protected against Indians by troops of the Army. Finally, when the time came to link these outposts to our eastern civilization, it was the Army that located and constructed the railroads. Only after the railroads had developed engineers of their own and the country had become safer for travel, did the Army relinquish its tasks and turn elsewhere for its missions. The troops of the line remained on the frontiers. The engineers of the Army began then to develop the great waterways, improving our rivers and harbors, to surpervise public parks, and to construct and administer our public buildings.

Up to 1855 there was scarcely a railroad in this country that was not projected, built, and operated in large part by the Army. Army engineers located, constructed, and managed such well-known roads as the Baltimore & Ohio; the Northern Central; the Erie; the Boston & Providence; the New York, New Haven & Hartford; and the Boston & Albany. Practically all of the transcontinental railroads were projected by the Army. An Army officer built the best locomotive of his time, after his own design. So widespread was his fame that when the Czar of Russia desired to build a railroad from St. Petersburg to Moscow he chose the American officer for the task. The officer, Lieut. G. W. Whistler, died before completing the work, but he passed it to another Army officer to finish. Americans are proud of their railroads. They owe their early development to the Army.

If the listener is interested, he usually asks, 'What else do we owe to the Army in early development?'

So I continue. The Army built the Chesapeake & Ohio Canal and the Erie Canal. The most effective influence in opening up the Middle West was the old Cumberland Pike, running from Cumberland, Md., to St. Louis, Mo. This was built by the Army. Practically every boundary of the United States, and most of the State boundaries, were surveyed and marked by the Army. The famous Lake Survey was made by the Army. Because of engineering difficulties involved in its construction, the old lighthouse erected on Minot's Ledge in Boston Bay was one of the most prominent sea-rock lighthouses in the world. This, like most of our lighthouses, was erected by the Army. The old channel of Boston Harbor had a depth of only 18 feet. The Army engineers have increased the depth of this important waterway to 35 feet and widened it from 100 feet to 1,200 feet, and similar work has been carried on by them in all harbors and navigable streams of the United States.

When the American citizen visits our National Capital, the first sight to greet his eye is the stately Washington Monument, completed under great difficulties by the Army. He next turns to the Capitol, of which the wings and dome were built by Army engineers. The Army likewise built the old Post Office Building, the new Municipal Building, the Government Printing Office, the War College, the Agriculture Building, and the beautiful Library of Congress. Army engineers supervised construction of the new Lincoln Memorial and practically all of the park system in the District of Columbia. They built the Washington Aqueduct, and are even developing the playgrounds in our Capital City.

I now will discuss the present work of the Army engineers, developing and maintaining our great waterways, including the Panama Canal, which the Army largely built. You gentlemen are familiar with this work and I will not bother you with its details. In addition to the present work itself, there is the planning and projection of future activities. The Board of Rivers and Harbors has recently instituted extensive studies of the port development in our country, concerning their present commercial facilities, the hinterlands which they can serve, their proper development, and factors which advance or retard their progress. Two of these studies for the ports of Boston, Mass., and Portland, Me., have already been published and are attracting enthusiastic attention among the railroads, shippers, and commercial interests generally. It is felt that this work is meeting a long-felt want.

Then there is another direction of interest. One of the most critical points in our transportation system is at the terminals of transfer between land and water carriers. Because of the antiquated facilities, the transfer costs are often greater than the cost of transport over hundreds of miles by rail or by ship. The Board of Rivers and Harbors is conducting a thorough investigation of terminal conditions and is giving very valuable advice to the local communities which can profit by improvement in this important respect.

A striking example of this is the project for the development of the port of New York, which presents a most difficult problem. While the Army engineers are not actually physically developing the project, it is being done under their supervision and with their coöperation. The Army engineers are rendering most valuable assistance in developing the ports of Houston, Texas, and Los Angeles, California, which are becoming great terminals. The Army is actually constructing the ship channels entering these ports, and is coöperating and advising with the local authorities regarding the construction of terminals, docks, etc. In short, the Army engineers are working with a zeal that is excelled by no other public organization, to adapt their various projects to a coördinated scheme for the entire country — one that will fit properly into the industrial and transportation fabric of our national life.

It was not long after the railroads had bound our country into a unity that was further cemented by reconciliation, after the Civil War, when we were faced with the problem of colonization of acquired territories; the problem that is perhaps the severest test of the ideals of any nation. Alaska, Hawaii, Cuba, Porto Rico, the Philippines, Guam, and the Canal Zone — one by one these burdens were thrust upon us. We have done this successfully and the major part of the task has been the work of the Army. When our citizens began their mad rush into the Klondike, it was the Army that opened the harbors and built the roads and trails leading to gold. When the gold was discovered or lost, men remained in this new land, and they were protected from mob rule and lawlessness by the Army. The Army surveyed their lands and policed their frontiers. Their only link with civilization was the cable, constructed and operated by the Signal Corps, which also operates 600 miles of telegraph overland. Army engineers projected the railroads which are beginning to open the country to intensive culture. Even today, a large part in the administration of this great territory is played by Army officers. Business to the extent of over $100,000,-

ooo annually is transacted over the 57 cable and telegraph offices and 17 inland radio stations, all operated by the Signal Corps. Alaska knows the Army as a friend in need. And as it was in Alaska, so also in the other colonies or territories which we have acquired.

The Philippines, Hawaii, Cuba, Porto Rico, and Panama all have histories of achievement, history in which the progressive forces of civilization have struggled against reaction and decadence. That civilized forces are triumphant is due primarily to the intelligent administration and constructive talents of the American Army. Building up public utilities, eradicating terrible diseases, educating the children, attending even to the spiritual needs, creating the institutions of self-government and protecting these institutions from aggression — in all these has the Army left its seal upon our possessions and protectorates and proven itself once more the pioneer of the American pioneers.

Then this question is asked: 'You say that the Army is responsible for our colonization — just what is their success?'

In the Philippines, where strife between tribes was almost continuous, we have built roads, and railroads, and schools, as well as churches, and have done more in 20 years to make the Filipinos a united people than was done before in centuries. Do you realize that we have taught practically all of the children to speak one language — the English language?

In Panama, our predecessors were unable to remain. Our work there is a conspicuous example of what can be accomplished, under the worst tropical conditions, in sanitation, municipal engineering, and construction. The American occupation has exerted and will continue to exert a powerful influence upon all of the near-by countries in Central and South America. These are stimulated to undertake much-needed improvements for which the means are derived from the increased prosperity which the canal has brought. For the last four months the tolls collected by our own Government have exceeded a million dollars per month. Seventy-five lines of vessels, serving the great trade areas of the world, ply through the waterway. The equipment of the Panama Canal as a base for fueling, supply, and repair is complete. It is, incidentally, a military asset of the greatest importance. Its use increases our ability in defense at least 50 per cent, although its total cost is no more than the cost of 10 modern battleships, which would be doomed to obsolescence in 20 years.

Americans do not believe in conquest of territory. The average citizen feels, perhaps, that our pioneering days are over. We cannot admit, however, that we have reached the end of our constructive abilities. There are other methods in which a civilization makes itself an influence for good. We have barely emerged from a war in which we fought for our convictions. It was our purpose to fight not only bravely and with determination, but also fairly and with mercy toward the weak and helpless. 'American relief' has acquired as much significance as a slogan of American progress, as once attached to the cry of 'westward ho.' The average citizen knows and loves Mr. Hoover for his part in American relief in Europe. Does the average citizen know that, except for the titular head of the organization and a few clerical assistants, the American relief in Europe was the Army and its individuals? Five colonels of the Regular Army acted as Mr. Hoover's principal assistants, either in Paris or at the head of more important missions, such as those which were sent into Poland and Armenia. There was a military personnel of 320 officers and 464 enlisted men who constituted the missions and agencies which distributed American relief. In addition, there was a vast amount of work, such as providing convoys and courier service and unloading supplies, performed directly by the American Expeditionary Force itself. In other words, the American relief was merely one of the activities of the American Expeditionary Force. The Russian relief is similarly an organization of Army officers and enlisted men carrying on the work of American civilization as pioneers.

We are obviously on the eve of perhaps the greatest period of construction and progress that we have yet known. The War Department is already playing its accustomed rôle of constructive pioneering. I have mentioned the work of the military engineers. There is a very significant influence in standardization of manufacture exerted by the department in its planning for the mobilization of industries for war. Military experiments in design of tanks and artillery tractors were influential in stimulating the development of the new tractor industry. The pioneering activities of our Air Service are preparing the way for an aviation industry, in stimulating manufacture and in projecting or advising on projects for airways and communication facilities for air traffic. In the near future aerial activity will play a great part in our national existence. The aerial development of the Army is not only for the purpose of war preparation but an extension of the service to commercial life. The department encourages the construction and development of new and better airplanes and is furnishing every aid practicable, within appropriations, to develop air lines which will be beneficial commercially. If this were not done, I venture to say that there would be years of delay in obtaining any commercial results worth mentioning. I have no doubt that, within the next 10 years, we will see many air routes established and doing a prosperous business; in fact, it would not be an extreme statement to make that the development will be comparable to that of the automobile.

The Army has likewise had a pioneering part in the development of the radio. Although the primary task of the Signal Corps is the modification of commercial apparatus to suit military purposes, its research and development experts are continually presenting to the scientific world solutions of vexing problems. Among these may be mentioned the loop, which superseded the cumbersome outside antennæ, and which led the way to the radio compass, and General Squier's remarkable invention, which applies radio principles to commercial telephone systems and makes possible the utilization of existing telephone, telegraph, and even power lines for the sending of private messages and for broadcasting and reception. The Army has to-day 72 radio stations, comprising its radio nets, installed to cover the United States. Last month these handled official messages employing more than 230,000 words and accordingly saved the Government a considerable sum of money that would otherwise have been spent on these communications. Does the average citizen realize that the Signal Corps to-day operates approximately 400 telephone systems, half of which are owned by the Government, and that the Army is, accordingly, a telephone organization second only to the Bell telephone system, which is, of course, the largest telephone organization on the Western Continent? 'Just what,' he asks, 'is the value to the country of these systems?'

To answer this I look back first to the construction of the transcontinental railroads and point out that the continual progress of the Army, in development work, was always followed by elaboration through civilian activities and that it was the elaboration of what the Army began that gave us what we call our civilization to-day. A great impetus to the expansion of our telegraph system was given by the Signal Corps of the Army just after the Civil War. As late as 1877 there were more than 3,000 miles of telegraph service throughout the South operated by the Signal Corps as an outcome of their service in the war. These wires provided the framework for building up the telegraph service in the South that exists to-day, just as the activities of the Army, in early pioneer days, resulted in settlements which later became great cities, such as Pittsburgh on the site of Fort Pitt and Chicago on the site of Fort Dearborn. So we can now look upon the activities of our Signal Corps with realization that they provide us with an enormous addition to our other available means of communication and with full expectation that in our coming development these means will prove of inestimable value.

The invention of the Chief Signal Officer of the Army in applying radio principles to commercial telephone and telegraph systems has greatly multiplied the capacity of existing telephone and telegraph lines and increased, many fold, our facilities for electrical communication. By utilizing the principle embodied in this invention, it is now possible to send simultaneously over the same line a number of telegraphic messages and at the same time carry on several telephone conversations. The system is now in actual practical use by the large commercial companies, and it is the present practice to send eight two-way telegraph messages and three two-way telephone channels, these being in addition to the messages transmitted by the usual practices. It might be remembered that this new system is just coming into use and its full possibilities have not as yet been worked out, but it is fairly certain that this method offers tremendous possibilities for increasing our facilities for communication. This method is particularly adapted for long-distance telephone transmission, and in all long-distance telephone communication this system is now used to a very large extent. The old-fashioned battery telephone method is quickly becoming obsolete, and the newer methods employing radio principles are rapidly taking its place.

It was also found that, by the utilization of the same principles, it is possible to transmit telephone and telegraph messages over power transmission lines, and these are being now utilized for broadcasting. As a result of experiments carried on in the Signal Corps a new method of broadcasting, which consists of transmitting speech or music over the lighting circuits, is now being introduced, and it is hoped that, before very long, it will be possible to receive broadcasted material, whatever its character, by connecting a small suitable receiving set to the light sockets in your homes.

It is interesting to appreciate that our Army has actually been a veritable 'vanguard of American civilization' just as the Roman armies left behind many of the most imperishable monuments to that earlier Republic.

I proceed to other little-known activities, such as those of the Chemical Warfare Service. Does the average citizen know that the deadly mustard gas, as well as several other war gases, is being employed, experimentally, with great hopes of its proving a valuable retardant in the treatment of tuberculosis?

'Why,' the citizen exclaims, 'I thought that war gases caused respiratory diseases.'

I inform him that, on the contrary, it has been established that they tend to prevent such diseases. Among the employees of large war-gas factories influenza and similar diseases were practically unknown, during the period of the plagues that swept our country at the close of the World War. Extensive arrangements are being made in the laboratories of the Chemical Warfare Service to conduct research into the fields of medical employment of war gases and by-products.

One of the greatest problems of modern sanitation is that of effective and safe fumigation. It is necessary to wage continuous war against the rats and other vermin which carry plagues. Only recently, in the fumigation of a ship in San Francisco, several men were killed and many injured by the fumes of hydrocyanic acid. The Chemical Warfare Service offered their coöperation and have already given promise of solving this problem. Tear gas was finally selected by them as the best possibility for use in fumigation. Near the end of October a test was made with a concentration of one-eighth the strength which would injure human life. Several officers spent the night in a room adjoining the kitchen, which was selected for the test. The gas was projected into the kitchen in the evening, and the officers in the next room reported that they were not inconvenienced thereby. In the morning it was discovered that every mouse, fly, cockroach, and other insect was dead. The gas was then projected into a large warehouse, killing hundreds of pounds of rats, mice, bats, and other vermin. The experiment was repeated in fumigating a ship, and the results were beyond expectations. The Public Health Service are enthusiastic about this work and the possibilities seem limitless.

Tear gases have also been demonstrated as very effective in employment against barricaded criminals and in attempted jail deliveries and other riotous actions. The gas mask is becoming very valuable for use in mining activities. The Chemical Warfare Service has produced the only substance suitable for protection of miners against the deadly carbon-monoxide gas. In their development of gas masks and suitable materials therefor, the scientists of the Chemical Warfare Service have made another valuable contribution to the industries in the form of a very active charcoal which is useful in manufacturing gasoline from natural gas and coal-tar products.

It is becoming recognized that any effective control of the boll weevil and similar pests must come from the adaptation of these poisonous compounds. The Air Service is coöperating in experiments by spraying the fields and orchards with the vapors. Experiments are being conducted by the Chemical Warfare Service, in coöperation with the Navy Department, in hope of producing a non-fouling paint and thereby avoiding the results of barnacles which gather on ship bottoms. Gases are being used in experiments with the hope of destroying the teredo and limnoria, which bore into submerged timbers in our southern waters. Finally, in addition to all of these constructive activities, one must recognize that the work of the Chemical Warfare Service has led the way to the foundation of an American dye industry that should one day be one of our most valued assets.

Do you know that the Army started our steel industry, guided it through its early development, and, in coöperation with the Navy Department, stimulated it throughout its expansion to the present gigantic proportions? Our Interior Department was an outgrowth of the activities of the War Department; in fact, the latter once consisted of three parts which are now the War Department proper, the Navy Department, and the Interior Department. The Bureau of Public Roads grew out of the work of the Corps of Engineers. The Signal Corps can be said to have played a major part in development of the telegraph industries. The development of our Life-Saving Service was possible, largely through the coöperation of hundreds of miles of governmental telegraph lines, operated by the Signal Corps. The Lighthouse Service that plays such an important part in coastwise and terminal-ocean traffic, was built up by the Army and turned over to civil agencies, only after its success was assured. In all of these ways the Army has proved that it can lead the way as a pioneer, not only through forests and over prairies but also through the fields of science and industry.

The dominating influences in building up 'steel' have been the provision of markets, the increasing adaptation in employment, and the specifications for design. The Army was the original market for steel products — offered an ever greater field for the use of steel — and led the entire industry in specifications for design. High-grade steel, as we know it to-day, dates from the Civil War, when the Army called for superior quality in gun metal. In 1880 the requirements for high-carbon steel, in making guns, were fully 50 per cent more severe than were the general industrial specifications. The Ordnance Department introduced alloy steels in the manufacture of Army material, and prescribed the use of nickel steel at a time when there were very few commercial uses for nickel steel in the entire country and when only two or three commercial concerns were capable of its manufacture. In 1875 the board of investigation at the Watertown Arsenal established a program of investigation and built an emery-testing machine that was the largest in the world — this machine is still in daily use, and was only recently superseded in its rank as the largest in the world. The work of Watertown Arsenal was truly pioneer work in this country, and it had a tremendous influence in stimulating similar investigators on the part of technical schools and colleges. Until the creation of the Bureau of Standards, the arsenal was recognized leader in metallurgical study and it is even to-day doing very original work which must have a noteworthy effect in the future.

When the American citizen takes his family out for a day in the country he frequently meets with a mishap, perhaps breaking a part of his automobile. Does he seek a country blacksmith or a machine shop to repair his Ford? Not he. Proceeding to the nearest garage he finds a stock of spare parts which meet his wants and enable him to go 'flivving' off in short order. He might, if he is scientifically inclined, utter a brief prayer to the inventor of 'interchangeable manufacture' which produces spare parts. If he were historically inclined, as well, he could look back over a century and discover that he owes this happy development to the filling of a contract for 10,000 muskets in 1798. That was the beginning of interchangeable manufacture. When the War of 1812 was forced on us the art was so well established that interchangeability had become a normal contract specification of the War Department. One of our contracts in that year contained a clause which reads as follows: 'The component parts of pistols are to correspond so exactly, that any limb or part of one pistol may be fitted to any other pistol of the 20,000.'

It is natural that out of this early development in Army arsenals, should have come some consideration for the problem which we now call 'scientific management.' We feel that America leads the world in the art of the efficiency expert. Does my inquiring friend know that in this field as in so many others the Army appeared as a pioneer?

I refer him to Doctor Taylor, who is well known as a noted protagonist of scientific management and who makes frequent mention of the work of the Army in this respect. In one of his books he observes that the card system of shop returns was invented and introduced as a complete system, for the first time, in the Government shops of the Frankford Arsenal, and that this was a distinct advance in the art of efficiency management. My prospect is thus brought once more to appreciate that the by-products of our national defense cannot sensibly be ignored.

It is common knowledge that one of the greatest developments ahead of us must be that of effectively utilizing our great resources in water power. It is necessary to harness this cheap energy, and yet to do it in such a manner as not to interfere with our navigable waterways, with the growth of our national forests, and with the public enjoyment of our national parks. In the second year of the power commission it has had to study projects for proposed developments of water power in excess of 20,000,000 horsepower, or more than twice the existing power development of this country and more than the combined potential resources of Norway, Sweden, Finland, and the Arctic and Baltic drainages of Russia — the principal water power region of Europe. In two years its engineers have had to study projects for development greater than double the resources of France and Italy and six times the aggregate of projects for development of resources under Federal control in the preceding 20 years. The greater part of this work of examination and study has fallen to the War Department, and the Chief Engineer and his assistants and the chief counsel of the power commission are officers of the Regular Army.

Does the citizen know that the Army organized the Weather Bureau and that during Army control this bureau gave out information that was of tremendous interest throughout the scientific world? Does he know that the Army has played a prominent part in diverting our explosives production into fields that offer great hopes of building up a great American nitrate industry which would be of inestimable benefit to the farmer? Does he know what the Army has done in helping to conserve our resources? The Army Engineers have led us in flood prevention and have assisted greatly in forest protection. At the present time the Air Service is coöperating, as much as funds will permit, in the work of the Department of Agriculture concerning forest-fire prevention. In the past year over 100,000 square miles of forest lands were covered by fliers. Of 1248 fires occurring in the national preserves of California in three months, the aerial patrols reported 664 and were first to report 376.

'Why must such products come from the Army?' I am asked. 'Why cannot some other agency do all of this work?'

I reply that neither the Government nor any individuals could afford to maintain a great pioneer organization with no other functions. Such benefits can come only from the work of an organized and trained public force which can produce them virtually as by-products and still perform its primary tasks. About the middle of last April the Mississippi River rose to the point of threatening disaster to thousands of families along its banks. Members of Congress from that region visited the War Department for advice, and varying degrees of concern were manifested by officials of the States affected. It was apparent that there was no organization other than the Army that could drop its routine tasks and handle such an emergency. The War Department had experienced this situation in the past and had prepared detailed regulations to govern the forces which might have to operate under these conditions. It was necessary only, to put the existing machinery into motion. The governors of four States were notified that certain military authorities would be assigned districts in their States. Military authorities were informed of depots which would furnish supplies needed. Commanding generals of corps areas were advised of the situation, and they made arrangements for utilizing troops, that might be necessary. Our fears were not realized. The danger passed. There was an excellent illustration, however, of the potential value of an organization like ours.

This potential power has unfortunately been called upon many times in our past. After the San Francisco earthquake and fire in 1906, it was the Army that took charge of disorder and administered the forces of order. In the Galveston disaster of 1915 the Army made a record for heroic achievement. Similarly the constructive value of the War Department was felt in the Mount Pelee disaster and during the Ohio and Mississippi floods of 1912. There is a huge file of grateful letters received by the department for its work, in these instances and others similar, of which the following is an example:

'Whereas the relief extended to our people during the recent flood ... has minimized the great loss and damage ...

'*Be it resolved by the Harrisonburg flood relief committee* ... That we hereby extend an expression of our thanks and appreciation for the prompt and efficient manner in which the said relief has been given by the War Department....' (1912 floods, Mississippi.)

Last year, in the coal fields of West Virginia, a situation arose that promised untold difficulties for the industry and for the community. The subsidence was so sudden that few citizens were able to appreciate the firm yet friendly manner in which the Army took control and insisted that the rights of the public must be maintained against the actions of any particular class or classes. In a very short time they assured peace, without making a single aggressive move and without antagonizing any party to the pending disputes. It is scarcely too much to state that these incidents alone justify the investments which we have made in a national force organized and trained for the national defense against outlawry. It is amazing to discover how little our citizens understand of this dramatic history of purely civic accomplishment. It is equally amazing to most of them when they do learn the facts.

There is a tendency to think of military men as hard-boiled masters of red tape and inefficiency. My own interest in the matter has led me to investigate the individual civil records of officers, to determine the effects of their military training. Their records are brilliant. In spite of the fact that their training has been for war, the influence of the high ideals of the Army and its spirit of teamwork have been enough to counteract the handicaps and enable officers to compete on fair terms. During the first century of its existence, West Point sent 2371 of its graduates into civil life, most of them after some years of military service in the Army. Even a very small college would graduate as many as 2371 in a few years. Yet where is there a small or great college or university that can excel the record of these 2371 graduates in civil life? Here is their record:

President of the United States..........................	1
President of the Confederate States......................	1
Presidential candidates................................	3
Vice-presidential candidates	2
Members of the Cabinet...............................	4
Ambassador..	1
Ministers to foreign countries..........................	14
Chargé d'affaires to foreign countries....................	2
Consul generals and consuls............................	12
Members of Congress..................................	24
United States civil officers of various kinds................	171
Presidential electors..................................	8
Governors of States or Territories.......................	16
Bishops..	1
Lieutenant governors..................................	2
Judges...	14
Members of State legislatures...........................	77
Presiding officers of State senates or houses of representatives..	8

'Where do officers gain the administrative knowledge that is necessary to make such records as these?'

After all that I have told of the achievements of the Army at home and abroad my questioners still fail to appreciate that the War Department and the Army is one of the greatest administrative concerns in the country. That it is criticized for adherence to 'red tape' is true, but the critics often fail to appreciate that this is because such a huge organization, open as it is to criticism from any citizen of this country, must be conservative and 'safe,' both of which qualities demand recognized forms of procedure. In the files of the Adjutant General are records of more than 30,000,000 individuals, nearly 10,000,000 of whom have had military service. I could make some picturesque comparisons, such as that the cover sheets of draft records alone would, if placed side by side, reach from the Atlantic to the Pacific, etc. The records of the Adjutant General are accommodated in 83,000 filing cabinets and occupy 450,000 square feet of floor surface.

The very citizen who criticizes us for 'red tape' might have sent us one of the countless queries which we receive daily, such as, 'Did George Washington throw a silver dollar across the Potomac River?' and 'Who originated the term "Buddy?"' If the citizen makes these inquiries in good faith, we are required to answer him, for it is his business even more than ours.

During May, 1919, the average number of pieces of mail received daily in this one office of the Adjutant General was over a half-million. In 1919 over 80,000,000 pieces of mail were received. I give these figures to the curious one in order to convince him that there is plenty of opportunity for the Army officer to learn administration. The Adjutant General's is but one of a great number of offices maintained by officers of the Army. There is every known phase of human life involved in their administrative calendars. Does the citizen realize that the Army must train thousands of young men not only for war but also in vocational and educational features? We have a continuous school problem and a normal provision for training men in the following occupations:

Horseshoeing, tractor drivers, dynamo tenders, steam-engine tenders, firemen, oilers, carpenters of all kinds, concrete workers, photographers, lithographers, painters, stonemasons, brick masons, blacksmiths, plumbers, pipe fitters, welders, printers, linemen, radio operators, telegraph operators, switchboard operators, auto mechanics, chauffeurs, battery repairmen, tire repairers, ignition and carburetion experts, sheet-metal workers, canvas workers, tailors, butchers, clerks, stenographers, typists, bookkeepers, instrument repairers, machinists, foundry men, pattern makers, farriers, pharmacists' assistants, X-ray operators, buglers, bandsmen, surveyors, topographers, highway construction men, bridge builders, draftsmen, interior wiremen, riggers, radio electricians, telephone electricians, telegraph electricians, motion-picture operators, bakers, cooks, cargadors, teamsters, wagon masters, wheelwrights, shoemakers, saddlers, laundrymen, and storekeepers.

Officers must pay the Army, keep accounts for the Army, feed the Army, give spiritual guidance for the Army, and in a word administer the Army according to the most civilized concept of human administration. Every officer must understand the military law.

Incidentally, in the face of all criticism which has been leveled at our system of military jurisprudence, it has been pronounced excellent by some of our best civil lawyers. The citizen sometimes asks me about the hard-boiled methods of prison administration prevalent in the Army. I invite his attention to various comments which indicate that our military prisons have donated many valuable contributions to the science and art of prison management. Everything possible is done to humanize our prisons and to develop the unfortunate occupants so that they can practice trades upon release and, even more important, so that their criminal tendencies might be lessened or completely eradicated. In each of our prisons there is a board of psychiatry and sociology which has for its purpose to modernize our treatment of this problem. Does the citizen realize all this?

'No, indeed,' he replies, 'and I am intensely interested by your exposition.' 'I begin to see what you meant when you claimed that your policy of national defense was of the participating type.' 'Nevertheless,' he frequently adds, 'it costs too much, doesn't it, Mr. Secretary?'

It is indeed a serious objection, at this trying time, that national defense should be so costly, or rather that it is made to appear so costly. As a matter of truth, it is not costly. In 1921, in the City of Boston, Massachusetts, from each dollar paid by the citizen for taxes 3½ cents went for military preparation and 3.7 cents for naval preparation. In other words, his policy of national defense (which he admits to be a participating policy) cost only 7.2 per cent of his total taxation. This is astonishingly small. The citizen is so often misled into charging up against his policy of insurance, the cost of a war which his insurance failed to guarantee against. He should rest assured that in a defenseless State he would be continually attacked by predatory forces, and his insurance is only against these potential attacks. The World War is costing us a great amount, it is true. A comparatively small investment in preparation, before the war would, however, have greatly decreased the present cost of our unpreparedness.

This accusation that the War Department wastes its money extravagantly is, of course, rather easy to refute. I do not know where this idea started — that the Army wastes its money so lavishly — unless it is from the knowledge that when we rush into war unprepared there is great general inefficiency of spending at a time when we must 'spend or take the consequences.' I do not desire to inject a political atmosphere into this discussion, and accordingly I hesitate to discuss, in detail, our efforts to save money. I believe that the operations of the Budget Bureau have, however, been approved by all parties. It seems safe to mention that during the past fiscal year the War Department withheld from expenditure about $85,000,000 which it might have spent. Of this amount, $35,000,000 represents projects that were postponed, while $50,000,000 was actually turned back into the unappropriated balance in the Treasury.

'Why, that is unheard of!'

Unheard of, perhaps, but true. It is difficult to appreciate the determination with which the entire Army has entered into our campaign of saving. Does the citizen know that the chief coördinator has been assisted by nine regular officers and that there would doubtless be more of them in the Bureau of the Budget if their numbers were not now so limited? Or that the present coördinator is himself a retired officer of the Army?

I had occasion to remark a recent editorial in which surprise was manifested at the activity of the officials of the War Department in appealing for a minimum strength for our Regular Army (150,000–130,000). The editor remarked that we should follow the sensible policy of other American countries in spending our money for peace organizations instead of for warlike preparation. I wondered if he knew what policy he was advocating? The United States maintains a smaller per-capita strength of Army than that of any other American country except Canada, which is protected by its participation in the British Empire. If we followed the average policy of the Americas we should maintain a Regular Army of 200,000. If Canada is excluded as a part of an Empire whose per-capita strength is much greater than ours, we should raise this figure to 250,000. If we determine our policy upon a basis of national wealth the figure would be still higher. If we followed the average policy of the world we should have approximately a million men constantly under arms. The editor, no doubt, didn't know all of this. It is to the advantage of all of us that we know these facts about the country in which we live, or else that we do not distort facts for purposes of argument.

I mentioned that Canada is maintaining a smaller army than we are. She is, however, manifesting an interest in military preparation in another direction that can be gauged by one brief comparison. During the past summer we trained about 22,000 men in our citizens' training camps. Canada trained about 100,000 men in hers. With less than one-tenth our population she is training five times as many citizens for national defense. Her 'sensible policy' of pacification (to quote the editor) involves fifty times the intensity of effort that we exert in preparation for defense. What a striking contrast this is. Canada evidently believes in the principle expressed by Thomas Jefferson: 'None but an armed nation can dispense with a standing army.'

'But how does Canada afford this training?' inquires my curious prospect.

I might reply that it is by cutting down on her use of chewing gum. We are a nation of gum chewers. In a year we spend three times as much for 'chewing gum and candy' as we spend for military preparation. For soda and confections we spend more than three times; for tobacco, more than four times; for perfumery, jewelry, and other items of adornment, nearly five times; and for theaters, cabarets, and similar amusements, more than three times. In other words this military preparation, that appears to cost so much really costs us about one-eighteenth of what we spend for mild vices and 'harmless amusements.'

During and after the Conference for Limitation of Armament last fall, I frequently heard the remark, 'Why doesn't this country set an example in practice, as she does in words, for the reduction of military forces?'

I reply that although we are one of the greatest of powers, our Army stands sixteenth on the list of the armies of the world. If we had taken the average of military strength, of the powers in that conference, we should raise our strength to about 450,000 men. If we based our strength upon population we should have, roughly, 1,000,000 men. Yet we reduced recently to a strength of 125,000 men.

'Oh,' is the reply, 'but we could quickly throw 4,000,000 men into the field.'

Really, the Army cannot take the field without materials and supplies. The proceedings of the conference would have shown that whereas Great Britain was prepared to throw a force of 6,000,000 men into immediate service, France more than 5,000,000, Italy more than 3,000,000, and Japan more than 1,000,000, we could with difficulty outfit an army of a bare million, even if these were available, officered and freshly trained for service. 'No, my friend,' I reply, 'there need be no fear that we might fail to lead the way to reduction. By every conceivable method of comparison, you can find that we have set the example in limitation by a very pronounced inferiority to the strength of any civilized power of great importance in the world.' The greatest fear is that we might lead too far and tempt other nations before they are prepared for the trust which reduction implies.

The response sometimes comes, 'Would not our trust cause other nations to disarm rather than to take the aggressive?'

I reply that I would like to believe it. There are few exceptions to the general rule that all peoples desire peace and decry war. No country has made more determined efforts to remove possible causes of conflict and to lighten burdens of preparedness. For further developments we must, however, wait until the world follows the example already set. We damage other peoples by placing too much trust in them — a trust that we cannot even place in our own population.

'What do you mean, Mr. Secretary, by saying that we cannot trust our own people?'

I reply that we cannot bare our own institutions to the citizens of the country — that we must provide a guard that protects not only the institutions, but also unfortunate individuals, against their own worst tendencies, which might lead them to crimes destructive alike to the public weal and to their own happiness. The 1920 census discloses that there were in this country, at least 32,314 marshals, sheriffs, and detectives; 82,214 policemen; and 115,553 watchmen, guards, and doorkeepers — a total of 229,981 employed for protection against dangerous impulses. Added to this there were 50,171 firemen, making a total of 280,152 engaged in protection of our institutions against the elements, which force us to insure our private affairs. Yet we maintain less than half the number as our share of the police of the world — against peoples at most no more law-abiding than are we. In one year the insurance companies of the United States paid out to policy-holders as insurance against death, fire, marine losses, and industrial loss over $1,125,000,000. It is presumable that policy-holders paid at least as much for insurance. Added to this amount is the amount paid to the police and watchmen for protection. We invest in a military preparedness policy, accordingly, less than one-fifth of the amount paid for internal insurance and protection.

'These figures are very remarkable,' he says, 'I am impressed with the logic of your position — but something still makes me dislike to spend money for military preparations.'

If I cannot defend myself against the imputations of militarism I turn back to my predecessors for support. John C. Calhoun remarked many years ago when he ran afoul of similar objections, 'If our liberty should ever be endangered by the military power gaining the ascendancy, it will be from the necessity of making those mighty and irregular efforts to retrieve our affairs, after a series of disasters, caused by a want of military knowledge, just as in our physical system a state of the most dangerous excitement and paroxysm follows that of the greatest debility and prostration. To avoid these dangerous consequences and to prepare the country to meet a state of war, particularly at its commencement, with honor and safety, much must depend upon the organization of our military peace establishment.' My immediate predecessor also observed that 'I know of no war in which America has been engaged, offensive or defensive, which was brought about by army pressure, or, indeed, stimulated by military desire.' This deep belief has been manifested by practically every public official in close contact with this department, and it has been, perhaps, the most common thought of our Chief Executives that we must look well to defensive plans if we would accomplish best our peaceful programme. One has but to look over the face of the earth to-day to realize that even those nations who have adopted the most fantastic theories of idealistic organization continue impressed with their need for national defense.

'Perhaps this is all true,' replies the citizen, 'but why is it, then, that the officials of the War Department and of the Army are always talking and thinking about national defense and about war, when the rest of us are thinking about peace?'

The citizen so often forgets that we pay these officials to think about war and about defense. The policemen are supposed to be on the lookout for thefts and the firemen for fires. The householder thinks only of the robberies in his own block. I ask the citizen a question, 'How many wars have we Americans been through in our history?'

'Oh, about five or six,' is the reply.

I then point out to him that while he counts war on the fingers of one hand the War Department numbers its actual calls to active service at more than 100.

'Why, I didn't know that! What were these calls?'

I observe that there has actually been an average of one call every year and a half, as follows:

1775. The Revolution.
1782. Wyoming Valley insurrection.
1786. Shays's rebellion.

1790. Northwest Indian War.
1791. Whisky insurrection.
1798. War with France.
1799. Fries's rebellion.
1801. Tripolitan war.
1806. Burr conspiracy.
1806. Sabine expedition.
1807. Chesapeake Bay affair.
1808. Lake Champlain affair.
1811. Northwest Indian war.
1812. Great Britain.
1812. Seminole war.
1813. Peoria Indians.
1813. Creek Indians.
1817. Second Seminole.
1819. Yellowstone expedition.
1823. Blackfeet Indians.
1827. Lefevre Indian war.
1831. Sac and Fox Indians.
1832. Blackhawk war.
1832. South Carolina nullification.
1833. Cherokee war.
1834. Pawnee Indians.
1835. Third Seminole.
1836. Second Creek Indians.
1837. Osage Indians.
1838. Heatherly Indian war.
1838. Mormons.
1838. New York–Canada frontier.
1846. Doniphan's Mexican expedition.
1846. Mexican War.
1846. New Mexican expedition.
1848. Cayuse war.
1849. Navajo.
1849. Comanche Indians.
1850. Pitt River expedition (California).
1851. Yuma expedition.
1851. Utah Indian.
1851. Oregon and Washington Indians.
1855. Snake Indians.
1855. Sioux Indians.
1855. Yakima expedition.
1855. Cheyenne Indian.
1855. Florida war (Seminoles).
1856. Kansas border troubles.
1857. Gila expedition.

1857. Sioux Indians.
1857. Mountain Meadow Massacre.
1857. Utah expedition.
1858. Northern Indian expedition.
1858. Puget Sound expedition.
1858. Spokane Indian troubles.
1858. Navajo expedition.
1858. Wichita expedition.
1859. Colorado River Expedition.
1859. Pecos Expedition.
1859. Antelope Hills Expedition.
1859. Bear River Expedition.
1859. San Juan Imbroglio.
1859. John Brown Raid.
1859. Cortina troubles.
1860. Pah Ute Expedition.
1860. Kiowa and Comanche Indians.
1860. Carson Valley Expedition.
1860. Navajo Expedition.
1861. Apache Indians.
1861. Civil War.
1862. Indian Massacres (Minn.).
1862. Sioux Indians.
1863. Cheyenne War.
1865. Northwestern Indian War.
1865. Fenian Raid.
1867. Mexican Border Indian War.
1868. Canadian River Expedition.
1871. Yellowstone Expedition.
1871. Fenian troubles.
1872. Yellowstone Expedition.
1872. Modoc Campaign.
1873. Yellowstone Expedition.
1874. Indian Territory War.
1874. Sioux War.
1874. Black Hills War.
1875. Nevada Expedition.
1876. Sioux War.
1876. Powder River Expedition.
1876. Big Horn Expedition.
1876. Sioux War.
1877. Nez Perces Campaign.
1878. Ute Campaign.
1878. Snake Indian.
1890. Sioux.
1891. Mexican Border (Tin Horn War).

1895. Bannock Indian trouble.
1898. Spanish American War.
1898. Chippewa Indians.
1899. Philippine Insurrection.
1900. Boxer Insurrection.
1912. Nicaraguan Expedition.
1913. Haitian and San Domingo.
1914. Vera Cruz.
1916. Punitive Expedition in Mexico.
1917. Germany.

The Army remembers these incidents by the loss of friends or predecessors and, generally, by the augmentation of the difficulties, in each case, due to lack of previous preparation. The country should remember them as events in the evolution of our very active nationality, during which our principles and our possessions were defended or our possessions actually increased. We can accordingly find, in this history, what is a very great dividend in return for the comparatively small investment made by our country for its defensive preparation, and yet a very great cost for our lack of such preparations. When I have reached this conclusion my prospective supporter for national defense generally becomes very silent and thoughtful and leaves me — no doubt to pore over his histories in hopes of finding something wrong with my story. Since he never returns with refutation, I assume that he has accepted my statements and been somewhat instructed.

I trust, gentlemen, that I have not wearied you with this quite expansive treatment of what is to me an intensely interesting subject. I hope that you will forgive my method of attacking the problem, and that if you are wearied you will appreciate that it is because I lack the graphic powers of an Edward Bok, and not because my purpose is less important than arousing an interest in the Empire of the Netherlands. I feel convinced that this chamber understands the merits of the policy which I have endeavored to present in its true light to the citizens of our country. I did not come before it to sell insurance to you gentlemen, for you have always been co-workers for reasonable defense. I do hope, however, that you may, individually or collectively, from time to time remember my little discussion and pass it along. Knowledge of our country and of its institutions we must have. We are united in our ideals; we must be united in our methods of defending those ideals. Regardless of our political affiliations or beliefs, we can always join in wholehearted response to the appeal of Theodore Roosevelt when he cried, 'Our voice is now potent for peace, and is so potent for peace because we are not afraid of war. But our protestations upon behalf of peace would neither receive nor deserve the slightest attention if we were impotent to make them good.'

INDEX